DELTA QUADRANT

The Unofficial Guide to *Voyager*

DELTA QUADRANT

The Unofficial Guide to *Voyager*

David A. McIntee

First published in Great Britain in 2000 by

Virgin Publishing Limited
Thames Wharf Studios
Rainville Road
London
W6 9HA

A catalogue record for this book is available from the
British Library.

ISBN 0 7535 0436 7

Typeset by Galleon Typesetting, Ipswich
Printed and bound in Great Britain by
Mackays of Chatham PLC

Contents

Acknowledgements

Many people were helpful in the writing of this book. Some knew what it was, and others are ones who spared me a few words at conventions or the like, but all deserve equal thanks. So, thanks, in alphabetical order, to:

Allie Andrews, Robert Beltran, Ken Biller, Brannon Braga, Roxann Dawson, John de Lancie, Anthony de Longis, Lolita Fatjo, '415Man', Bryan Fuller, Robert Duncan McNeill, Kate Mulgrew, Maria Nausch, Robert Picardo, Andrew Robinson, Tim Russ, Eric Stillwell, Jeri Taylor, Keith Topping, Robert Wolfe . . . And the cast and crew of *Star Trek: Voyager*, some of whom I've no doubt missed out when I shouldn't have.

Voyager's Roots

Those wishing a detailed look at the creation of the series should pick up the excellent *A Vision Of The Future – Star Trek Voyager* by Stephen Edward Poe, which covers absolutely everything you could possibly imagine.

Voyager's genesis was in 1994. *The Next Generation* was due to end with its seventh season, and *Deep Space Nine* was finding its feet.

The team assembled to create a syndication package of 100 episodes consisted of three experienced *Trek* producers. Rick Berman had produced *The Next Generation* from the start, and was officially Gene Roddenberry's heir to the franchise. He had also co-created *Deep Space Nine*. Michael Piller, the other *Deep Space Nine* co-creator, had also been a producer on *The Next Generation* for several years. Jeri Taylor, who had started her producing life on *Quincy*, before overseeing *The Next Generation*'s final year, completed the team.

In an attempt to get away from the familiar Klingons and Romulans, it was decided the new show would see a ship flung to the opposite side of the galaxy, and meet new races as it made its way home. To counter the problems posed by lack of conflict within Starfleet crews, the ship would carry a mixture of Starfleet and Maquis crewmen, forced to work together.

Just as *Deep Space Nine* (henceforth *DS9*) had gained a springboard from *The Next Generation* (*TNG*) by having some episodes (notably 'Ensign Ro') foreshadowing the new show, so *Voyager* would be foreshadowed. A two-part *DS9* episode, 'The Maquis', would set up who the renegade crewmen were – vigilantes fighting the Cardassians in breach of Federation treaty.

Ironically, the conflict among the crew would largely be forgotten very quickly once the series started, and *DS9* made far more capital out of the Maquis concept by not being afraid to portray the Federation as a Stalinist dictatorship.

With the concept approved, and the art department working hard on designing a new, smaller and sleeker ship, it was time to choose the characters, and actors to play them.

Kate Mulgrew as Captain Kathryn Janeway

Kathryn Janeway was originally envisioned as Elizabeth Janeway, to be played by Genevieve Bujold. However, Bujold walked out after only one day of shooting. The official reason for her quitting is that she was unprepared for the punishing schedule of TV work. However, the word is that she simply had a change of heart about appearing in a science-fiction show, and found the make-up and costumes 'silly'.

Janeway herself is very much a creation of Jeri Taylor, who has often described the captain as her alter ego. Janeway is a scientist and explorer, but first and foremost a Starship captain.

Kate Mulgrew is probably best known prior to *Voyager* for appearing as Mrs Columbo, in *Kate Loves a Mystery*, and in films and shows as diverse as *Roots: The Gift* and *Remo: Unarmed and Dangerous*.

Robert Beltran as Chakotay

Chakotay was originally envisioned as being from the planet seen in *TNG* episode 'Journey's End', though this has never been stated on screen. At first his ancestors and background were from the Four Corners area of the US, but he has subsequently become some kind of Aztec or Mayan descendant. He was to be the strong, silent and spiritual type, but also a man whom people would trust and follow.

Robert Beltran had previously appeared in movies such as *Eating Raoul* and *Night of the Comet* as well as the BBC drama *Runway One*.

Roxann Dawson as B'Elanna Torres

B'Elanna is the half-Klingon engineer, always fighting against herself. In many ways she was intended to be the junior end of a mother–teenage daughter relationship with Janeway, but her part in that has subsequently been taken by

Seven of Nine. She was cast as an engineer in order to make a change from the usual Klingon warriors.

At the time of her casting, Dawson was married to Casey Biggs, who played Damar in *DS9*. Prior to her role in *Voyager*, she appeared in the likes of *NYPD Mounted* and *Greyhounds*. She also appears in *Darkman III: Die Darkman Die*.

Jennifer Lien as Kes

Kes was imagined as the one-year-old girlfriend of Neelix, and has telepathic abilities, allowing her to be the sensitive one in the crew. Sadly, she doesn't come into her own until Season Three, shortly before leaving the show.

Before joining the cast, Lien was mainly a voice artist, in cartoons such as *The Critic* and *Duckman*. Since leaving the show, she has been a regular voice in the animated *Men In Black* series, and appeared in *American History X*.

Robert Duncan McNeill as Tom Paris

Originally Tom Paris was going to be Nick Locarno, McNeill's character from *TNG* episode 'The First Duty'. Jeri Taylor says this changed because Locarno was 'beyond redemption', which is odd as his back-story is identical to Tom's.

Robbie McNeill (the three Roberts are known on set as Robbie McNeill, Bob Picardo and Robert Beltran) made his big break in the film *Masters of the Universe*, and guest starred in such series as *Quantum Leap*.

Ethan Phillips as Neelix

Neelix was essentially planned as an attempt to repeat the tongue-in-cheek success of Quark, but sadly the former trader-turned-chef doesn't have that effect. Fortunately, he later began to get more dramatic episodes, better suited to Phillips's talents.

Ethan Phillips is one of those character actors whom you know you've seen before, but can't place. You most likely saw him in *The Shadow*, or indeed *Masters of the Universe*, with Robbie McNeill.

Robert Picardo as the Doctor

The EMH (Emergency Medical Hologram) is the show's answer to Data – the character in search of what it means to be human. It was originally planned that he would choose Zimmerman as his name, but this was dropped, and given to his creator instead. Nevertheless, some pre-publicity mistakenly called him that before the show's launch. Picardo, incidentally, auditioned for the role of Neelix at first.

Bob Picardo is probably the most familiar face in the crew, having appeared in almost all of Joe Dante's movies, most notably *Gremlins 2* and *Innerspace*. He was also a doctor in the medical drama *China Beach*, set in the Vietnam War, and guested as a patient, for a change, in *ER*.

Tim Russ as Tuvok

Jeri Taylor's original intent for Tuvok was for him to be an older, visibly middle-aged, Vulcan, to be a paternal Obi-Wan sort of figure for Janeway, and Taylor wasn't best pleased when the screen version was a younger man with a quite different sort of chemistry.

Tim Russ was cast largely because Rick Berman remembered him from his audition for the part of Geordi LaForge eight years earlier, and his roles as Devor in *TNG* episode 'Starship Mine' and a Klingon in the *DS9* episode 'Invasive Procedures'. While filming Season One of *Voyager*, he also found time to be a human officer on the bridge of the *Enterprise-B* in *Star Trek: Generations*, which marked the end of the mythology of TOS (The Original Series). Russ had also appeared with Mulgrew in *Roots: the Gift*, and is an accomplished singer and art-house film-maker.

Garrett Wang as Harry Kim

Harry would be the baby of the crew – young and eager to please, but inexperienced. Of all the character concepts, his is the one that stayed closest to the original plan.

This was Garrett's first major role.

The Episode Guide

Each episode entry will give the production number and episode title, writer credits, director credits, music credits and US air date, followed by some choice comments in the following categories:

Plot: A brief synopsis of the story, with stardate where known (not all episodes are given stardates, and so we've only mentioned stardates that have been spoken on screen).

Déjà Vu?: Many episodes are remakes of other *Trek* stories, or inspired by other media. This bit will tell you whether each episode owes its origins to a previous *Trek* episode, or a different show altogether.

Behind the Scenes: Authorial intent, notable locations and occasional anecdotes from cast or crew. Also ideas dropped, added or cut from script development. Trivia, basically.

***Voyager* Database:** What new information about the *Voyager* universe is given.

(Lack of) Continuity: Brannon Braga, writer and producer, is also notorious for actively fighting against continuity, so this part would cover all the screw-ups (such as whether or not the Doc can be backed up, or how many people are aboard . . .) and all the follow-ups.

Ye Canna Change the Laws o' Physics: This is where we keep the technobabble. Sometimes praising or debunking the science in the show, but also noting any other references to reality (references to historical events, use of contemporary projectile weapons and so on).

Puzzles: Unanswered questions, plot threads left hanging, and general sloppiness.

Bloopers: Notable mistakes on show.

Learn Your Lines: Any memorable snippets of dialogue, with comments where appropriate.

Highs: A purely subjective note of any particularly fine effects, dialogue, scenes etc.

Lows: An equally subjective note of any really cringeworthy bits.

Verdict: A brief summary review on whether the episode is any good (or not) and for what reasons, with a score out of 10.

Well, it's been five seasons of videos compressed into a few weeks. In many ways I'll be delighted not to have to watch another episode for a while, but . . .

I still love it . . . It may be the least impressive of the *Trek* series, but I still prefer it to most other shows.

Now, this is going to be something of an informal chat. Just pour yourself something nice, and imagine you're sitting at a convention bar, discussing *Star Trek: Voyager* . . .

First Season

Regular cast:
Kate Mulgrew as Captain Kathryn Janeway
Robert Beltran as Commander Chakotay
Roxann Biggs-Dawson as B'Elanna Torres
Jennifer Lien as Kes
Robert Duncan McNeill as Tom Paris
Ethan Phillips as Neelix
Robert Picardo as the Doctor
Tim Russ as Tuvok
Garrett Wang as Harry Kim

Recurring cast:
Martha Hackett as Seska
Josh Clark as Lt Carey

#101/102: 'Caretaker'

**by Michael Piller and Jeri Taylor
from a story by Piller, Taylor and Rick Berman**

Directed by Winrich Kolbe
Music by Jay Chattaway
US air date 16-01-95

Plot: Stardate 48315.6. Chakotay's Maquis ship, with Chakotay, Tuvok and B'Elanna as the command crew, disappears while hiding from a Cardassian ship in the plasma storms of the Badlands.

Captain Janeway of USS *Voyager* enlists the services of a Maquis convict, Tom Paris, to help find the ship, as her security chief was on board undercover. After a stop at DS9 to pick up the ops officer, Harry Kim, *Voyager* follows the Maquis ship's last-known heading, and is hit by a coherent tetryon beam. Half wrecked and with many deaths, it ends up outside a large array in the Delta Quadrant, 70,000 light years from home. The Maquis ship is there too. The crew are abducted and find themselves in a holographic Earth farm, before being rendered unconscious and biologically tested. They then find themselves back aboard ship three days later, but with Harry missing from *Voyager*, and B'Elanna missing from the Maquis ship. Both crews team up to visit the array to demand answers, and Tuvok reveals himself to be the security chief who had been spying on the Maquis. On the array, the old man they find refuses to help them, and teleports them back to *Voyager*. Janeway promises to get Tuvok home to see his family again.*

Making for the fifth planet of the system, *Voyager* encounters the trader Neelix, who offers to help the crew find the missing pair. He leads them to meet the Kazon, who are holding his girlfriend, Kes – an Ocampa who has left the city where Harry and B'Elanna are being held. She offers to help the crew get into the city. Harry and B'Elanna, meanwhile, learn about the Ocampa, and discover that they have been infected with an unknown but fatal disease. An Ocampa nurse helps them to escape. Janeway and company catch up with them, and the Emergency Medical Hologram cures them back on the ship. The array begins firing at the surface to seal the Ocampa off from the Kazon, and Janeway and Chakotay beam over to find out why. It transpires that, as Tuvok had theorised, the Caretaker is dying, and trying to protect the Ocampa until they can be rescued. The Kazon would enslave the Ocampa if they gained control of the array, and a space battle is already in progress, in which Chakotay sacrifices his ship to give Janeway time to destroy the array – even though it was the only thing that could send them home. The Maquis, Neelix and Kes all join the depleted crew, and Janeway orders a course set for Earth.

Déjà Vu?: Tom's frustration over the soup echoes Arthur

---

* In the two-part version for reruns and syndication, this is where Part One ends.

Dent's attempts to get the *Heart of Gold*'s drinks machine to make him proper tea in *The Hitch-Hikers' Guide to the Galaxy*.

The super-powered alien looking after some less advanced species nearby isn't exactly unusual either (for example 'The Apple' and 'Return of the Archons' in TOS).

Tom's back-story is very reminiscent of the events that happened to Nick Locarno, also played by Robbie McNeill, in *TNG* episode 'The First Duty'.

Behind the Scenes: Location shooting for the Ocampa city took place in the LA Convention Center. The desert at El Mirage Dry Lake near Victorville served as the planet surface (Kazon camp etc.) while the farmhouse scenes were filmed in Norwalk. The shaft that allows escape from the Ocampa city appears to be the cave set from *TNG* episode 'Second Chances', where the alternate Riker was created.

The Caretaker's array is a rebuild of the Floating Office model from *Star Trek: The Motion Picture*, which had also been used as the Regula 1 station in *The Wrath of Khan*, and has appeared as various starbases throughout *TNG* and *DS9* (most recently in the *DS9* episode 'The Valiant').

Ethan Phillips has a prosthetic chest for his bath scene, with a Y-shaped ridge over the front of his collarbone.

Tim Russ is the only one of the regular cast to have actually shot a scene with the original Janeway, Genevieve Bujold (she promises to return him to his family).

The tricorders and phasers here are the versions used in *TNG* since Season Three. The compression rifles are new.

Voyager Database: *Voyager* is an Intrepid-Class ship, with variable-geometry warp nacelles, a sustainable cruise velocity of warp 9.975, fifteen decks, and bioneural circuitry.

Lt Stadi lists the crew complement as 141. It's uncertain whether this includes Paris (who is aboard as an observer, therefore technically just a passenger) or Tuvok, who is a crew member but is not aboard at the time.

Tom Paris had caused the deaths of several crewmen through reckless/negligent piloting some time in the past, and had tried to cover up his responsibility – just like Nick Locarno in *TNG* episode 'The First Duty'.

Janeway served under Tom's father on the USS *Al-Batani*.

B'Elanna made it to the second year of Starfleet Academy. Ocampa are telepathic and live for only nine years. It's implied that they had other psi powers in the past, which they no longer need and which have therefore disappeared through evolution. They have lived in their underground city, cared for by the Caretaker, for 500 generations.

Confirmed killed are the helmsman (Stadi), first officer (Cavit), chief engineer, doctor and nurse. The overall casualty figure is not stated, and nor is the number of Maquis who join from Chakotay's ship.

(Lack of) Continuity: *Voyager* is presumably named after the series of space probes of which V'Ger (*Star Trek: The Motion Picture*) was a part.

The *DS9* regular Quark appears, as does Gul Evek (*TNG* – 'Journey's End'; *DS9* – 'The Maquis').

Harry's tricorder in the barn recognises only one Vulcan (Tuvok) among a bunch of humans held comatose in the array. Not only does it not detect the other aliens among the crew seen later in the series (Vorik, Suder, Seska etc.), but it overlooks B'Elanna too.

There's a famous tendency, dating from *TNG*, for the number 47 to appear an inordinate number of times in small roles in modern *Trek*. They start showing up here: between *Voyager*'s arrival and their discovering Neelix, the interval between energy pulses directed at the fifth planet from the array decreases by 0.47 of a second.

Harry's infection is just the first of many unfortunate fates to befall him in his role as *Voyager*'s whipping boy. He's obviously a descendant of Kenny McCormack from that little town in Colorado . . .

Tetryons are apparently particles that are stable only in subspace, and were first mentioned in *TNG* episode 'Schisms'.

There's mention of another Caretaker, which doesn't appear here. That being is destined to show up in the second-season episode, 'Cold Fire'.

Ye Canna Change the Laws o' Physics: Both *Voyager* and the Maquis ship are brought to the Delta Quadrant by a large displacement wave made of 'some kind of polarised magnetic variation' after passing through a coherent tetryon beam. Magnetism, of course, can be polarised only one way or the other.

According to Lt Stadi, the bioneural gel packs process data faster and more efficiently than conventional circuitry. By 'conventional' she presumably means isolinear optical circuitry. Certainly the human brain can process basic information (for autonomous functions) faster than any artificial computer.

The Caretaker itself is a 'sporocystian life form' – which suggests that it's some kind of fungus! However, when it dies, it shrivels up into a piece of crystal.

The Ocampa planet's atmosphere contains no nucleonic particles, and apparently that's why rain is impossible there. Nonsense of course. The phrase suggests a lack of particles containing nuclei – which leaves one to wonder where all the matter came from (sand, metal, Ocampa . . .), since all atoms contain nuclei.

Apparently the Kazon are able to build warp-capable ships, but can't synthesise water from hydrogen and oxygen. Given that this is something we can do on Earth today, it's hardly realistic.

Puzzles: Since the Doctor is generated by the ship's computer, why does he need a holographic combadge in order to talk to it, or to access the communications systems?

So, what was up with Harry and B'Elanna getting infected with a disease anyway? It's cured in an instant by the holodoc, and there's no explanation as to what it was, or why only those two contracted it.

Bloopers: Chakotay's tattoo is slightly different here, and slopes back at a much more rakish angle.

When B'Elanna is struggling with the Ocampan doctors and nurses, there is one shot in which the front of her gown starts opening up to reveal a rather nice, non-Starfleet, lacy bra. Perhaps we can speculate that it's this incident that prompted the obsession with emphasising Seven of Nine's dimensions, which becomes apparent throughout Seasons Four and Five. (And, incidentally, all the *Voyager* women have padded costumes.) There's a cut, and then you see her again – still struggling – only now her gown is tightly closed up front, right to the throat. Apparently she popped out of it and they had to cut and close her gown and splice together the pieces of film . . . What do you mean 'trust me to notice something like that'? Later, when she thumps the door, there's a large hole where the sleeve meets the rest of the gown.

In one of the shots of Neelix on the main viewer, in his first conversation with *Voyager*, there's a wider view of the set of his ship. In this shot, the shadow of a stagehand is visible moving around on the far left of the screen.

Ethan also pronounces Maje (the Kazon rank) as 'Mah-jay' here rather than as 'Maj'. It's hard to tell whether this is a deliberate idea that got dropped in later episodes, or whether he's goofed by starting to say 'Jabin' too early.

Kes's clothes . . . Once she is rescued and beamed up, presumably she goes to sickbay (next scene) to have her bruises treated. Only . . . she must have had a shower first and changed clothes: when she arrives in the transporter room, she's wearing the drab Ocampan clothes, but in sickbay she's wearing the yellow-red ensemble.

Learn Your Lines: Janeway: 'Mr Kim, at ease, before you sprain something.'

Tom: 'The ghosts of those three dead crewmen showed me the true meaning of Christmas.'

Highs: The conversation between Janeway and Tuvok at the end of part one.

The opening and closing battles.

The theme tune.

Lows: The banjo music, and in fact the whole farmhouse party.

Neelix.

The sudden cure of Harry and B'Elanna's infection being such an anticlimax.

Verdict: When 'Caretaker' first aired, I remember thinking that it was probably the best stand-alone of the *Trek* pilots. Watching it again five years on has only cemented that view. Where 'The Cage' has dated, 'Encounter at Farpoint' was hideously dull, and 'Emissary' requires reading the novelisation to understand fully, 'Caretaker' is a straightforward *Trek* story that both engages the interest and does a nice job of introducing the concept and some of the characters. The other nice thing about 'Caretaker' is that it isn't about a superior being judging humanity. What a nice change!

It does have its flaws, of course. For one thing, the whole subplot of Harry and B'Elanna's disease is shameless padding that is eventually dispensed with without a word of explanation – they're just suddenly cured by the Doctor without even revealing how they came by the infection.

In terms of acting and performances, Kate Mulgrew (Janeway) and Tim Russ (Tuvok) are notably at the forefront, though Garrett Wang (Harry Kim) and Robbie McNeill (Tom Paris) are also pretty good. The others don't really get their chances until later. In fact, watching it now, I find it astonishing how little Chakotay has to do, and doubly astonishing to see how much Tuvok gets, before they forgot him. From the pilot alone, *Voyager* actually looks like being very good indeed, but it has already made at least one big mistake – Tom Paris's character arc, from mercenary to redemption, is pretty much covered within this first episode, leaving little room for development later (and that will be covered early in Season Two).

All in all, the story is a simple one of courage in the face of adversity. It has some engaging characters, and some as-yet unknown ones. Any doubts about a female captain are settled right from the start, as Mulgrew makes her mark. 8/10.

#103: 'Parallax'

by Brannon Braga
from a story by Jim Trombetta

Directed by Kim Friedman
Music by Dennis McCarthy
US air date 23-01-95

Plot: Stardate 48439.7. B'Elanna has put acting Chief Engineer Carey in sickbay with a broken nose over a technical disagreement. Chakotay both reprimands her for this, and wants Janeway to make her first officer, as some of the Maquis crew have suggested they'd back him if he tried to take over the ship. Meanwhile, the ship receives a distress signal from a vessel trapped in a quantum singularity. Only once *Voyager* itself is trapped do the crew realise that the signal they received was their own. Chakotay irritates Janeway by putting B'Elanna in charge of the engineering team to deal with the problem.

Déjà Vu?: The Disney film *The Black Hole* also features a ship trapped in a similar situation, though that one doesn't meet itself, and doesn't escape either.

Behind the Scenes: The first bottle show of the season. 'Bottle show' means one taking place entirely on standing sets – in this case the regular ship sets.

***Voyager* Database:** The hydroponics (called Airponics in later episodes) garden is in Cargo Bay 2, because it was designed for organic cargoes and has variable environmental controls. Replicator power is down and rations have run out. More on this in the entry for 'Scorpion' Part II.

The USS *Voyager* is 116 metres wide. (Flying through a 120-metre-wide channel leaves it with a clearance of only two metres on each side.)

B'Elanna had four disciplinary hearings and one suspension in her two years at Starfleet Academy. She was taught by Professor Chapman, who considered her one of his most promising students, even though they always fought.

Seska makes her debut, but in a blue uniform rather than the yellow one she wears for the rest of her appearances.

The transporter chief is confirmed as having been killed in the previous episode.

Tom is assigned to train as a field medic, having taken two semesters of biochemistry at the Academy.

Security is relocated to Deck 7 so that Deck 9 can be shut down to redirect its energy to propulsion.

(Lack of) Continuity: Hitting a fellow officer was established as a court-martial offence in TOS episode 'This Side of Paradise'.

A quantum singularity is defined in *TNG* episode 'Timescape' as a very small black hole.

Ye Canna Change the Laws o' Physics: Holodeck power systems aren't compatible with those for the rest of the ship, which is why they can still be used when everything else has to be rationed. Convenient, that. Unlikely, too, given that the holodeck largely operates in the same way as the replicators, and *they're* on rations.

The anomaly that traps the ship is described as a 'type-four quantum singularity'. Neelix describes a singularity as a black hole (rather than a point inside a black hole), and calls the event horizon an energy field – which is nonsense: it's a boundary surrounding the singularity. And, if the ship on the monitor really is inside the event horizon, then how are they seeing it? No signals or light would be able to get out.

The laws of physics take more of a battering later, as Janeway and B'Elanna work out that they can escape through a 'crack' in the event horizon.

Puzzles: There's no good reason whatsoever why B'Elanna should be made chief engineer. If I were Carey I'd be very pissed off.

Tuvok is said to have given Starfleet the names of all of Chakotay's Maquis crew before the ship left DS9. In fact it must surely have been rather longer before – since the reason for leaving DS9 was that contact with Tuvok and the Maquis ship had been lost.

Bloopers: Seska appears to be in two places at once. She's at the bridge engineering station when Carey is being invited over the intercom to a briefing. However, when Carey turns (in Engineering) to invite B'Elanna to accompany him, Seska is standing behind her!

Learn Your Lines: Janeway: 'Sometimes you just have to punch your way through.' Tom: 'I'll have to remember that one . . .'
    Tuvok: 'I will never cease to be amazed at the human capacity for hyperbole.'

Highs: Chakotay is pretty good here, being a bit of a thug.
    Just about any scene between Mulgrew and Dawson.

Lows: The dodgy science, and the ludicrous means of escape.

Verdict: In spite of the above scientific absurdities, 'Parallax' is still a watchable episode – mainly due to the performances of Mulgrew and Dawson. It's possible to forgive the lame tech-nobabble side of the plot simply because it isn't the main thrust of the episode. Robert Beltran (Chakotay) is quite watchable in thuggish form and there's a nice animosity between Chakotay and Tuvok, which sadly has yet to be used as the springboard for a story. The main thing is picking up the pieces from 'Care-taker', and setting up who will do what for the rest of the season. 7/10.

#104: 'Time and Again'

by David Kemper and Michael Piller
from a story by David Kemper

Directed by Les Landau
Music by Jay Chattaway
US air date 30-01-95

Plot: Stardate 48498.7. The ship detects a huge polaric explosion laying waste to the surface of a nearby planet. Taking an away team down, Janeway and Tom find themselves caught by a drifting subspace fracture, and sent back in time to the day before the polaric explosion. Passing themselves off as travellers from another province, the pair acquire native clothes and try to send a signal to the away team. At first Janeway doesn't want to break the Prime Directive by preventing the explosion, but soon changes her mind. The pair are captured by rebels opposed to polaric energy, and Janeway follows them into the power plant, which she believes they intend to sabotage.

Déjà Vu?: The attempt to prevent a huge explosion in the past turning out to be the very thing that caused it is probably best known from the 1972 *Doctor Who* story, 'The Day of the Daleks'.

Kes's supernatural knowledge seems to echo that displayed by Guinan in *TNG* episode 'Yesterday's Enterprise'. Apart from being very similar to a certain scene featuring Alec Guinness . . .

Behind the Scenes: Although the episode is set on some alien planet with futuristic technology, the power plant guards are armed with Calico Liberty 3 semiautomatic carbines (also seen in *Dark Angel* and *Total Recall*), and the rebels have what appear to be H&K P9s.

There's a large door in the town square, which appears to be the one hiding Soran's solar probes aboard the Amargosa observatory in *Star Trek: Generations*.

***Voyager* Database:** Harry has a girl back home (Libby, whom we'll see in 'Non Sequitur'), while Tom claims to have five. Harry points out that he intends to see his again.

The Doc speculates that Kes's increased mental abilities are a result of chemical changes that all organic bodies make in order to adjust to space travel. In her case this has meant chemical changes in the brain that allow her to regain some of the abilities mentioned in 'Caretaker', which the Ocampa people as a whole had lost over time in the underground city. According to Kes, nobody had really believed those stories about the Ocampa ancestors. Neelix compares her new abilities to the visions of 'the Drakian Forest-Dwellers'.

Combadges are designed to self-activate if the casing is destroyed, to help rescue teams home in on victims or survivors.

This is the first instance of what will rapidly become Janeway's *massively* inconsistent attitude to the Prime Directive.

(Lack of) Continuity: The Romulans and Prime Directive get name-checked.

Ye Canna Change the Laws o' Physics: 'Differentially charged polaric ions' are 'a sign of a massive detonation'. Apparently the planet suffered a chain reaction in subspace due to the explosion of one or more polaric-ion devices. Subspace is a fictional layer of space beyond normal relativistic space, in which faster-than-light travel is permissible. I'd assume 'polaric ion' refers to whether an ion is positive or negative (a positive ion is an atom that has lost an electron, and a negative ion has gained one).

This has caused subspace fractures to drift across the surface, causing temporal flux where the subspace shockwaves have gone back in time instead of forward. Other than temporal flux simply meaning that time is being jumbled up, this can't even really be translated, let alone explained scientifically.

Phasering the polaric generator causes 'Adion particle resistance'. No, I don't know what any of this means either.

Puzzles: What exactly were the terrorists up to, if not sabotaging the power plant?

More importantly, why *did* Janeway decide to tell all? She hadn't yet figured out the truth about the explosion's cause, and so the only reasonable explanation is that she just got scared of being killed there. But aren't Starfleet officers supposed to be willing to die to protect the Prime Directive?

Bloopers: B'Elanna mispronounces Chaltok as Shontok.

When Terla shoots Tom, the slide on his gun jams back, proving that it's empty after just one shot. Janeway then pauses to grab a gun from the body of the guard they've also shot, and follows them in. However, once inside, she's carrying one of the generic energy-weapon props that have been around since *TNG*, despite the fact that the locals on the planet have only contemporary weapons.

Learn Your Lines: Tom (re Harry's girl at home): 'Let her go. Let her have a husband and kids, and a good life . . . While you and I have the Delaney sisters!'

Doc: 'It seems I've found myself on a voyage of the damned.'

Highs: Tom winding up the young boy.
The Doc's new-found line in one-liners.

Lows: Technobabble overload! Help!

Verdict: *Voyager* quickly became notorious for overuse of technobabble, and it's probably down to this episode. It also doesn't help that the idea of effect preceding cause was the thought behind the previous episode too – well, it is one of Brannon Braga's favourite schemes. On the good side, the Holodoc is starting to get funny lines. The kid on the planet isn't actually that bad, and the basic plot is OK too. In other words, it's forgettable but harmless. And I always loved time-travel episodes anyway. 7/10.

#105: 'Phage'

by Skye Dent and Brannon Braga
from a story by Tim DeHaas

Directed by Rick (Winrich) Kolbe
Music by Dennis McCarthy
US air date 06-02-95

Plot: Stardate 48532.4. While exploring a moon for signs of dilithium, Neelix is attacked by an alien. Back on the ship, it turns out that his lungs have been transported out of his body. The Doctor keeps him alive by giving him holographic lungs, though this will mean he has to remain motionless in sickbay for the rest of his life, unable to move more than two microns while in the requisite isotropic restraint. This soon begins to drive Neelix over the edge, and he begins to suspect that Tom has designs on Kes.

Meanwhile, an away team find an alien hideout on the moon, filled with medical equipment, and vital organs from many species. The owners are the Vidiians, who are ravaged by a disease called the Phage, which forces them to replace their own decaying body parts with other people's.

Déjà Vu?: Basically 'Spock's Brain' without the laughs.

Behind the Scenes: The Vidiian corridor hidden behind the force field on the planet is the corridor that was hidden behind the holographic barn in 'Caretaker'. Also, the Vidiian ship appears to be a conversion of the freighter model from *Star Trek III: The Search for Spock*. At the very least, the four engines are certainly from that model.

The characteristic *Voyager* flashlights – a pair of small flashlights mounted on a wristband – debut here when the away team explore the moon for signs of dilithium.

***Voyager* Database:** Ration Pack 5 contains stewed tomatoes and dehydrated eggs.

Neelix's kitchen is in Cabin 125-alpha, on Deck 2. This room, which is attached to the mess hall, was the captain's private dining room until he hijacked it.

The USS *Voyager* weighs 700,000 tons. It's unclear whether this is in metric tonnes or Imperial tons, but the latter is more likely, since metric tonnes were *specified* as such in reference to the amount of dilithium the crew hoped to find on the planet.

There are three transporter rooms.

Ylethians have three spinal columns, according to Neelix.

B'Elanna converts the auxiliary impulse reactor to a dilithium reactor. Apparently this sort of modification is particularly frowned upon by Starfleet, even though it's necessary.

Neelix discovered the planet, with 500–1,000 metric tonnes of dilithium, three years ago.

The Doctor can be made solid or not, according to adjustments of his magnetic containment field.

Kes volunteers to be trained as a medical assistant – an arrangement the Doctor finds more suitable than training Tom.

(Lack of) Continuity: Neutronium was introduced as an impenetrable metal in TOS episode 'The Doomsday Machine', in which the planet-killer's hull was made of pure neutronium.

The Vidiian organ collection includes a Kazon liver, as well as unidentified pulmonary and epidermal organs.

Ye Canna Change the Laws o' Physics: The Vidiian weapon is a combined energy weapon, medical scanner and surgical instrument. It uses a neural resonator to stun victims, then begins a microcellular analysis of the entire body, and can transport selected parts out to another location. If it is fired at someone, the user will instantly know everything about the victim's body, down to the DNA sequence. In fact parts of this concept are quite reasonable – certain sonic or electromagnetic frequencies can be used to interrupt normal brainwave functions and cause nausea, or even fainting.

A KLS stabiliser compensates for warp-core fluctuation. Which doesn't mean much if we don't know how a warp core fluctuates, or what KLS stands for.

The means that Chakotay thinks of, and Tuvok implements, to detect the real Vidiian ship in the 'hall of mirrors' asteroid is quite simple, straightforward and thoroughly scientifically accurate – a laser (or in this case minimal-power phaser) beam will indeed keep bouncing off the reflective surfaces until it hits something more absorbent.

Neutronium is a conjectural name for the metallic material of a neutron star – a material that has been collapsed so far that the nuclei are actually touching, with no electrons separating them.

Puzzles: There's a sort of water-bubble tank in sickbay which isn't seen in any other episode. It is unclear whether this has something to do with the equipment to keep Neelix alive, or whether it's simply a set decoration that was decided to be unsuitable after this one experiment.

Learn Your Lines: Neelix (re Tom): 'He's just one big hormone walking around the ship.'

Tuvok: 'I could describe to you in detail the psychological

observations I've made about you over the past four years, which lead me to conclude that you are about to take this ship inside the asteroid. But suffice it to say, I know you quite well.' Janeway: 'One of these days I'm going to surprise you, Tuvok – but not today.'

Highs: The sequence in which the Doctor demonstrates his magnetic containment field to Tom.

Lows: Neelix's overacted paranoia about Tom and Kes.

Verdict: Well, the appellation 'Spock's Brain without the laughs' is probably a little too cruel – this episode isn't *that* bad. The basic hook of the story is supremely silly, but the concept of organ-stealing degenerate aliens is a creepy one, which will be used to far better effect in their second episode, 'Faces'. It's strange that the Vidiians have so much gunk on their faces, mind you; wouldn't they be more likely to be scrawny and, well, unhealthy looking? The episode is neither particularly exciting nor character-based, but it holds the attention reasonably well, all things considered. 5/10.

#106: 'The Cloud'

by Michael Piller
from a story by Brannon Braga

Directed by David Livingston
Music by Jay Chattaway
US air date 13-02-95

Plot: Stardate 48546.2. Searching for omicron particles – which are needed for something to do with the fuel system – *Voyager* heads for a nebula which shows high concentrations of them. To the annoyance of Neelix, who thinks that going around nebulae is more sensible, the ship enters, and promptly encounters resistance from, organic particles.

Meanwhile, Tom introduces Harry to the new recreation area – a holodeck representation of a bar in Marseilles called Sandrine's, filled with pool hustlers and gigolos.

After blasting a hole in an energy wall and doing various other bits of damage, B'Elanna and the Doctor realise that the nebula was a living organism which they have injured, and must now heal . . .

Déjà Vu?: The life form large enough for a starship to enter is reminiscent of the space amoeba from TOS episode 'The Immunity Syndrome', but in this case the ship is trying to heal it rather than kill it.

Voyager **Database:** Harry sleeps with an eye mask because of a roommate at the Academy who sat up studying all night. Said roommate did at least get Harry through fourth-year quantum chemistry, so it had its compensations.

Chakotay's medicine bundle contains a blackbird's wing, a stone from a river and an akoonah.

The Doctor's creator is a man named Zimmerman, at the Jupiter Station Holoprogramming Centre. He 'looks a lot like' the Doctor.

Neelix nominates himself morale officer, and cooking helps him unwind.

Janeway's notorious caffeine addiction first becomes apparent here.

Ye Canna Change the Laws o' Physics: The nebula in which the valuable omicron particles have been detected is seven astronomical units across – that's seven times the distance from the Earth to the sun: 651,000,000 miles, or 1,041,600,000 kilometres. It doesn't look anything like that big in exterior shots.

Apart from omicron particles – whatever they are – the nebula mostly comprises hydrogen, helium and hydroxyl radicals, which are reasonable substances to expect.

The magnetised dust backing the barrier to the interior of the nebula has a 'return force of 4.1', whatever that means – since there's no scale named.

The nebula's molecules are isolinear, with no polycyclic structures. Its nature as a life form is revealed by its nucleo-genic peptide bonds, which B'Elanna erroneously suspects are phospholipid fibres. In a nucleogenic life form, nucleonic radiation promotes regeneration of wounded areas. In reality, peptides are any compounds consisting of two or more amino acids linked end to end, and can be artificial as well as natural. As for 'nucleogenic', that's just a standard piece of *Trek* technobabble which really means 'produced or generated by or through nuclei'. If the Doctor is trying to say what I think he's trying to say, he should have said 'the peptide bonds in these nucleotide sequences', and not 'nucleogenic peptide bonds'. Oddly enough the Doctor says that the bonds are not phospholipid fibres, but, more interestingly, are signs of life. This is bizarre, considering that phospholipids *are* organic compounds, including triglycerins, phosphates and one or more fatty acids. Perhaps his and B'Elanna's technobabble got swapped round for aesthetic effect.

The akoonah in Chakotay's medicine bundle is a technological replacement for the peyote or other psychoactive drugs historically used by shamans and vision questers to allow an altered state of consciousness. Although it works by one's putting a hand on it, it would make more sense if it were pressed against the temples, as it is known in real life that electromagnetic stimulation of the temporal lobes can produce altered consciousness. See any book on or by Michael Persinger for examples.

According to Chakotay, animal guides are what Jung thought he invented with his 'active imagination' technique in 1932.

Puzzles: The Doctor suggests that, if he were given the ability to reprogram himself, he might create a family or raise an army. He does the former in 'Real Life', so will he ever do the latter?

Bloopers: When Chakotay brings his medicine bundle to Janeway, he says he's never shown it to anyone before. However, when B'Elanna interrupts them, it's clear she has seen it, as Chakotay says that, when she tried to learn about animal spirit guides, she tried to kill hers!

Learn Your Lines: Harry: 'There's an ancient Chinese curse – may you live in interesting times. Meal times are always interesting now that Neelix is in charge of the kitchen.'

Janeway: 'There's coffee in that nebula!'

Janeway: 'Dismissed. That's a Starfleet expression for get out.'

Highs: Just about any scene with Mulgrew being utterly in charge.

The scene in which the bridge crew switch off the audio while the Doctor is talking to them.

Lows: Neelix's selfish whining.

The unnecessary bumpy-foreheaded alien in Sandrine's.

Verdict: Another bottle show (i.e. one set entirely on the ship) of which there are many in the first two seasons. The plot is basically quite simple, but strangely likable. In particular, it's a good *tour de force* for Mulgrew to show all the different sides of Janeway; in this episode she really makes the role her own. Sandrine's quite nice too, though there's no need for the European gigolo to be a bumpy-foreheaded alien of the week. There's some humour from the Doctor too – particularly the scene in which the bridge crew turn the sound off while he's talking to them. On the downside, Neelix maintains his status as the show's pain in the arse. 5/10.

#107: 'Eye of the Needle'

by Jeri Taylor
from a story by Hilary Bader

Directed by Rick Kolbe
Music by Dennis McCarthy
US air date 22-02-95

Plot: Stardate 48579.4. Kes is shocked that people are so rude to the Doctor. Meanwhile, Harry has discovered a microscopic wormhole, into which a microprobe is launched. The probe becomes stuck in a gravitational eddy, but acts as a relay to a ship on the other side – in the Alpha Quadrant. Unfortunately, the other ship is a Romulan science vessel, whose sole crewman disbelieves them. After some convincing, he agrees to try an experimental transport, and beams to *Voyager*.

Déjà Vu?: In the *Space: 1999* episode 'Journey To Where' the crew find a possible way back to Earth, which turns out to have a temporal problem attached, though in that case the other end of the journey was in the fourteenth century.

Behind the Scenes: Telek R'Mor's chair is from *TNG* episode 'Face of the Enemy' and has been seen as a piece of Romulan furniture in many episodes.

***Voyager* Database:** Microprobes (mentioned in the previous episode) are just under 30 cm (one foot) across. This compares with normal probes, which in previous episodes of other *Trek*s have been shown to be modified photon torpedo casings about six feet long and two feet across.

The current year is stated to be 2371. Telek R'Mor died in 2367.

(Lack of) Continuity: Transporter test cylinders were seen in the original series – boxes wrapped in reflective material. The new version is much smaller, transparent, and has lights flickering in it.

Ye Canna Change the Laws o' Physics: Verteron emanations in subspace, and secondary tunnelling particles, alerted Harry to the wormhole. It has microscopic gravitational anomalies, extremely constricted spatial dimensions, and a strange phase variance in its radiation stream (this turns out to be the temporal variance – a good bit of clue-setting). It is ancient and has probably been collapsing for centuries. Though Harry describes it as 'almost microscopic', it is about 30 cm across. Such wormholes are thought to exist in real science – and in real science it is believed they would be microscopic, or perhaps even subatomic in size. I doubt they'll have verteron emanations, though, unless a fan gets to name them.

Harry can determine the other end of the wormhole by its verteron X-effector, whatever that means.

Puzzles: Did Telek R'Mor make arrangements in his will for *Voyager*'s fate to be passed on to Starfleet? Apparently not, as Starfleet had no idea that the ship was still around when they finally make contact in the fourth season.

Bloopers: When R'Mor first steps off the transporter pad, a woman is suddenly behind Tuvok and Harry at the console. She wasn't there in the previous shot. We can't see her face, but it may be Martha Hackett as Seska, who operates the transporter when R'Mor leaves.

Learn Your Lines: Kes: 'I enjoyed studying anatomy – it'd be interesting to see an autopsy someday.'

Highs: B'Elanna and Harry working so well together. The scene in which they discuss their loved ones (or lack thereof) back home is a definite highlight.

Neelix not being in the episode.

Lows: A lack of really moving/funny/thoughtful/exciting dialogue. None of the dialogue is actually bad – it just isn't at all memorable.

Verdict: One of the best episodes of the first season, by virtue of the clever way that the chance of getting home is first presented, and then removed. For once it isn't a last-minute cheat that kills their hopes, but a well-thought-out twist that is hinted at from the beginning. It's very clever and quite sad. The performances are all decent here too, and there's real chemistry between Wang and Dawson that ought to be played upon more. 9/10.

#108: 'Ex Post Facto'

by Evan Carlos Somers and Michael Piller

Directed by LeVar Burton
Music by Dennis McCarthy
US air date 27-02-95

Plot: Stardate not given. An injured Harry returns from an away mission to report that Paris has been found guilty of murdering a leading scientist on the planet Banea. His punishment is to relive the last moments of the victim every fourteen hours. Tuvok investigates, discovering that Tom had had a fling with the man's wife. When complications threaten brain damage, Tom is moved to the ship, and a rival race, the Numiri, attempt to kidnap him. Tuvok must investigate and discover the real killer.

Déjà Vu?: Punishment by implanted memories was also the theme behind the *DS9* episode 'Hard Time'.

Just about every cliché of film noir – the chain-smoking *femme fatale*, warm rain etc. – also puts in an appearance in this acknowledged pastiche.

Behind the Scenes: The Numiri ships appear to be modified Bajoran ship models from *DS9*.

The alien dog is a Chihuahua whose hair has been teased and blow-dried.

There's a nice out-take from the scene where Tuvok mindmelds with Tom: Tim Russ throws back his head without warning and, in his best James Brown impression, yells 'I'm feeeeelin' *gooooood*!'

***Voyager* Database:** Tuvok has been married for 67 years.

Tom Paris's middle name is Eugene – after Eugene Roddenberry, of course.

Memory engrams from murder victims are used both as evidence at trial, and as punishment.

The old Maquis trick used against the Numiri (see below) was previously used by Chakotay and B'Elanna against two Federation Runabouts (the enlarged shuttles used in *DS9*) near Teluridian IV.

Director Burton was Geordi in *TNG*.

(Lack of) Continuity: Tuvok was presumably married at his first pon farr, as it was established in TOS episode 'Amok Time' that this is when Vulcan arranged marriages are performed. This makes Tuvok due his pon farr in Season Four. Every seventh year of his adult life, a Vulcan male must endure the pon farr (mating cycle). Though able to mate at any time, in this period their hormones are so imbalanced that they *must* mate, or die. The concept was introduced in TOS episode 'Amok Time'.

Ye Canna Change the Laws o' Physics: The Banean heart is best attacked through the intercostal gap between the eighth and ninth right ribs. Third and fourth left for humans.

Memory engrams . . . The concept of using the victim's dying memories is probably a modern updating of the old belief that if you looked in a dead person's eyes you would see the reflection of the last thing he or she saw.

The old Maquis trick used against the Numiri is to vent the LNZ exhaust conduits along the dorsal emitters, and cut engine power to lure the attackers into a false sense of security. The idea of faking damage is an old one, beloved of submariners, who would vent excess oil to make an enemy believe the vessel to be more severely damaged (or destroyed) than it was. None of which explains what the LNZ stands for . . .

Puzzles: The Doctor claims to have asked the captain for a name a week ago, when in fact he asked Kes.

Is the doctor who was a Numiri agent the only one who performs these punishments? If a different man had been picked for the trial, Tom would have been cleared and he'd never have got to implant the stolen data.

Bloopers: When the victim's point of view looks down to see the knife hilt sticking out of him, you can see that McNeill is barefoot. This is presumably to lower his height, because one of the clues is that the real killer is shorter than Tom.

Learn Your Lines: Lidel (on smoking): 'Maybe I kill myself slowly because I don't have the courage to do it quickly.'

Chakotay: 'Out here in the Delta Quadrant, every old trick is new again.' (And more than a few old episodes are 'new' as well!)

Highs: Tuvok out-frosting the ice maiden *femme fatale*.

Lows: A few clichés too many.

Verdict: A straightforward murder mystery of the kind done on just about every weekly drama from time to time. Lidel is a full-fledged *femme fatale*, straight out of film noir – right down to the sultry looks and cigarette. The revelations of the clues and what they mean are all quite clever – though when Tuvok introduces the Chihuahua as a witness it's amusing to imagine him trying to mind-meld with it. It's a nice ensemble piece, and the narrated flashbacks are a nice touch too, but film noir doesn't really work in such a brightly lit show. Still, it was nice of them to try. 7/10.

#109: 'Emanations'

by Brannon Braga

Directed by David Livingston
Music by Jay Chattaway
US air date 13-03-95

Plot: Stardate 48623.5. While investigating habitable asteroids for a new element, Chakotay, Harry and B'Elanna find caves full of dead bodies. A subspace anomaly suddenly deposits another corpse, and takes Harry away in the process. He finds himself in a parallel dimension, whose people believe that our reality is the afterlife, and that he has returned from the dead. Harry also discovers that people are sometimes expected to go to the afterlife while healthy, for the sake of their families, and that his presence – and his tales of caves full of corpses – are upsetting the status quo. Meanwhile, corpses begin arriving on *Voyager*, and one is Patera, a woman brought back to life by the Doctor.

Déjà Vu?: Survival after death has long been a theme in SF and fantasy writing, of course.

Behind the Scenes: Some of the wall panels in the Vhnori rooms are leftover mouldings from the *DS9* sets. Jerry Hardin (Neria) played Samuel Clements (Mark Twain) in *TNG* episode 'Time's Arrow', but is best known as Deep Throat in *The X-Files*.

***Voyager* Database:** On his first away mission, Chakotay accidentally desecrated a grave on Ktaria.

The Ocampa bury their dead, and call the soul the 'comra'.

(Lack of) Continuity: Though not stated, we can assume that Ktaria is the homeworld of the Ktarians from *TNG* episode 'The Game'. This race is not to be confused with the Ktarans, of which race Ensign Wildman's husband is a member.

The Doctor revives Harry with 2 c.c.s of cordrazine – the stimulant that caused so much trouble when Dr McCoy overdosed on it in TOS episode 'City on the Edge of Forever'. Usually in modern *Trek* the updated version, tricordrazine, has been used since *TNG* episode 'Shades of Gray'.

Ye Canna Change the Laws o' Physics: As of 2371 there are 246 known atomic elements (today there are 114, if I recall correctly).

The web surrounding the bodies in the cave is 'some kind of bio-polymer residue'. This turns out to be a result of cell breakdown, having been excreted through skin pores.

The bodies are delivered – and Harry is abducted – by means of a subspace vacuule. A vacuule deposits a body somewhere in the asteroid ring every two hours, although the corresponding ones appear on the Vhnori world every six hours. The vacuules are natural, not created by the Vhnori, who merely take advantage of them, and call them 'spectral ruptures'.

The Vhnori are 'Class 5 humanoids', but there's no indication of what the different classes are. Each body that arrives on *Voyager* releases a burst of neural energy through the hull that is of the same frequency as the ambient radiation in the asteroid belt – perhaps related to the morphic field theorised to be generated by living beings.

Puzzles: So, is there an afterlife, then? At least for the Vhnori? The question is deliberately left open – much of the episode's power derives from the shock of discovering that deeply held and comforting beliefs are untrue, but there is the matter of the energy discharges that flow out to the ring system – suggesting that perhaps something does survive.

Bloopers: The Doctor has a dead body ready to be revived – yet he dresses her first?

The ceremonial shroud, which is reminiscent of mummy bandages, is passed down from generation to generation. But how come? When the cenotaph first pulls Harry in, his uniform comes with him, even though the (presumably shroud-wrapped) bodies are delivered naked. Then, when Harry goes through again, wrapped in the shroud, he arrives naked too (or at least bare-shouldered).

There's plenty of room in the cenotaph for Harry to avoid the little poles that touch his neck to kill him, so why doesn't he?

Learn Your Lines: Janeway: 'What we don't know about death is far greater than what we do know.'

Highs: Harry's conversations with the thanatologist, and how quickly he realises his error in this first-contact situation, and attempts to make good.

Most of the dialogue about the possibility (or lack) of an afterlife.

Lows: Patera is disposed of rather carelessly, as if Braga was unsure how to write her out.

Verdict: Wow. Another candidate for the best episode of the season, if not the series. Garrett gives a great performance while Jerry Hardin is a very likable character, despite his sinister job. Best of all, the script is extremely thoughtful and intelligent, with less technobabble than usual. The debate over what happens after death is well handled, with adequate cases being made both for and against an afterlife. This episode may not quite be up there with *TNG*'s 'The Inner Light' or *DS9*'s 'The Visitor', but it's pretty close. 10/10.

#110: 'Prime Factors'

by Michael Perricone, Greg Elliot and Jeri Taylor
from a story by Perricone, Elliot, David R. George III
and Eric Stillwell

Directed by Les Landau
Music by Jay Chattaway
US air date 20-03-95

Plot: Stardate 48642.5. The ship is greeted by the Sikarians, who offer the crew shore leave and gifts. When Harry discovers that the Sikarians possess a spatial trajector that could get the ship at least halfway home in an instant, things look up for the crew. However, when the Sikarians refuse to allow this, the stage is set for some crewmen to take matters into their own hands to get the technology.

Déjà Vu?: An ancient race seeking the newest fads to keep them amused was also seen in the *Doctor Who* story 'The Greatest Show in the Galaxy', though the Sikarians are rather friendlier than the Gods of Ragnarok.

Voyager **Database:** One of the Delaney sisters is called Jenny. She is now seeing a crewman called Murphy, after Harry fell out of the gondola ride they were taking on the holodeck.

Because of the spatial trajector's requirements (see below) it could never be compatible with Federation technology.

(Lack of) Continuity: Ships' deflector dishes were originally meant to clear micrometeoroids out of the ship's path. In modern *Trek*s, however, they've become a catch-all tool, used as a weapon (*TNG* – 'Best of Both Worlds') and a more general power tool (*Star Trek: Generations*). Throughout the series it will become as much a handy get-out-of-jail-free card as Seven's nanoprobes.

According to Seska, fighting is still going on in the demilitarised zone between Federation and Cardassian space, as seen in the *DS9* story 'The Maquis' and other episodes.

Ye Canna Change the Laws o' Physics: Alastria is a binary system 40,000 light years from Sikaris, or 2.5 billion Sikarian AUs – which tells us that Sikara is 94.08 million miles from its sun.

The atmospheric sensor operates on nonlinear resonance, adjusting to atmospheric resonance. Its chimes indicate atmospheric conditions.

The spatial trajector works by space-folding. This leaves a subspace residue – a neutrino dispersion pattern – from forming a neutrino bubble around the object to be transported. Carey thinks that using the deflector dish to generate phase neutrinos might form a bubble around the ship, which would allow it to be trajected. Tetrahedral quartz crystals in Sikara's mantle are needed to generate a sufficient neutrino envelope. Antineutrinos are an unexpected catalyst for space-folding. The process raises the warp plasma temperature to 50 million Kelvin.

In real life, neutrinos are chargeless, massless particles which can go straight through practically anything. Their spin is important, because in beta-decay the energy, momentum and spin of neutrinos are not conserved, in violation of the expected laws of physics. Presumably, in *Trek* science, forming a bubble of them around the ship eases transport by space folding, which itself remains unexplained.

Puzzles: If the trajector needs the quartz in Sikaris's mantle to work, then how is it still able to return Harry and Eudana from Alastria? Even if Alastria has an identical mantle, there would have been no guarantee of that until someone installed the trajector, and tried it.

Why isn't B'Elanna given thirty days in the brig, as Tom will be in Season Five? Their offences are comparable.

Learn Your Lines: Eudana: 'Stories are an essential part of every person's being. I would never share one without permission.'

Janeway: 'You can use logic to justify anything. That's its power – and its flaw.'

Highs: The way in which Seska, B'Elanna, Carey and Tuvok all come to the right conclusion.

Lows: Janeway simpering over Gath. She does something like this once a season, and it always goes hideously wrong.

Verdict: This was actually the first episode I saw, before the series reached British shores. A bit of a mixed bag. Slow to start, with the real point of the episode – the conflict over the Prime Directive – not addressed until the last couple of scenes. This means that the consequences of their actions aren't fully dealt with, because there isn't enough time left in the episode. The episode does succeed, however, in the way its narrative flow introduces and uses the characters: Gath invites Janeway to Sicaria; Janeway invites the crew, which leads Harry to discover the trajector; Harry leads to B'Elanna; B'Elanna to Seska and Carey; then eventually to Tuvok. It's all very well handled, but ultimately a triumph only in the technical aspects of storytelling, rather than the creative ones. 5/10.

#111: 'State of Flux'

by Chris Abbott
from a story by Paul Coyle

Directed by Robert Scheerer
Music by Dennis McCarthy
US air date 10-04-95

Plot: Stardate 48658.2. A Kazon-Nistrim ship following *Voyager* is damaged by an explosion, and investigations reveal that the disaster was caused by the failure of an attempt to integrate a Federation replicator into their systems. It soon looks like Seska has been selling *Voyager*'s technology to them – but is she guilty, or is she being framed? Either way, she seems to have lied about her medical background.

Déjà Vu?: A Kazon warrior is fused into the wall on the damaged ship, in a prop reminiscent of the Cyberman fused into the door in the *Doctor Who* story 'Earthshock'.

Seska's red face after trying to get at the console on the Kazon ship is very like Richard Dreyfuss's two-face look in *Close Encounters of the Third Kind*.

Behind the Scenes: Anthony de Longis thought from his few lines with Janeway in the script that his character Culluh would be romancing Janeway. In spite of learning otherwise very quickly, there is a sexual tension between them, which is sadly absent from later episodes.

***Voyager* Database:** Leola root – the basis for Neelix's famous stew (and, in fact, most of his dishes) – debuts in this episode, found on the nameless planet. The taste of the thing is bad enough to make even Chakotay change his facial expression. Genevieve Bujold plays a character called Leola in the film *Pinocchio* – it's possible the revolting root was named for her!

Kazon ships use 'masking circuitry', not a cloaking device. Mushroom soup is Chakotay's favourite.

Neosorium composite is used only in Federation technology. Bioneural fibres in the pattern buffer relays prove the components must be from *Voyager*. (Since it's a new ship, with the first use of bioneural gel packs, no other Federation ship would have them.)

Tuvok is an expert gin player, beating Chakotay by 94 points.

(Lack of) Continuity: Though the Kazon overall were introduced in 'Caretaker', this episode introduces both the Kazon-Nistrim sect and First Maje Culluh of the Nistrim, who will become recurring villains until the opening of Season Three. Neelix says the Nistrim are one of the most violent sects in the Kazon Collective.

The Cardassians had previously altered Kira's DNA to appear Cardassian in the *DS9* episode 'Second Skin'. The truth of Seska's origins is a follow-on and reversal from that precedent.

Transporter pattern-enhancers debuted in *TNG* episode 'Power Play' and make their first *Voyager* appearance here.

When Tuvok suggests the possibility of another Federation ship having preceded them to the Delta Quadrant, Janeway says that none have been reported missing, to her knowledge. She is, of course, wrong: we'll later discover that the private vessel *Raven* and the science ship USS *Equinox* were drawn to the Delta Quadrant by the Borg and the Caretaker respectively, both prior to *Voyager*'s arrival.

Ye Canna Change the Laws o' Physics: Fluctuating nucleonic radiation is postulated as a sign of the Kazon reactor breaking down, and may be what fused one Kazon into the wall. It turns out that the Federation technology given to the Kazon was a food replicator. The interior shielding was too thin, and, when nucleonic radiation leaked out, a cascade reaction was inevitable. Again, all radiation produced by matter-to-energy conversion is nucleonic.

The Kazon survivor's cells have mutated, bonding with metallic compounds. A complete pyrocyte replacement and cytological screening are performed on him by the Doctor in an attempt to save him. Cytology is the study of cells in medicine.

Puzzles: Seska is merely said to be a Cardassian agent. It's not explicitly stated whether this means she's simply a soldier sent undercover, or that she is a proper member of the Obsidian Order.

How come we were never told of her and Chakotay's relationship before? That would have gone a long way to making her treason more of a shock.

Edible mushrooms grow on an alien planet in the Delta Quadrant? Even that makes more sense than the idea of using highly radioactive technology to produce food from replicators.

Bloopers: Robert Beltran audibly has a bit of a cold in the scene where he confronts Seska in sickbay.

Learn Your Lines: Chakotay (to Tuvok): 'You were working for her, she was working for them . . . Was anyone on board that ship working for me?'

Janeway: 'I'm really pretty easy to get along with most of the time. But I don't like bullies, I don't like threats, and I don't like you.'

Highs: The scenes between Tuvok and Chakotay – especially the closing one.

The caves are more realistic than usual – complete with dripping water.

Lows: Chakotay and Seska being unconvincing as old flames.

Neelix's demonstration of the effects of the kaylo.

Verdict: The beginning of *Voyager*'s first real story arc, which will stretch through until the Season Three premier. It's certainly an intriguing enough story, with emphasis more on mystery than technobabble, and some reasonable characterisation. Sadly, Seska's guilt is obvious thanks to Martha Hackett overacting somewhat.

The Kazon still aren't much of a threat, looking like little more than intergalactic tramps, though Mulgrew and de Longis play their scene in sickbay with almost sexual tension – just watch the tilt of her head. It's also nice to see a Vulcan being brought into a game less 'intellectual' than chess.

The highlights of the episode are certainly the Tuvok/ Chakotay scenes. There's a definite sharpness between the pair that causes not sparks but the sort of ominous feeling of an approaching storm. It's still very much a bottle show, apart from a brief foray out to the usual patch of desert (the equivalent of *Doctor Who* and *Blake's 7*'s sandpit), and some leftover sets made to look trashed, but the obvious launch of an arc is still an exciting moment. And Seska's 'to survive we must make alliances' is something that Janeway will eventually come to agree with. 7/10.

#112: 'Heroes and Demons'

by Naren Shankar

Directed by Les Landau
Music by Dennis McCarthy
US air date 24-04-95

Plot: Stardate 48693.2. Harry, Chakotay and Tuvok disappear from the holodeck while a holonovel of *Beowulf* is running. An outside influence is affecting the program and threatening the ship and crew, and so it falls to the Doctor to enter the holodeck and find out the truth. Once there, he discovers that the fictional monster, Grendel, poses some real dangers, even to a hologram.

Déjà Vu?: The holodeck goes wonky, trapping crew

members inside with all the safeties off. Like that never happened before. Or since . . .

Behind the Scenes: Bob Picardo describes the episode as '*Alice in Wonderland* with a bald, middle-aged, cranky, arrogant Alice . . .'

Marjorie Monaghan (Freya) is best known as number one in *B5*.

Selections from the music score are available on the GNP/Crescendo CD *The Best of Star Trek*, GNPD 8053.

When Tom transfers the Doctor to the holodeck, the sound effect starts off with the beginning of the transporter dematerialisation, and segues into the usual Doctor deactivation sound.

For the first time, the faint melody before the main theme is absent from the closing credits.

Voyager **Database:** Holodecks are an outgrowth of transporter matter/energy-conversion technology.

The Doctor chooses Schweitzer as his name, but then abandons it, because he doesn't want to be reminded of the painful time it was last spoken – by the dying Freya.

The Doctor also seems to have working tastebuds, when he samples elk in the Vikings' hall. But it *is* holographic elk . . .

It seems that the Doctor and Freya are definitely flirting, though he doesn't know how to handle it. This question of holograms romancing will be further addressed several times later in the series.

(Lack of) Continuity: Tuvok says there are no demons in Vulcan lore. This contradicts several (noncanon) novels.

Ye Canna Change the Laws o' Physics: Freya claims to be the daughter of Hrothgar, the Danish king in *Beowulf*. In fact she was the twin of Frey, and both were the offspring of Njord and Nerthus. Freya was said to be still alive in the thirteenth century, and was the goddess of love affairs in Alfheim. In this respect she's probably another avatar of the Faerie Queen. In the episode, she claims to have burned Scyld the Gardane's hall to the ground, and fought the Heatho-bobs. The latter is perhaps an in-joke about 'Bob' Picardo, since the script says 'heatho-bards' and that's definitely not what she says.

While the costumes and set of the hall create atmosphere, the swords are way off. They're very much post-Norman swords of the early Middle Ages (big, six-foot things), and not the type of short stabbing weapons that would be right for Norse culture in the sixth to eighth centuries.

Freya says the mushroom Attuta is taken for 'berserking'. The Doctor identifies this as *Amanita muscaria*, a poisonous fungus, and proceeds to give (quite correct) highlights of its effects. Otherwise known as the Fly Amanita, this mushroom produces ibotenic acid and muscarine. If consumed, it causes abdominal cramps, nausea, vomiting and violent diarrhoea, eight to twelve hours after consumption. Jaundice and potentially fatal cyanosis are also possible within three days. It is also, however, a hallucinogenic, and Freya was correct about warriors of the period consuming it in the hope of giving them berserk qualities.

Photonic energy has leaked into the holodeck matter/energy nodes. If the disappeared crewmen's molecular patterns still exist, then they can be restored. It turns out they had been converted to energy and held in a photonic lattice, which is either a shelter or a ship.

The photonic Grendel is recognised as a life form by having synaptic patterns. In fact synapses are gaps *between* neurons, across which signals are sent. If this was supposed to mean it has a recognisable brain, the Doc should have said 'neural patterns'.

Grendel's taking the Doctor's arm seems unlikely – surely it would drain energy from him equally all around.

Puzzles: Why does the Doctor need to read *Beowulf* from a PADD (Personal-Access Display Device)? Can't he just download it into his memory, as was done with all the various medical texts he knows? (We see this being done in 'Message in a Bottle'.) For that matter, why does he need to tap his combadge to speak to someone in any episode? Since the computer generates him and routes communications, and his combadge is illusory anyway, he should just be able to direct speech to whoever or wherever he wants.

Why does Tom transfer the Doctor to the holodeck from

sickbay? Surely this is a job for B'Elanna, who arranged the technology in the first place.

Bloopers: The *Beowulf* holonovel is set in winter – both Hrothgar and Freya describe the season as such. However, the forest is lush and green, and neither Tuvok nor Chakotay seem troubled by the night-time temperature. (If it really is mid-winter in Scandinavia, it should be well below freezing.)

Learn Your Lines: Freya: 'He was like no other. Hair straight and raven-black; eyes bright with fierce fire – the burning gaze of a hero.' Tuvok: 'Grand eloquence notwith-standing, that would qualify as a description of Mr Kim.'

Highs: The first really noteworthy musical score since the pilot episode – it's quite heroic and rousing, and makes a nice change from the homogenised *Voyager* in-house style that has permeated the series so far.

The Doctor's version of telling tales of his exploits to impress the warriors is also worth seeing.

Lows: Actually, there aren't any cringe-inducing moments that spring to mind.

Verdict: The Doctor's first away mission is good fun. Despite some iffy accents and mangling of myth, this is a hugely suc-cessful episode. The acting is pretty good all round. More importantly, the Doctor is developed, with the first real chance for Picardo to shine. And, as holodeck-malfunction stories go, it has a nice line in surprises and plot developments. 8/10.

#113: 'Cathexis'

by Brannon Braga
from a story by him and Joe Menosky

Directed by Kim Friedman
Music by Jay Chattaway
US air date: 01-05-95

Plot: Stardate 48734.2. A shuttle returns from a nebula, bearing an unconscious Tuvok (who recovers) and a brain-dead

Chakotay. As Janeway tries to investigate, something begins possessing members of the crew, and sabotaging all attempts to investigate what happened in the dark-matter nebula. Meanwhile, Janeway has also begun indulging in a holonovel, where she's the governess to a pair of rather odd children in a spooky nineteenth-century mansion.

Déjà Vu?: The body-hopping incorporeal alien that turns out to be Chakotay's consciousness is handled in a manner very similar to that in 'Lonely Among Us', way back in *TNG*'s first season. The Komar, the evil entity, bears some resemblance to the RedJac entity in TOS episode 'Wolf in the Fold'. There's a similar struggle for the *Enterprise* in *TNG* episode 'Power Play', in which Riker, Troi and O'Brien are possessed. Likewise, *DS9* has its share of personality takeovers, first in 'Dramatis Personae' and then later in 'The Assignment', and subsequent episodes dealing with the battle between Pah Wraiths and Prophets.

Not forgetting the 1980 version of *The Thing*, and the original story it was based on, *Who Goes There?*

Behind the Scenes: The holonovel scene was originally written and shot for 'Eye of the Needle' but that episode was overrunning, so the sequence ended up in this episode.

When the ship leaves the nebula, the crewman standing behind Harry looks to be Alexander Enberg, who will later play Vorik. It's hard to tell, as his back is to us.

No reason is given for Tuvok's now wearing lieutenant's rank pips – it's an unofficial retcon (and officially a 'correction') because some people had been confused at his not being first officer when he technically outranked Chakotay. From here, we're supposed to take it as read that he was always just a lieutenant.

Carolyn Seymour (Mrs Templeton) has twice played a Romulan in *TNG* and was Abby Grant in *Survivors*.

***Voyager* Database:** Janeway's holonovel debuts. In it, she plays Mrs Davenport, the governess to Henry and Beatrice, the children of Lord Burleigh, whose household has a skeleton in the cupboard. For the most part, Janeway is confused by the kids, fancied by Lord Burleigh, and resented by housekeeper Mrs Templeton. She is instructed never to go to the fourth floor.

Tom used to read holo comic books.

A magneton scanner is the most thorough sensor on the ship.

(Lack of) Continuity: Kes's psi powers, first apparent in 'Time and Again', are developing further: as well as knowing that a Lt Hargrove had been in sickbay a few hours before her, she also senses the intruder.

From here onwards, until his promotion in Season Four, Tuvok wears only a lieutenant's two pips, rather than his previous Lieutenant-Commander's pips.

When the warp core is shut down, it takes two hours to regenerate the dilithium matrix. In the old days it would take a day or so.

Ye Canna Change the Laws o' Physics: The Doctor diagnoses Chakotay as brain-dead. Neural energy has been drained from every axon and dendrite right down to the synapses. Axons are large nerve fibres in the brain, and dendrites are their smaller branches.

Tuvok claims the shuttle was attacked by a ship that came out of a 'dark-matter nebula'. Dark matter is a theoretical substance proposed to explain the fact that there isn't enough known matter in the universe to account for all of its mass.

The medicine wheel is said to represent the universe and mind. Vision quests or dreams are walking the wheel, but when someone is in a coma they're lost outside the wheel. The Doctor – who has been programmed with psychospiritual medical systems – says that B'Elanna's misplacing of the Coyote Stone on the medicine wheel will lead Chakotay's soul into the mountains of the antelope women.

The ion trail Tuvok claims to have found shows no subspace distortions, which means that whatever made it had no engines. (And by implication that it therefore didn't exist, and the trail is a fake.) Why ions should affect subspace is unknown to me.

The Komar, the alien villains of the piece, are highly coherent energy pulses with a biomatrix. According to the magneton scan, the Komar are trionic-based energy, and feed on neural energy. Apart from the neural-energy bit, that's all made-up science. Essentially, though, they're psychic vampires.

Puzzles: What the hell does 'Cathexis' mean anyway?

It takes three neural transceivers, two cortical stimulators, and fifty gigaquads of computer memory to reintegrate Chakotay's consciousness with his body. Despite the mention of the equipment used to re-embody Chakotay, there's no indication of where his consciousness physically was for the Doctor to have worked with it. It can't have been in the computer memory, or he wouldn't have needed to possess people to operate consoles. Presumably he more openly took over some volunteer, and delivered himself to sickbay so the Doctor could do a personality transplant.

Bloopers: Tom refers to Kes having received a Vulcan neck pinch rather than a Vulcan nerve pinch (though TOS scripts often referred to it as the FSNP – famous Spock neck pinch).

When Harry picks up energy pulses heading towards *Voyager* from the nebula, he is actually looking at a clearly visible display of the ship, on which the words 'vehicle status' are legible.

Learn Your Lines: Doc (re Tom's childhood): 'Other than his irritating lapses into nostalgia, I see nothing wrong with him.'

Highs: Some genuine paranoia, even if it is ripped off from *The Thing*.

Lows: The usual fish-eye lens for dreams/hallucinations/disembodied aliens from *TNG* reappears, though at least they've added a disguising filter over it.

Verdict: Quite a fun story, if spectacularly unoriginal. The alien presence could take over anyone at any time, and it's quite a surprise when the true nature of the sabotage – and the presence of a second intruder – become apparent. The mystery is maintained relatively well, though when Kes is attacked it's obvious that damage to the neck when in the presence of a Vulcan is down to the Vulcan nerve pinch. It's rather let down by a lack of motivation for the aliens, and a real mishmash of beliefs where Chakotay's spirit is concerned. Tim Russ is good, giving a subtly different, edgier performance. Given the attention paid to trying to make Chakotay look good in later episodes, it's quite amusing to see that this is one of his finest moments. 6/10.

#114: 'Faces'

by Ken Biller

Directed by Rick Kolbe
Music by David Bell
US air date 08-05-95

Plot: Stardate 48784.2. An away team consisting of Tom, Lt Durst and B'Elanna has been captured by the Vidiians. Tom and Durst have been put to work in the mines, but B'Elanna has been split into two halves – one complete Klingon and one complete human – by a scientist who thinks that Klingon DNA may provide a cure for the Phage. While Chakotay attempts a rescue, the two B'Elannas must work together to escape.

Déjà Vu?: Splitting people into two isn't unusual in *Trek*. TOS episode 'The Enemy Within' (which introduced the Vulcan nerve pinch) had two Kirks – one good, one evil – later spoofed in the *Red Dwarf* episode 'Demons and Angels'. *TNG* episode 'Second Chances' has a duplicate Riker. Even the novels had two Spocks in *Spock Must Die*.

The Avery system may refer to Avery Brooks.

Like the Daleks, the Vidiians prefer living slaves to dig tunnels, when machines would be more effective.

Behind the Scenes: 'Faces' was actually Ken Biller's second script, though it aired first. It's his favourite of his three first-season scripts. The original draft involved no Vidiians, but was set on a 'Nazi' planet, where the natives force B'Elanna into the genotron as part of a programme of genetic purification. He also feels that the Vidiian scientist, Sulon, falls in love with B'Elanna, in a Beauty-and-the-Beast thing.

The Vidiian security console in the main lab appears to be a revamp of the Klingon Bird of Prey weapons console often used in *DS9*.

Voyager **Database:** Neelix has been experimenting with the crew's native foods. Apart from the Plomeek soup, he has made corn salad for Chakotay, and peanut butter and jelly sandwiches for Tom.

The crew are searching for magnesite deposits on the third planet of the Avery system.

The first symptoms of the Phage are excruciating joint pain, from which some sufferers die.

B'Elanna and her mother were the only Klingons on Kessik IV at a time of tension between Klingons and the Federation. Her father left when she was five, and B'Elanna tried to hide her forehead with hats and scarves, hoping he'd return if she didn't look Klingon. Tom hid his head too, to conceal the haircuts his father made him have on the first day of summer.

Ayalla is in Harry's station.

Klingon females are renowned for their sexual appetites as well as physical prowess. (And that's just at conventions.)

Tuvok displays an unexpected talent for tailoring, as he makes Vidiian clothes for Chakotay's disguise. Hmm. 'Plain, simple Tuvok, the tailor . . .'

B'Elanna admires her Klingon half's strength and bravery – but not her social skills.

(Lack of) Continuity: Lt Durst was introduced with a large role in the previous episode, thus making his fate here more effective, as he isn't just a nobody that we never saw before.

Plomeek soup here is red, as opposed to green in TOS episode 'Amok Time'. Whether this is a blooper or a deliberate indication of Neelix's dubious culinary skills is open to debate. However, he does admit to changing the recipe, so I'll give it the benefit of the doubt.

Ye Canna Change the Laws o' Physics: Magnesite is magnesium carbonate – it's used for the refractory lining in furnaces, and for insulation.

The fully Klingon B'Elanna is made by a device called the

'genotron', running a biomatrix. To reconstitute her genome, it converted her Klingon matter to energy, promoting cell division and enhanced mitosis, which then rematerialised as a pure Klingon. This sounds like some kind of hybrid transporter/replicator.

Lack of Klingon DNA compromises the ability of B'Elanna's cells to synthesise proteins – which would obviously be fatal.

Puzzles: Is Janeway amnesiac? In 'Phage' she warns the Vidiians that if they mess with *Voyager* again she'll kick their asses halfway across the quadrant. Here they mess with *Voyager* again, killing a crewman, and she . . . does absolutely nothing!

Why extract all of B'Elanna's Klingon DNA when a single cell would have done the job?

Why do the Vidiians use slaves to dig their tunnels, instead of machines? Worse still, why use strong slaves, and take organs from the weak. The other way round would make more sense, if they wanted to have long-lasting organs!

Learn Your Lines: Sulon: 'I think Klingons are the most impressive species I've ever seen.'

Doctor: 'If you think this is remarkable, you should see me remove a bunion.'

Tom (to B'Elanna): 'Sometimes fear can be a good thing: it keeps you from taking unnecessary chances. Courage doesn't mean that you don't have fear. It means that you've learned to overcome it.' This is particularly noteworthy with hindsight after the fifth-season episode 'Extreme Risk'.

Highs: Roxann's performance as a human.

The scene in the cave where the two B'Elannas work out their differences.

Lows: Dawson's performance as a Klingon. Sexy as hell, but that delivery is excruciatingly stiff.

Verdict: A much more successful and nasty outing for the Vidiians than 'Phage'. A point in the show's favour is that the main Vidiian isn't exactly evil per se, but he does such terrible things in pursuit of his goals. A bit like certain real-life researchers down through the centuries. Roxann Dawson, usually reliable, is variable here. As a human, with a deeper part to play, she's very good; sadly she's hopelessly stilted as a Klingon. Brian Markinson is also excellent, being quite a contrast to his role as Durst in the previous episode. The actual plot is no great shakes – crew get captured, tortured and escape – but it's well handled, and brings out some good themes. 6/10.

#115: 'Jetrel'

by Ken Biller

Directed by Kim Friedman
Music by Dennis McCarthy
US air date 15-05-95

Plot: Stardate 48832.1. The ship is greeted by Ma'bor Jetrel (James Sloyan), inventor of the weapon that destroyed Neelix's home colony, who is seeking help with a cure for a disease Neelix may have. As the pair learn about each other, and themselves, it becomes apparent that both have secrets, and neither is quite telling the truth.

Déjà Vu?: The plotline of a scientific war criminal offering aid to the crew is reminiscent of the *Babylon 5* (*B5*) episode 'Deathwalker', though this version is superior.

Much of Jetrel's doubt and search for redemption is clearly based on opinions expressed after World War Two by scientists who worked on the Manhattan Project, which created the atomic bomb. The descriptions of the victims of Rinax are similar enough to nuclear blast victims to reinforce this.

The 'Ka'Ree' of course, are the Narn government in *Babylon 5*, misspelling notwithstanding . . .

Behind the Scenes: Ken Biller conceived the idea as 'what if a Nagasaki survivor confronted Oppenheimer?' He feels that Neelix lies when he forgives Jetrel at the end, just to give him peace in his last moments.

James Sloyan played Dr Mora Pol (Odo's 'father') in *DS9*.

***Voyager* Database:** Sandrine's pool table rolls a little to the east, according to the hustler, though he may just be winding Tuvok up.

The Haakonian Order conquered Talax 15 years ago, after a twelve-year war. Neelix lived on the moon colony of Rinax, which had a temperate climate before the metreon cascade. The metreon cascade wiped out 300,000 colonists, including all of Neelix's family, vaporising them by biomolecular disintegration. Neelix was one of the rescuers who went there afterwards, to find the moon clouded with a perpetual nuclear winter.

Metraemia is a degenerative blood disease caused by exposure to metreon isotopes, whose decay rates are highly variable. It causes blood cells to undergo fission.

(Lack of) Continuity: This is the first time we see the Doctor use the ability to deactivate himself, using the command, 'Computer: override command one EMH alpha, and end program.' In future episodes he will generally just say 'Computer, deactivate EMH.'

Ye Canna Change the Laws o' Physics: Electrostatic properties in the nuclear-winter cloud around Rinax hold disassembled biomatter – the vaporised victims – in animated suspension. Jetrel believes that the transporter can be used to effect regenerative fusion, and restore the victims. However, the attempt fails, as the degree of fragmentation is too great for the transporter's biogenic field. In other words, bits of the victims are scattered in a dust cloud, but it would be too much of a strain for the transporters to put them back together again.

Puzzles: Why was Jetrel given voice command over the computer to the extent of being able to deactivate the Doctor?

Is Haakon a separate planet or not? Jetrel describes it as his country, rather than his planet.

Shouldn't Jetrel have disintegrated upon death, if metraemia does in fact cause cellular fission, akin to the way the cascade's victims were vaporised?

Bloopers: The transporter has a biogenic field? Usually in *Trek* that phrase is an indication of life in whatever object has such a field. Presumably it was slipped in by mistake when they meant biofilters, an oft-referred-to piece of the transporter's mechanism.

Learn Your Lines: Neelix: 'Peace of mind is a relative thing, Captain.'

Jetrel: 'Something as large as science will not stop for something as small as man.'

Jetrel: 'It's good to know how the world works. It is not possible to be a scientist unless you believe that all the knowledge of the universe, and all the power that it bestows, is of intrinsic value to everyone. And one must share that knowledge, and allow it to be applied. . . . And then be willing to live with the consequences.'

Highs: The whole scene in sickbay where Jetrel explains his motivations to Neelix, and Neelix replies with his definition of 'consequences'. I could have quoted Neelix's definition in the **Learn Your Lines** section, but it really does need the performance for full effect.

Lows: Neelix didn't have the disease. It would have been more powerful still if he had.

Verdict: A total revelation. To date, Ethan Phillips's Neelix has been an unsuccessful and somewhat irritating attempt to replicate the success of Quark in *DS9*. The idea of giving him a solo heavy-drama episode is a recipe for disaster . . . yet somehow it works. Phillips proves to be very good in this emotional character-drama type of scene. There's nothing wrong with Phillips's or Sloyan's excellent performances, which really touch plenty of emotional nerves. Some of the dialogue is downright poetic, and delivered perfectly. 9.5/10.

#116: 'Learning Curve'

by Ronald Wilkerson, Jean Louise Matthias and Jeri Taylor

Directed by David Livingston
Music by Jay Chattaway
US air date 22-05-95

Plot: Stardate 48846.5. While a series of breakdowns plague the ship as a result of a viral infection in the bioneural gel packs, Tuvok is put in charge of a group of Maquis crewmen who need extra training in Starfleet protocols – which is an uphill struggle, to say the least.

Déjà Vu?: Well, take your pick from *Stripes*, *Full Metal Jacket*, *Private Benjamin*, *Police Academy* . . .
   In Janeway's holonovel, Henry is Viscount Timmin, perhaps a reference to Timmin in the *Doctor Who* story 'The Caves of Androzani'.

Behind the Scenes: The backpacks are the ones that debuted in *TNG* episode 'Chain Of Command' Part I.
   The faint intro melody to the closing theme is heard again.

***Voyager* Database:** Janeway's holonovel is filed as 'program Janeway lambda-four', and the holodeck is stated to be on Deck 6.
   The bioneural gel packs run half of the ship's essential systems, and are 'virtually impossible to damage'. They operate in energy grids: grid beta-four runs the holodeck, while the 'forward grid' controls replicators, which are inoperable when that grid is off line.
   Tuvok taught at Starfleet Academy for sixteen years. Academy specifications for training include physical training, academic studies and holodeck simulations.
   Plasma gas from ruptured EPS conduits is toxic in minutes.

(Lack of) Continuity: Tuvok insists that Gerron's Bajoran earring is against the Starfleet dress code. However, he is mistaken, as both Ro in *TNG* and Kira in the final season of *DS9* wear the earring with the uniform.
   Degaussing the transporter room with the microresonator takes 26.3 hours, as opposed to five minutes with the magneton scanner. This contradicts 'Cathexis', in which the latter device was described as the ship's most powerful internal sensor.

Since Cargo Bay 2 is the airponics bay, presumably the one we see here is Cargo Bay 1.

Ye Canna Change the Laws o' Physics: The virus affecting the gel packs is small enough to reside inside bacteria. In fact, all viruses are small enough to live within bacteria – the largest known viruses are poxviruses, only 450 nanometres across.

To cure it, a plasma burst from a symmetric warp field is needed. This entails setting the warp drive to 80 per cent power while remaining stationary, and inverting the warp field to affect the inside of the ship. Given that previously we were told the warp field is a huge electrical field that would fry everything, and that plasma is superheated ionised gas, this would surely be self-destructive to the ship and crew.

Puzzles: The phrase 'a symmetric warp field' is odd. Do they mean 'a symmetrical' warp field, or 'an asymmetric' one? Either way, somebody probably goofed.

Bloopers: When the temperature on the bridge is 360 Kelvin, and Tom claims to be 'ready to pass out', nobody is breaking a sweat. They do so after the symmetric warp field has taken effect.

Learn Your Lines: Possibly the worst line in *Star Trek* history as B'Elanna says, 'Get the cheese to sickbay – the Doctor should look at it as soon as possible.'

Tuvok: 'The strongest tactical move is always the one in which you will reap the highest gain at the lowest cost.'

Highs: A few teensy smiles from the team of losers, and Tuvok's exasperation with them. The Doctor's bedside manner with the cheese.

Lows: Spectacular in its lack of originality.

Verdict: There is some good here, and Tim Russ is particularly fine. Unfortunately, it's exactly the same as any military boot-camp comedy drama you've ever seen. All of the Maquis trainees are utterly one-dimensional stereotypes (the loudmouth troublemaker, the quiet one, the fat one, the lone woman among men), and you can see every twist coming a mile away. Well shot and acted, but unimaginative and derivative. The B story about the malfunctioning gel packs is at least mildly original, albeit leading to some utter silliness where the cause is concerned. At least Picardo saves those scenes too. 6/10.

The next four episodes were produced as part of Season One, but held back to air at the beginning of Season Two in the US. Since the UK video releases grouped them with Season One, this is a UK-published book, and the stardates were not redubbed to fit into Season Two, I'm including them in this section.

You'll notice the airdates are out of order. In the US, the schedule for the first five episodes of Season Two went: 'The 37's', 'Initiations', 'Projections', 'Elogium', 'Twisted', 'Non Sequitur', and then the rest of Season Two.

#117: 'Projections'

by Brannon Braga

Directed by Jonathan Frakes
Music by David Bell
US air date 11-09-95

Plot: Stardate 48892.1. The Doctor is activated to discover that the ship has been overrun by the Kazon, and the crew have abandoned ship. His puzzlement increases when he is wounded, and discovers that he is human while everyone else is holographic. Before long, he is joined by Reg Barclay, who insists that the Doctor is Lewis Zimmerman, and that *Voyager* is a holosimulation to test the new EMH, but that it has gone wrong and affected Zimmerman's memory. More bizarre still, Kes is his wife! Barclay tells him that to shut down the simulation he must destroy the ship. But what is really going on?

Note that since almost the entire episode is a delusion of the Doctor's, entries in the **Database**, **Continuity**, **Laws o' Physics**, and **Bloopers** sections below may not be binding!

Any contradictions or problems can be written off as a corruption of the Doctor's program while he's in trouble.

Déjà Vu?: *TNG* episode 'Frame Of Mind' also featured hallucinations within hallucinations.

Behind the Scenes: Bob Picardo says that, between him and Dwight Schultz, shooting this episode was like having a party. Schultz is best known as Murdock in *The A-Team*.

***Voyager* Database:** The EMH is auto-initiated by a shipwide red alert.

There is a mention of sewage and waste reclamation, as a section on the ship. This is probably *Trek*'s first open mention that humans still need toilets in the twenty-fourth century.

The full designation of the EMH program in sickbay is 'EMH program AK-one, diagnostic and surgical subroutine omega three-two-three.'

The holographic memory core for the ship is in Engineering, on the far side of the warp core from the main doors.

Barclay was in reality part of the Holodoc design team, and was in charge of testing the Doctor's interpersonal skills.

(Lack of) Continuity: Reg Barclay was previously a member of the *Enterprise-D*'s engineering staff, and was somewhat neurotic, preferring to hide in the holodeck rather than face his fears.

The stardate is said to be six months after 'Caretaker'. Normally each season equates to one year for the characters. The Doctor also says that he was activated on Stardate 48308.2 – he's wrong. *Voyager* set off on Stardate 48315.6. If the Doctor had said 48318.2, it'd match up.

Even at maximum setting, it would take a phaser a sustained burst to punch through the warp core's duranium casing. Maximum was set in *TNG* as Level 16, which would blow out the wall of a room, or even level a building. In *Star Trek: First Contact*, Picard says a phaser on maximum would vaporise him.

Ye Canna Change the Laws o' Physics: A kinoplasmic radiation burst is blamed for everything by Barclay. The etymology suggests a mobile form of radioactive gas.

If Neelix was allergic to tomatoes, it could theoretically kill him by anaphylactic shock – there has been quite a scare over fatal cases of peanut allergy in recent years.

Puzzles: Why would the Doc imagine Kes as his wife?

When was Barclay part of the Holodoc design team – he was still on the *Enterprise* at least until *First Contact*, which was contemporary with the early episodes of *Voyager*'s third season.

Bloopers: When the Doctor goes to the computer terminal after touching a gauze pad to his head, his wound disappears with the change of shot.

Learn Your Lines: Neelix (looking at a large red stain on his jacket): 'Am I going to die?' Doctor: 'Not unless you're allergic to tomatoes.'

Chakotay: 'It doesn't matter what you're made of. What matters is who you are.'

Highs: Any of the scenes between the Doc and (the fake) Barclay.

Lows: None, really. Even the redoing of bits from 'Caretaker' is accurate.

Verdict: Once again Braga ponders on the nature of reality. It's largely a two-handed show, between the Doctor and Barclay, who spark off each other very well. Unfortunately there's no real suspense with regard to who and what the Doctor really is, as we know that he must turn out in the end to be the holodoc. It's also strange that Barclay should be so apparently villainous in tone towards the end, as he's just a hallucination. Nevertheless, it's an entertaining and strongly performed episode, even if not exactly original. 8/10.

#118: 'Elogium'

by Ken Biller and Jeri Taylor

Directed by Rick Kolbe
Music by Dennis McCarthy
US air date 18-09-95

Plot: Stardate 48921.3. The ship wanders into a cloud of spaceborne organisms which want to mate with it, and are generating electrophoretic activity which is swamping it. This in turn sparks the elogium in Kes – a combined puberty and mating cycle that Ocampa go through only once. She must decide whether she is ready to have a child, and Neelix has a similar decision to make.

Déjà Vu?: Generation starships are a long-established SF invention, originally postulated by the rocketry pioneer Konstantin Tsiolkovsky. The first one used in SF is probably *The Voyager that Lasted 600 Years* by Don Wilson, published in 1940. Probably the best-known generation starship is the one in Heinlein's *Orphans of the Sky*. *Trek* itself has had *Yonada* in 'For the World is Hollow and I Have Touched the Sky'.

Behind the Scenes: The original storyline was a seven-page treatment by Jeri Taylor. Ken Biller's reaction was 'a show about eating and sex – these are things I know a lot about . . .' At this point in the show there was no writing staff; Biller was given rewrite notes by Taylor, rather than his script simply being rewritten. On the basis of the second draft, he was offered a staff position. Most of the stuff relating to the elogium itself – Kes locking herself in the office, her dialogue with the Doctor, and subsequent foot massage – were added to the story by Jeri Taylor. The cloud of organisms attracted to the ship is Biller's part.

The optical effect for the cloud is partly composited out of magnified footage of sperm, and it shows. Closer up, they're CGI.

Trek has had several spaceborne organisms before, but the particular nature of these ones (draining power from the warp nacelles) is vaguely reminiscent of the behaviour of the mynocks in *The Empire Strikes Back.*

Though Ethan Phillips has always said he thought Kes and Neelix were at it like rabbits behind closed doors, this episode seems to imply they weren't!

Voyager **Database:** Ocampa females can conceive only once, during the elogium. There is a fifty-hour window for mating to start, and then she must stay in intercourse for six days! (And she develops the adhesive on her hands to make sure the man stays too. That's the ipasaphor, and is the beginning of the fifty-hour window . . .) She also develops the mitral sac on her back, where a baby will incubate. Before mating is the roli-sisen, where one of the parents – or in this case the Doctor – massages her feet for an hour. This nerve stimulation causes hormone changes leading to glandular effects in the tongue. The ritual also helps the young Ocampa accept her new adulthood. The word 'elogium' means 'time of change' when the body prepares for fertilisation. It usually happens at age four or five, though Kes is less than two. You didn't really want to know all that, did you? In Kes's case it was a false elogium brought on by the electrophoretic effects of the creatures, and the Doctor thinks she'll go through it properly later.

Janeway intends to be home before Mark (her fiancé) gives her up for dead. As we'll discover in Season Four, they don't make it in time.

Ensign Samantha Wildman debuts.

Kes's craving leads her to eat six bowls of mashed potatoes with nitrogenated soil – and some beetles ('spawn beetles' according to the script).

Klingons put Targ scoops on their ground-assault vehicles. These are high-frequency tone projectors that disperse Targ herds in their path.

Chakotay drinks from a square bowl, which can't be very tidy, and thinks they'll need replacement crew in 'half of' 75 years – i.e. 37 years. That would make *Voyager* a generation starship.

Voyager's mission to the Badlands was supposed to last three weeks.

Tuvok has three sons and one daughter.

(Lack of) Continuity: The Hydroponics bay ('Parallax') is now called the Airponics bay.

The magnetic anomaly is a cloud of under 2,000 spaceborne organisms. Individuals are moving at up to 3,000 k.p.s., but the cloud as a whole is moving at 1,000 k.p.s. These aren't the first spaceborne organisms in *Trek*: previous ones have included the Farpoint giant jellyfish and its mate in *TNG* pilot 'Encounter at Farpoint'; *Gomtuu*, the organic ship in *TNG* episode 'Tin Man'; and the creature in 'Galaxy's Child'. The creatures attached to the warp nacelles drain power from impulse, guidance, navigation and tactical.

A Targ was seen in *TNG* episode 'Hide and Q', while the Breen have a surprising part to play in the last few episodes of *DS9*.

Ye Canna Change the Laws o' Physics: Spaceborne organisms including bacteria are considered by scientists to really exist. Bacteria could survive in hibernation, and the theory is called 'panspermia'. The noted astronomers Sir Fred Hoyle and Chandra Wickramasinghe have proved that bacteria exist in nebulae.

The organisms flagellate to move, like protozoa. This just means they swim like sperms.

The creatures pull the ship deeper into the cloud by creating a magnetic wake, or EM resonance field. The large creature has a substantial magnetic mass, and emits an electrically charged plasma stream of the same subspace frequency as the warp emissions. This attracts the smaller creatures for mating, as Chakotay correctly deduces. This is all perfectly reasonable, if unlike anything known on Earth.

Chakotay fears that warp exhaust can harm the creatures. Exhaust? What exhaust?

Kes's cravings and fever are a sign of increased electrophoretic activity. Apparently this is caused by the creatures that are swarming around the ship. Electrophoretic activity in real life is the movement of charged particles through a medium, caused by an electric field formed between electrodes immersed in that medium. What medium transmits it between the space creatures and Kes is anybody's guess –

unless one of them gets aboard and into the atmosphere, or Kes steps out of the airlock into the cloud, there should be no effect on her.

Chakotay expects *Voyager* to become a generation starship – this is a ship where the crew is gradually renewed by births on board, the children taking on the parents' roles in continuing the journey. Though he expects replacements to be needed in 37 years, it's generally accepted that a generation of time is 25 years, or approximately a third of the average life span, rather than half of it. A race who can have only one child per couple will find its population halved every generation (Biller's answer to this is that maybe male Ocampa can get pregnant too).

Puzzles: Kes asks Neelix to mate with her. You mean they haven't yet?

Why would navigation and tactical systems be run from the warp nacelles? You don't put your car's map under the bonnet.

Will Kes ever undergo the elogium for real? If she did, we were spared it.

Bloopers: Samantha Wildman discovers she's pregnant by her husband, whom she last saw at DS9. Six months ago. It should definitely have become obvious long before that.

Learn Your Lines: Kes: 'Isn't that why we have minds? To look beyond biological urges; to consider their consequences?'

Janeway (to Chakotay): 'Well done, Commander. In the future if I have any questions about mating behaviour, I'll know where to go.'

Highs: The conversation about fatherhood between Neelix and Tuvok.

Fetishists may get a kick out of Kes getting a foot massage, but, other than that, everything here is utterly forgettable.

Lows: Just about everything else. The utterly cringe-inducing way that everything in the episode is centred around reproduction in such a dull and unsophisticated manner.

Verdict: Starts off intriguingly, with Kes eating bugs. Unfortunately this is rapidly forgotten, and it turns into sickeningly cheesy attempts at making sexual-politics statements, all of which fall utterly flat. It gets through every cliché of puberty, PMS, pregnancy, abortion and menopause, without really saying anything about the personal effects of any of them. The acting's workmanlike, and the script is just dull. Chakotay somehow comes off best, for actually using his brain – it must be down to all that wilderness knowledge. Jennifer Lien is good at freaking out when the sac develops, though. In the end, the theme seems to be that all women really want to be mothers and all men are immature bastards, rather than the intended theme of teen pregnancy. 1/10.

#119: 'Twisted'

by Ken Biller

Directed by Kim Friedman
Music by Jay Chattaway
US air date 02-10-95

Plot: Stardate not given. The ship encounters a spatial anomaly which causes some areas and corridors to loop back on themselves, making it impossible to move around. At the same time, some kind of energy field is encroaching on the holodeck, where the crew must plan their escape from the anomaly.

Déjà Vu?: Anybody who has seen the last two episodes of the *Doctor Who* story 'Castrovalva' will get a severe case of déjà vu at some points!

Behind the Scenes: The episode was a budget-saving one when money ran out at the end of the season, and it underran by eight minutes. Little character pieces such as the hologram trying to chat up the Doctor were added to pad it out.

Though there are two holodecks (at least) in the series as a whole, there is only one corridor set with a holodeck door.

***Voyager* Database:** It is Kes's second birthday. Her blue birthday cake from Neelix is made of seven layers of Jimballian fudge. Her favourite dessert, though, is purée of l'maki nuts.

Kes's quarters are on Deck 8. Hargrove and Ayalla are on Deck 7. Kyoto is on Deck 6, and Nicoletti on Deck 4. Holodeck 2 is on Deck 6. It's unclear whether this means both holodecks are on Deck 6, as the one in 'Learning Curve' isn't given a number, though it is on Deck 6.

There is a small cargo hold directly behind the bridge (though there doesn't appear to be any room for one on the blueprints).

The ship's database has been copied and downloaded by the entity, which has also deposited 20 billion gigaquads of new data into the computer. Which is never mentioned again, and so we don't know what it all was.

(Lack of) Continuity: 'Puss-hog' must be Neelix's favourite insult – after saying it to the Kazon in 'Projections', he calls Tom one here.

Though not explicitly stated, the mess hall is strongly implied to be on Deck 6 (Baxter can't get off Deck 6 but passed the mess hall). We know from 'Phage' that it's on Deck 2. This may, of course, be a symptom of the ship's spatial dimensions being scrunched up.

Ye Canna Change the Laws o' Physics: The anomaly is a spatial distortion ring putting out a lot of EM, which collapses the ship's warp field, making warp speed impossible. Just about everything interferes with warp – and, if EM radiation does it, you'd think they'd never get a warp field started, since the universe is full of electromagnetic radiation.

A shock pulse to invert the implosion ring might be achieved by raising the pressure in the warp core to near critical, 50 megapascals – but might also cause a subatomic particle shower that would blow up the whole ship. A shock pulse of what?

Puzzles: Chakotay and B'Elanna hold hands as the distortion ring approaches. This may be a sign of potential developments, but it doesn't last long.

Bloopers: Looking at the door to Sandrine's from outside, we see that the holodeck door was previously – in 'The Cloud' – to the right. In the teaser to this episode, Kes enters from the left. Harry later comes in from (and leaves through) the correct side.

When B'Elanna first reaches Engineering, the lighting to show the active warp core isn't on. Either that or it's supposed to be off line altogether, though that isn't supported by any on-screen dialogue, and it is illuminated in later shots.

Learn Your Lines: Sandrine (re the Doc): 'If he won't play pool with you, and he won't make love to me, then as far as I am concerned he can mop the floor.'

Chakotay: 'You know, Tuvok, I may not get another chance to say this: I sometimes find you arrogant and irritating, but you're a hell of an officer.' Tuvok: 'And, since we are speaking candidly, may I say, sir, that I have not always been partial to your methods either.' (I think that's Vulcan for 'the same to you, with knobs on.')

Highs/Lows: The Doctor fending off Sandrine's advances is a high.

The resolution turns out to be 'do nothing and it'll go away'. I'm not sure whether to count that as a high for sheer guts, or a low for sheer laziness in failing to get out of a corner one has written oneself into.

Neelix's jealousy, and the first real instance of gratuitous Tuvok-bashing (from Chakotay) are definite lows, though.

Verdict: Actually a decent episode for the most part, with a clever scientific dilemma as the ship is spatially distorted. Everyone in the cast gets something important to do, and there's a genuine sense that they may not get out of this one. The main real complaint here is that the anomaly turns out to have been an entity communicating in this manner – it might actually have been a better hard-SF show if it were really just an anomaly (perhaps a result of the warp engines . . . well, warping the place). 6/10.

#120: 'The 37s'

by Jeri Taylor and Brannon Braga

Directed by Jim Conway
Music by Dennis McCarthy
US air date 28-08-95

Plot: Stardate 48975.1. After finding a pick-up truck floating in space, the ship follows a radio SOS to a nearby planet, where the ship lands near a Lockheed Electra aeroplane. Exploring, they find several humans from 1937 – including Amelia Earhardt and Fred Noonan – in suspended animation. The planet turns out to be occupied by the descendants of humans who were abducted by aliens centuries ago, but who have made this world their own. These humans also have an offer the *Voyager* crew could find hard to refuse.

Déjà Vu?: Blue alert – I wonder if that means changing the bulb. It's the emergency alert aboard *Starbug* in *Red Dwarf*.

Behind the Scenes: The location used is the same desert location as in 'State of Flux'.

The weapons used by the human inhabitants of the planet are stock ones originally seen as Romulan weapons in *TNG* episode 'Unification', and later used by the terrorists in 'Starship Mine' and the mercenaries in 'Gambit'.

David Gray was a Klingon in *DS9* episode 'Soldiers of the Empire', and is best known as Tackleberry in *Police Academy*.

Voyager Database: Starfleet doesn't routinely monitor radio frequencies, as signals travelling at the speed of light are too slow for interstellar communications.

Blue alert is the call to landing stations.

The universal translator is built into the combadge, as demonstrated when the Japanese office thinks they're all speaking Japanese.

The inhabitants of the planet use deflection technology to trick sensors.

The 37s are: Earhardt and Noonan, a Japanese army officer, a black American farmer, an Indian woman, a Russian peasant, a boy in a flat cap and a woman in a green smock.

The Briori abducted 300 people 15 generations ago for slaves. The slaves revolted, and now there are 100,000 of them, living in three 'beautiful' cities.

Chakotay refers to the Arizona desert and Gulf of Mexico as his home.

The ship cannot be operated by fewer than a hundred people.

Janeway says war and poverty simply don't exist on Earth.

(Lack of) Continuity: Baxter's first name is Walter.

Ye Canna Change the Laws o' Physics: Janeway is correct that oxidisation – rust – can't take place in space.

Gasoline includes complex hydrocarbons such as benzene, ethylene and acetylene – correct again.

The planet is L-class, with an oxygen/argon atmosphere. Trinimbic turbulence interferes with scans. Trinimbic surely means 'three clouds'.

Fifteen generations is roughly 375 years, or in 1996. Presumably the 1937 abductions were a scouting attempt, with the main slave raid in 1996. Which means the Briori could get from the planet to Earth in, at most, thirty years.

Warp 9.9 is 4 billion miles per second, or 47.73 years to get home.

Amelia Earhardt disappeared after taking off from New Guinea on 22 July 1937. She was secretly on an intelligence-gathering mission over Japanese outposts when abducted by the Briori. In fact she vanished while trying to cross the Pacific, on a leg from Lae in New Guinea to Howland island. Various theories have been proposed to account for her disappearance, including the romantic notion that she eloped with Fred Noonan, her navigator, or that she was executed for spying by the Japanese after having been brought down over Saipan. This is unlikely, as the Japanese would have made propaganda capital out of it. It's more likely that they either were forced down by a storm or lost course and ran out of fuel.

Puzzles: So, who are the Briori, then? Why were the 37s left in stasis by them, and not enslaved like the other humans?

Bloopers: Although the effects for landing show the ship passing through heavy cloud, all the location shooting has clear cloudless skies.

The ship, as seen in some of the shots of it on the ground, is incorrectly scaled, and would have to be bigger on the inside than out if it was to hold all the crew and rooms we've seen.

Learn Your Lines: Janeway: 'Am I the only one so intent on getting home? Is it just me? Am I leading the crew on a forlorn mission with no hope of success?'

Highs: Not much expense spared on the props and effects. Lovely shot of the landed *Voyager*, even if the scale is off.

Lows: Though we're told about the impressive cities built by the human inhabitants of the planet, all we see is the one little patch of scrubby land. It reminds me of the Frank Muir/ Denis Norden joke about doing *Zulu* on the BBC (two chaps sitting in a tent, saying, 'There's thousands of them out there . . .').

Verdict: Though this is a season finale, there isn't much sense of closure. Rather there's a sense of beginning: that all we've seen so far was just the start, and from here on in things will get really impressive, now that everyone is set for the journey home. The performances are all at least watchable, though it's impossible to accept that David Graf is supposed to be Fred Noonan, and not Eugene Tackleberry. For the most part it's the little vignettes that make up the best parts, such as Janeway's speech to Earhardt about what was thought to have happened to her, or B'Elanna and Harry talking about whether to settle on the planet or not. 6/10.

Interlude

Apart from the holding back of the last four episodes in the US, there wasn't much changed between Seasons One and Two.

A new story arc was introduced, to raise shipboard tensions and give a recurring enemy, but that was all.

Because of the two shows having different shooting schedules, Tim Russ was able to slip across to *DS9*, where he portrayed the Mirror Universe version of Tuvok, in 'Through the Looking Glass'.

Second Season

Regular cast:
As Season One

Recurring cast:
Martha Hackett as Seska
Anthony de Longis as
First Maje Jal Culluh of the Kazon-Nistrim
Raphael Sbarge as Jonas
Simon Billig as Hogan

#121: 'Initiations'

by Ken Biller

Directed by Rick Kolbe
Music by Dennis McCarthy
US air date 04-09-95

Plot: Stardate 49005.3. While on a shuttle trip to meditate, Chakotay is attacked by a Kazon boy, Kar (Aron Eisenberg), who must make his first kill to earn an adult name from his sect, the Ogla. When Chakotay not only defeats but saves the boy, the youngster is dishonoured, and both of them are forced to flee the Kazon-Ogla ship. Kar leads Chakotay to a moon where the Ogla train their warriors, and the pair must team up to survive the traps there.

Déjà Vu?: Two enemies have to team up to survive. That theme has been most famously handled in the films *Hell in the Pacific*, and *Enemy Mine*. In *Trek*, *TNG* episode 'The Enemy' is the closest match.

Terok, of course, is part of the Cardassian name for DS9 – Terok Nor. Presumably this is a nod to the fact that Aron Eisenberg is a regular on that show.

Behind the Scenes: The writer Ken Biller was inspired by the autobiography of an LA gang member, and wanted to base the Kazon culture on LA gangs.

The Kazon training camp is, of course, at Vasquez Rocks. You'll recognise the famous rock formations from TOS episode 'Arena', where Kirk fought the Gorn: they're the first location shot you see in this episode. You may also recognise the place from its equally famous sending up of that scene, in *Bill and Ted's Bogus Journey*.

Voyager Database: The pakra is the Day of Memories, a solitary ritual commemorating the anniversary of Chakotay's father's death. The ritual goes: 'Hakuche-moya, I pray on this day of memories, to speak to my father, the one whom the wind called Kolopak. Though I am far from his bones, perhaps there is a spirit in these unnamed skies who can find him, and honour him with my song.'

There are, on average, eighteen Kazon sects, but this is variable due to fighting between them. Sect borders also change every day.

The Kazon fought to gain independence from an oppressor who wore uniforms. They shared the Trabe homeworld until they revolted 26 years ago.

A *Voyager* shuttle is destroyed. The ship originally had two large shuttles and four shuttlepods. Keep note of these numbers – they'll soon lose more than they had to start with.

The Ogla train on Terok, a class-M moon of a Jupiter-type gas giant. The landscape is dotted with booby traps such as proton beams, biomagnetic traps and disruptor snares.

Starfleet medical Code White means the patient is dead but revivable, at least for two minutes after death.

(Lack of) Continuity: The Kazon-Ogla appeared in 'Caretaker', led by Maje Jabin. Now they are led by Maje Razik. The Nistrim appeared in 'State of Flux', and the Relora sect are also named here.

Kazon ships are made of polyduranide alloy, as opposed to the tritanium of Federation shuttles. However, according to the *DS9* episode 'Q-Less', Runabouts have duranium skins, as did shuttles in TOS episode 'The Menagerie'. A mixture of tritanium and duranium is used in Starfleet starship construction, according to the Okudas. Kazon ships are also less manoeuvrable at low speeds.

Ye Canna Change the Laws o' Physics: Radiothermic interference from weapons emplacements on Terok will jam communications. Waves of heat will jam them?

Puzzles: If Chakotay can perform this ritual in his quarters, then why not do so to start with, instead of losing another shuttle?

Why is Chakotay suddenly so proud of his Starfleet uniform, when he was a rebel against that organisation?

Learn Your Lines: Razik: 'Why did you save him? It's not a very effective way to wage war.'

Chakotay: 'For some reason that escapes me at the moment, I keep saving your life. If you want to hate me for it, fine, but I'd appreciate it if you'd keep it to yourself.'

Highs: The adult Kazon are all first-class complete bastards. Wonderful.

Nice to see the familiar formations of Vasquez Rocks again.

Verdict: A fairly average episode. Aron Eisenberg as Kar is good, but just too recognisably the same actor who plays Nog. If you've seen the *Red Dwarf* episode 'Polymorph' it's all too easy to view Kar as Nog with his nervousness removed. Neelix proves to be reasonable at negotiating with the Kazon. The first half of the episode suggests some culture-clash problems à la *Shogun*, but sadly the second half simply becomes another enemies-must-team-up-to-survive story. On its own terms, however, its watchable, and occasionally quite strong. 7/10.

#122: 'Non Sequitur'

by Brannon Braga

Directed by David Livingston
Music by Jay Chattaway
US air date 25-09-95

Plot: Stardate 49011. Harry wakes up next to his girlfriend Libby, back on Earth. Confused, he discovers that he never went on *Voyager* – his best friend went in his place. Instead, Harry is a rising star at Starfleet headquarters, working on engineering projects. It transpires that he was in a shuttle accident that intersected an alien realm, and the aliens rescued him by putting him in this altered timeline. Now he must break the law to recreate the accident and get back to his proper place. But for that he will need help.

Déjà Vu?: In *Trek* the alternative-timeline idea dates back to at least *TNG*'s 'Time Squared'.

It's a Wonderful Life should probably also get a mention here, as Harry sees what life would be like if he hadn't gone on *Voyager*.

Behind the Scenes: The usual backlot that served *DS9* as a New Orleans street 'Homefront'/'Paradise Lost' here serves as a San Francisco street.

The shots of Starfleet headquarters exterior are from *Star Trek IV: The Voyage Home*, as is the daytime footage of the Golden Gate. The night-time shot of the Golden Gate is from *Star Trek III: The Search for Spock*, and that building is Kirk's apartment!

The Spacedock doors aren't the doors from Spacedock in the movies. They're the doors from the Dyson Sphere in *TNG* episode 'Relics' in a recomposite of the shot of the *Enterprise-D*'s escape in that episode, replacing the *Enterprise* with the Runabout.

The monitor in the HQ conference room is from the *Enterprise D*'s briefing room.

Shuttlecraft *Drake* is presumably named after Frank Drake, the scientist who developed the Drake Equation, which sets out to prove mathematically the likelihood of life in space. It's unlikely to be Sir Francis Drake, as *Trek* tends to name starships after explorers, and shuttles after scientists.

***Voyager* Database:** Danny Byrd was Harry's best friend before he was assigned to *Voyager*. In this reality, Byrd was assigned to *Voyager* instead.

Harry left the Academy eight months ago.

Voyager's memorial service was held two months ago. Since Harry went straight to *Voyager* from graduation, we can presume that Starfleet wait six months before declaring a missing ship officially lost. This may be why Janeway didn't know of any lost ships in 'State of Flux', if the *Equinox* had been pulled to the Delta Quadrant less than six months before.

The head of Starfleet Security is female.

Harry won the Cochrane Award for excellence in warp theory, named for Zephram Cochrane, who invented the warp drive (TOS – 'Metamorphosis'; *Star Trek: First Contact*). He lives with Libby in a fourth-floor apartment (4G) of a building near Starfleet headquarters. Since he doesn't know his way to the building, it's presumably a place Harry and Libby got after the timeline diverged. In this timeline, he has a clarinet, which he will later take up once back in the real timeline.

The alternate Tom's parole was revoked when *Voyager* stopped at DS9, and Odo arrested him for fighting with Quark over the Lobi crystals ('Caretaker').

(Lack of) Continuity: The last contact Starfleet had with *Voyager* was on Stardate 48307.5. This, bizarrely enough, is before Chakotay's ship was lost, and *Voyager* was assigned to search for it!

The Nebula Class of starship, which pursues Harry and Tom here, first appeared in *TNG* episode 'The Wounded' as the USS *Phoenix*.

An Yridian (*TNG* – 'Birthright') is seen leaving Sandrine's.

Ye Canna Change the Laws o' Physics: Harry's new Runabout design is intended to overcome the problem of dilithium fracture and subspace damage in tetryon-plasma warp engines. Presumably dilithium fracture means the crystals themselves break up when you try to make an engine that uses plasma made of tetryon particles.

The aliens who put Harry here live in a temporal-inversion fold in the space-time matrix. Harry's shuttle intersected with one of their timestreams, causing history to be jumbled, and

Harry to end up in this alternate reality. I'm not even going to try explaining any of that jargon, lest my ears start to bleed . . .

Tetryon plasma emits multiflux gamma radiation, which disrupts subspace. (Venting it causes the engines of the following ship to stall.)

Harry was doing 140,000 k.h.p. with a polaron scan out to a quarter-million kilometres when he hit the timestream.

Puzzles: Did Harry actually return to the timeline of the previous episodes, or just one that was a lot closer, so he didn't notice any tiny differences?

Bloopers: When Libby tries to block the security guards as Harry ducks out of the apartment window, the skyscraper visible through the window is not part of the environment in the exterior location shots.

Although Tom says it will take security twenty seconds to lock on to their unauthorised presence, it actually takes only nine seconds.

Learn Your Lines: Harry: 'It was another lifetime; I'm doing the best I can.'

Highs: A reasonably different variation on the temporal anomaly. Garrett is well used.

Lows: A scene very obviously (and cheaply!) shot in the alley between two sound stages. Garrett and Jennifer Gatti don't really have much chemistry. Compare his chemistry with Roxann Dawson to see how it could have been done.

Verdict: As with 'Projections', it's obvious from the start that Harry is out of place, and will return to the right place by the end of the episode. Harry's confusion engenders sympathy, though it's strange that everyone else is so cold and hostile if they're supposed to be his friends. Tom's inclusion is somewhat gratuitous (though it does make sense if Harry was never at Quark's to get between them), and this is one episode where a guest appearance from, say, Riker or Dax would actually have made more sense within the context of the story. The ending is rather rushed as well, and once again we get the remarkable coincidence of rescue at the moment of destruction. 6/10.

#123: 'Parturition'

by Tom Szollosi

Directed by Jonathan Frakes
Music by Dennis McCarthy
US air date 09-10-95

Plot: While tutoring Kes in shuttle piloting, Tom Paris begins to develop romantic feelings for her. Although he keeps this to himself, and she doesn't reciprocate, Neelix is paranoid enough to start a fight with him over her anyway. Things come to a head when they have to go on a shuttle mission together, and the shuttle crashes, stranding them both on a hostile planet, with a baby alien.

Déjà Vu?: Two crewmen who share a grudge have to work together both to survive and to become friends. Not a new idea in *Trek*: Riker and Worf in *TNG* finale 'All Good Things' would qualify.

Behind the Scenes: The subspace anomaly in the shuttle training simulation is the micro-wormhole from 'Eye of the Needle'. The Jem'Hadar fighters are a stock shot from the *DS9* episode 'The Jem'Hadar', in which they destroy the USS *Odyssey*.

The planet being nicknamed Planet Hell is an in-joke, referring to the fact that, since *TNG* days, the alien planet sets built on Stage 16 at Paramount have been called Planet Hell by the casts and crews of all three modern *Trek* generations.

***Voyager* Database:** Alvarian hair pasta isn't just a name. It's made of the hair of mature Alvarians, harvested during the shedding season. And this is on the menu? It seems like a setup for the ultimate 'hair in my soup' gag, doesn't it?

Food reserves are at 30 per cent.

Tom's father taught the Starfleet Academy survival course

in Tom's year. His mother once fed a fallen chick with water
from an eye dropper.

(Lack of) Continuity: Harry is seen playing the clarinet,
which he has taken up following his alternate life in 'Non
Sequitur'. Apparently he ate Neelix's food for a week to save
up enough replicator rations for it.

Stellar Cartography is where the Delaney sisters work.

Apropos of falling for the women he can't have, Tom tells
Harry not to knock it till he's tried it. Harry will then do this
at least once a season from now on!

Ye Canna Change the Laws o' Physics: Planet Hell is
Class M, shrouded in cloud or trigemic vapour and electromagnetic storms, like a young planet such as the primeval
Earth. Actually it sounds even more like Venus. Sensors have
registered amino acids and proteins, which doesn't necessarily mean there will be plants there – there could just as
easily be primeval soup . . . The trigemic vapour turns out to
contain the amino acids and proteins, and is a nutrition
source on its own.

Dermal osmotic sealant protects Tom and Neelix from the
trigemic vapour. The skin does breathe through osmosis to a
certain degree, and presumably this prevents it. The Doctor,
though, should be aware of the dangers of skin suffocation
(obviously he's never seen *Goldfinger*).

The alien ship's weapons are comparable to *Voyager*'s, but
have a phase retraction in the shields when auxiliary power is
transferred to the aft weapons array. A co-variant phaser
pulse into the aft control systems would disable their
weapons.

According to Tom, most reptiles never return to their
hatchlings (well, it varies . . .) while Neelix knows that some
species abandon nests that have been tampered with.

Puzzles: Why does Harry visit Kes to keep her apprised of
the situation? Wouldn't it be Tuvok or Janeway, with whom
he has a closer relationship? Or does he fancy her too?

Is this race related to the Voth from 'Distant Origin'? In the
script it's merely called a reptohumanoid.

Why doesn't Janeway try hailing the reptohumanoids' ship?

Learn Your Lines: Tom: 'I'm famous for my dirty tricks, y'know.'

Tom: 'I think I'm in trouble.' Harry: 'What's new?' Tom: 'I think I'm in love.' Harry: 'What's new?'

Kes: 'On my homeworld it's so much simpler: You choose a mate for life. There's no distrust, no envy, no betrayal.' Doc: 'Your world must have very dry literature . . .'

Tom: 'If you hear muffled screams, consider that a request for a beam-out.'

Highs: Janeway chewing them out after their food fight?

Tom's confession and apology to Neelix. (They're definitely trying to turn him into Ace Rimmer and make us all say, 'What a guy!')

Lows: Neelix's insane jealousy. Again.

The baby dinosaur is so obviously a glove puppet.

Verdict: So soon after 'Initiations', another two-conflicting-persons-must-settle-their-differences-to-survive story. Unfortunately one of those persons is Neelix, so we know we're in for a lot of annoying whining. On the other hand it's an office-romance story. There isn't really much else to say. 4/10.

#124: 'Persistence of Vision'
by Jeri Taylor

Directed by James L Conway
Music by David Bell
US air date 30-10-95

Plot: The ship is about to enter what Neelix calls Bothan space – home of the secretive Botha. As the journey continues, members of the crew begin to have strange experiences: Janeway is attacked by a holodeck character in her quarters; Tuvok sees his wife; B'Elanna sleeps with

Chakotay . . . In fact the ship is under attack by a telepathic alien, who wants to make sure they never emerge from Bothan space.

Déjà Vu?: 'Many Bothans died to bring us this episode . . .' Well, not quite, but the name Bothan is from *Return of the Jedi*.

Behind the Scenes: A Kazon fighter is used in the illusory attack on *Voyager*.

Voyager Database: Janeway last had shore leave two months ago, and last did something pleasurable – i.e. take part in her holonovel – several weeks ago.

Starfleet protocol says the ship's doctor overrules the captain in health matters. The Doctor ordering Janeway to take some time off is the first time a hologram has ordered a captain.

Neelix gets information from other traders they meet. His contact on Mithren says that ships vanish in Bothan space.

Neelix serves Seltan wood fungus, brine-soaked nestle strips, devilled wood throck and fried myrt cake, which Janeway hallucinates to be a cucumber sandwich. Neelix doesn't know what a cucumber is.

Kes has been doing mental exercises with Tuvok to improve her telepathic abilities.

Janeway sees the Bothan as Mark; Tom sees him as his father; Harry sees him as Libby (not shown on screen); Tuvok sees him as his wife, T'Pel; B'Elanna sees him as Chakotay!

Tuvok has a Vulcan lute, which he used to play for T'Pel.

An escape pod would take a week to go the distance *Voyager* travels in a day.

The fake Mark claims to have vowed to wait for Janeway for as long as it took – unlikely for the real one, once the memorial service was held.

(Lack of) Continuity: One of the Doctor's hallucinations in 'Projections' was that his condition was a result of a failed attempt to set up holoemitters that would permit him to visit other areas of the ship. This is attempted here for real, though his imaging interface isn't properly stabilised, leaving him about six inches tall when he materialises in Engineering. ('Just a small oversight,' says Harry.) The spare holo-projectors used are from storage, not removed from the holodeck.

The photo of Janeway and Mark is in a different frame from that in 'Caretaker', though given the number of times the ship is knocked around it's inevitable some furnishings and fittings will have to change.

There was another T'Pel in *TNG* episode 'Data's Day', who was in fact a Romulan spy. Is there something Tuvok isn't telling us? The Vulcan lute first appeared in TOS, where Spock had one in 'Charlie X', and the Vulcan landscape is stock footage from the *Bird of Prey* takeoff scene in *Star Trek IV: The Voyage Home*.

Ye Canna Change the Laws o' Physics: Presumably Tuvok is easily affected by the attack, due to his telepathic affinities, though Kes is able to reflect their effect.

The Bothan ship is putting out bioelectric-field modulation on a delta-wave frequency. Delta waves appear during third stage sleep, and are higher-voltage brainwaves of between 0.5 and 2.5 cycles per second. During this stage, the neurons are firing faster and are more synchronised. The Bothan ship's field has a psionic complement for psychoreactive effect as well. (In fact all they'd need to do is attack the victims with the rhythms associated with REM sleep.)

A resonance burst will disrupt the psionic field. A resonance burst of what? Simply interfering with the frequency should do the job. Or switching it off would be best. Three million degrees Kelvin is a high enough temperature for the warp core to emit the resonance burst – that's almost a fifth of the temperature of the core of the sun, but supposedly not high enough to irradiate everyone on the ship (it'd just vaporise them!).

Puzzles: If adjusting whatever cut off the telepathic emissions, then how come the alien – who was himself an illusion – didn't disappear at the same instant?

How many Bothans are there – the implication seems to be

that there's just the one, making ships disappear because he can.

Since even the telepathic alien didn't really exist (maybe), then what was behind it all?

Was the alien a Bothan? He's not definitely identified as such.

Learn Your Lines: Mark (to Janeway): 'Someone else is in your thoughts now.' Actually Chakotay, though this won't be shown for a while.

Highs: Lots of very surreal scenes.

Lows: B'Elanna begging Chakotay to bed her.

Verdict: This one's a good one. The basic premise of something making the unreal real is nothing new in *Trek*, and at first it has the air of a holodeck-malfunction story. However, soon things get far more surreal, with fine acting from all the regulars. The outcome, though involving a bit too much technobabble, is pretty good, and leaves open the possibility of a worthy sequel. It doesn't advance the characters much – since the B'Elanna/Chakotay angle never reappears – but it is a very nice piece of surreal creepiness, which is appropriate, given that it aired the day before Hallowe'en. Almost *Doctor Who*-ish – in fact almost *Sapphire and Steel*-ish. 7/10.

#125: 'Tattoo'

by Michael Piller
from a story by Larry Brody

Directed by Alexander Singer
Music by Dennis McCarthy
US air date 06-11-95

Plot: When an away team searching for minerals find a symbol on a planet, it reminds Chakotay of when he saw the same symbol on Earth. On a quest with his father, Kolopak, to find a related tribe, the Chamusi, or Rubber Tree People, they had discovered that the Rubber Tree People's sky spirits had given them this same symbol, and the tattoo they wore was to honour those spirits. Chakotay was more forward-thinking, and not spiritual. Sure there is a connection to this planet, Chakotay strips off and goes native, looking for the sky spirits who had bred with the Rubber Tree People. Meanwhile, to learn to empathise with his patients, the Doctor gives himself the 29-hour Levodian flu.

Déjà Vu?: The search for the Rubber Tree People is reminiscent of John Boorman's film *The Emerald Forest*.

Behind the Scenes: The nude shot of Chakotay is a body double, not Beltran.

Mulgrew's hair is back in a bun.

Although the characters searching are on a good studio set, the bird that dives at Chakotay was filmed on location.

A variety of stock weapon props are seen when Kolopak's expedition is disarmed.

The first subtitles in the series are seen when Kolopak speaks to the Chamusi.

Voyager's descent through the clouds is footage from 'Parturition'.

Voyager Database: The symbol of the sky spirits is a blessing to the land for damaging it with a campfire.

Wildman's baby is lying in such a way as to press on the sciatic nerve.

Tuvok is a prizewinning orchid breeder, and Neelix also breeds them.

Captain Sulu sponsored Chakotay's application to the Academy.

Starfleet protocol instructs that away teams should remain armed and ready to defend themselves until contact has been – (at which point Chakotay interrupts Tuvok's speech on the subject).

The aliens visited Earth 45,000 years ago and bred with native women as they crossed the Bering land bridge. The Chamusi are their Inheritors – surviving hybrids.

Chakotay's father accepted the tattoo from the Chamusi as

a gift, and Chakotay took it after his father was killed fighting the Cardassians.

(Lack of) Continuity: Though Chakotay previously counted the US deserts as his ancestors' home, they've suddenly become a tribe in the Central American jungle. Chakotay's actual home is a colony on the Cardassian border. Chakotay was a breech-birth baby, and didn't share his people's beliefs until after the expedition to the jungle.

Ye Canna Change the Laws o' Physics: The crew are looking for polyferranide deposits, which are apparently needed to prevent the warp nacelles from burning up.

In fact, legends of beings from the sky who bred with Earth women are a common feature of Native American beliefs.

The flower native to both the planet and the Mexican jungle is an orchid: a rare variety of *saprepedium*, of the Asiatic genus *Papiopradillum*. Sadly I don't know enough about orchids to identify this species.

Thoron-radiation bombardment would decontaminate the surface. Nonsense – it would contaminate it with Thoron radiation.

The village building is made of alloy-polymer compounds.

The aliens took two generations to reach Earth, and last visited it twelve generations ago. In human terms those figures would be 50 and 300 years respectively, but there's no indication of the aliens' life span.

Puzzles: Is it just me, or does the face in the clouds look like a Son'a from *Star Trek: Insurrection*?

Bloopers: The 'village' on the planet appears to consist of only one building.

Learn Your Lines: Doc (displaying his great bedside manner): 'Well, Ensign, unfortunately pregnancy causes its fair share of discomforts and you'll have to learn to live with them. That's just the way it is.'

Doc: 'I feel like I'm fading – do you know what that means to a hologram?'

Highs: Henry Darrow is pretty good.

The Doctor's illness.

Lows: Chakotay's (well, a stand-in's) butt.

Verdict: Here's where it all starts to go wrong for Chakotay. From here on in, all the intriguing hints from Season One about what sort of person he is are shot down in flames. As if that weren't bad enough, the story is really about his father, and doesn't go anywhere. It's the sort of thing that would have made a reasonable B arc over a few episodes, like Janeway's holonovel, but doesn't stand up in its own right. And Beltran isn't good enough to carry it either, though Henry Darrow as Kolopak just about saves it from plunging into the abyss. 5/10.

#126: 'Cold Fire'

by Brannon Braga
from a story by Anthony Williams

Directed by Cliff Bole
Music by Dennis McCarthy
US air date 13-11-95

Plot: When the remains of the Caretaker start rattling around in their drawer, it becomes apparent that the ship may be in the vicinity of the female Caretaker. Soon, another array, smaller than that orbiting the Ocampa homeworld, is found, and an Ocampa named Tanis beams aboard so that Janeway can ask his help in contacting the female Caretaker. Tanis begins trying to seduce Kes away from Tuvok's tutelage and to the Dark Side, hoping she'll join the Ocampa community on the array.

When they reach the female Caretaker, Suspiria, it becomes clear that she's not in a helpful mood, believing Janeway and *Voyager* to have murdered the Caretaker.

Déjà Vu?: *Suspiria* is a horror film made by Dario Argento.

Tanis, of course, is named after the location of the Well of Souls in *Raiders of the Lost Ark*, though the city did really exist, southwest of Lake Manzila in Egypt (and not in fact just outside of Cairo!).

When Kes 'knows' the plants, they're shown as brighter and more garish – a demonstration of the Doctor's story about the flower in the *Doctor Who* story 'The Time Monster'.

Suspiria's true appearance is quite Lovecraftian, and reminiscent of the 'Star People' from *At the Mountains of Madness*.

Behind the Scenes: There is a recap of the events of 'Caretaker' – the first time this has been done for an episode other than the second half of a two-parter.

The new array is a revamp of the model of the original array, with lots of bits taken off.

Suspiria's voice is dubbed by Majel Barrett.

***Voyager* Database:** The toxin breaks down a specific enzyme in the sporocystian cellular structure, inducing temporary paralysis.

Suspiria should appear within 47 hours of being signalled by subspace carrier wave at the appropriate location.

Tanis's idea of heaven is Exosia – a subspace layer of pure mind.

(Lack of) Continuity: 'Caretaker' is stated to have occurred eleven months ago. Suspiria's array is a tenth the size of the Caretaker's one, and has 2,000 Ocampa aboard. It is 300 years old.

Tanis claims to be fourteen, and says his father was twenty. All the Ocampa on the station have had their life spans extended, by a means discovered three generations (fifteen years) ago.

Tanis explains that the Kazon have given *Voyager* a bad name – claiming the ship declared war on them, killed the Caretaker, and has been pillaging planets throughout the quadrant.

Suspiria incorporates as pure sporocystian energy, and takes form only when absolutely necessary.

Tuvok correctly bleeds green when Kes accidentally heats his blood by 37 degrees.

Suspiria's physical form is made out of plasmatic energy – not sporocystian energy. She's a pink gel-like column with grey tentacles, quite unlike the jellyfish-like Caretaker.

Ye Canna Change the Laws o' Physics: A hypnogogic state is that experienced when the brain is no longer fully awake, but not yet asleep, in which dreaming can nevertheless occur. The opposite of this is a hypnopompic state, so I'm not sure where hypergogic fits in. Presumably it means the senses are superactive.

Kes sees atoms burning like meteors when she heats the drink. A nice image, but utterly ludicrous. Atoms become agitated when heated, and zoom around faster.

Puzzles: Tuvok and Janeway think it's a good idea to develop a toxin against sporocystian life forms, just in case. All right, so it comes in handy, but what sort of people are they, to automatically think about biological warfare against a new species they discover? Other than knocking Suspiria back for an instant and scaring her off, the toxin doesn't work anyway.

In spite of all that happened, and the narrow escape, Janeway still wants to find Suspiria again after she flees into subspace.

Bloopers: There are only about six racks of small plants in the airponics bay – fewer than in the average suburban greenhouse – and this is supposed to feed around 150 people?

Kes fills the airponics bay with fire, yet only the plant material is damaged – not Tanis, not Kes, not even the shelves.

When Tanis asks Kes if she can hear Suspiria, you just make out Kes's left ear prosthetic starting to come away from the side of Jennifer Lien's head.

Learn Your Lines: Tanis: 'Focus on the goal, not the task.'

Tuvok: 'Without the darkness, how would we recognise the light?'

Highs: Kes being tempted by the Dark Side – I mean being tempted by powers she doesn't know how to control.

Her scenes with Tuvok.

Lows: The female Caretaker being a little girl.

Janeway's monumental stupidity in wanting to find Suspiria again, and her callous decision to develop biological weapons for no reason.

Verdict: A somewhat belated follow-up to the pilot, and strangely disappointing too. It's not that there's anything really wrong with it as such, it's just . . . well, it's just so inconsequential in the end. The female Caretaker decides that *Voyager* killed her mate, with no evidence, and then equally irrationally lets them go. Much that happens does so for no reason. This would be acceptable if the show were story-arc-based, and we knew that things would work out later, but it just seems to have been cobbled together from elements of two or three different scripts to fill an hour-long slot in the schedules. 5/10.

#127: 'Maneuvers'
by Ken Biller

Directed by David Livingston
Music by Jay Chattaway
US air date 20-11-95

Plot: Stardate 49208.3. A message from a Federation beacon lures the ship to a nebula, where a waiting Kazon ship attacks. A manned torpedo breaches the hull and steals a transporter module. Neelix points out that these are new tactics for the Kazon – a result of Seska's advice. Seska and Culluh plan to use the transporter to attract allies from the other sects, but instead end up using it against them. When *Voyager* finds the bodies, and the crew realise what's going on, Chakotay takes a shuttle on a suicide mission to destroy the transporter module.

Behind the Scenes: As well as writing the episode, Ken Biller wrote a 'Kazon Bible' for the writers, and developed the whole idea of their having been enslaved by the Trabe – a history that is told in 'Alliances', developed from this document.

De Longis particularly enjoyed working with Robert Beltran, whom he describes as a very strong and generous actor. For his part Beltran considers this his favourite episode of the first three years.

Kes doesn't appear at all in this episode.

The big door from the town square in 'Time and Again' is now a part of the Kazon bridge.

Voyager Database: Chakotay and B'Elanna play hoverball.

Starfleet officers and, on *Voyager*, Maquis ones – are given their security codes well in advance of the implementation date.

Cargo Bay 2 is on Deck 4.

Voyager's neural-assisted computers are twice as fast as Kazon ones.

Seska once disabled a Cardassian ship near Bajor, using an antiproton beam. Chakotay uses the same tactic to ruin the stolen transporter module.

The Kazon-Relora are more numerous and powerful than the Nistrim, who are their sworn enemies. The Relora and Ogla are the two supreme sects. Other sects include the Hobii, led by Jal Surat; the Mostral, led by Jal Lorat; and the Oglamar, led by Jal Valek; as well as the Ogla, whom we met in 'Caretaker' and 'Initiations'. Jal Sankur unified the Kazon to overthrow their masters, the Trabe.

Kazon booze is red and called 'enemy's blood'.

(Lack of) Continuity: There's no sign of Kes's airponic garden in Cargo Bay 2.

Seska is restoring her true Cardassian physiognomy.

The Kazon-Relora were mentioned in 'Initiations'.

Chakotay has been on *Voyager* for ten months – which is less time than he'd been there in the previous episode!

Ye Canna Change the Laws o' Physics: Protons and neutrons make up atomic nuclei. The antiproton, predicted by Dirac, was discovered by two American physicists in 1955.

Photon charges disable Chakotay's shuttle. Since bursts of light shouldn't harm it, these are presumably some technology related to photon torpedoes.

B'Elanna suggests beaming Chakotay out at warp by modulating the annular confinement beam to warp frequency. This is a force field that holds the transportee in the transporter beam for safe transit. The targeting scanners verify the position and state of the subject to be transported, while the pattern buffer holds the dematerialised molecules in suspension while any problems are ironed out. At the time, their warp speed is two billion kilometres per second. That's 1.25 billion miles per second, or 6,740 times light speed – far higher than the ship's maximum warp!

Puzzles: How can Janeway trust Chakotay – as Seska points out, he'll go off like a bull after a red flag at the slightest provocation, forgetting his responsibilities. This is hardly a desirable quality in a first officer.

Bloopers: The close-up of the shuttle after Chakotay drops power is a mirror image of a stock shot – you can see that the registry number is backwards.

B'Elanna says she's going to reinitialise the targeting scanners to match the relative phase of the dampening shield. A few seconds later she describes the same procedure as matching the pattern-buffer frequency to the dampening shield.

Learn Your Lines: B'Elanna: 'It's about Chakotay.' Janeway: 'That's not exactly my favourite subject right now, Lieutenant.'

Seska's verdict on Chakotay in bed: 'It was never *that* good.'

Highs: Chakotay getting beaten up.

Seska and Culluh are a good pair of villains.

Lows: The final plot twist, of Seska impregnating herself with Chakotay's DNA, is iffy.

Verdict: The return of Culluh, Seska and the Kazon-Nistrim marks an upturn in the story arc that will run throughout Season Two. Overall it's interesting that 'Initiations', 'Tattoo' and 'Maneuvers' were thought to have 'solved the Chakotay problem' by giving us his background, since these three episodes don't invoke Robert Beltran's best performances. 6/10.

#128: 'Resistance'

by Lisa Klink
from a story by Kevin Ryan and
Michael Jan Friedman

Directed by Rick Kolbe
Music by Dennis McCarthy
US air date 27-11-95

Plot: While trading on a planet, Tuvok and B'Elanna are arrested by the Mokra Order as suspected dissident sympathisers. Neelix gets back to the ship, while Janeway is knocked out. She wakes to find herself being looked after by Caylem, an old man who thinks she is his long-lost daughter, Ralkana. While Tuvok and B'Elanna are tortured, Janeway enlists Caylem's aid to contact the resistance and mount a rescue mission.

Déjà Vu?: It has the air of many wartime movies about the French Resistance, as the title implies.

The 85 phased ion cannon targeted on *Voyager* by the Mokra may be derived from the ion cannon in *The Empire Strikes Back*.

Behind the Scenes: Kevin Ryan is a former *Star Trek* novels editor at Pocket Books, and Michael Jan Friedman is a prolific *Trek* novelist.

Kes is totally absent from this episode as well.

The UK video sleeve misspells Ralkana (as it is in the script) as 'Rokana'.

The Mokra carry the same model of stock pistol as Janeway miraculously finds in 'Time and Again'.

The prison alarm is *TNG/Generations/DS9* red-alert sound from a Klingon Bird of Prey.

***Voyager* Database:** The crew are seeking tellerium.

The dissident group are the Alsaurian resistance.

Though Caylem believes Janeway to be his daughter, and his wife to be imprisoned, in reality his wife died twelve years ago, and his daughter was shot trying to break some rebels out of prison.

(Lack of) Continuity: The prison has metaphasic shielding, first introduced in *TNG* episode 'Suspicions'.

Tuvok correctly bleeds green again.

Ye Canna Change the Laws o' Physics: If the ship's anti-matter reduction rate drops below 9 per cent (of what?) the plasma injectors will fail, and the nacelles can never be reinitialised.

The main deflector can be modified to emit a Radion pulse.

Puzzles: It's unclear whether the Alsaurian resistance are named after the planet, a geographical region, or even a religion or a person.

How and when did Tom and Neelix get into the prison? They just suddenly show up when Caylem dies.

The only person who could have betrayed Janeway and Caylem's plan to the Mokra is their contact (because he's the only person they spoke to at all), yet at the end Janeway trusts him to spread the truth about Caylem's bravery! Is she too stupid to realise he must be a double agent?

Learn Your Lines: Neelix describes the Mokra as 'paranoid and hostile, with little use for diplomacy'.

Highs: Any scene with Joel Grey (Caylem) qualifies, but especially the point where he pretends to let himself be humiliated so that Janeway's contact can get away.

The scene where B'Elanna is shocked at Tuvok's torture.

Lows: The villains are just black-clad thuggish cyphers with no character or motivation.

The dodgy cardboard skyline seen at one point also qualifies.

The Mokra posing as a rebel is too dumb to change his jackboots to go with his disguise? Come off it!

Verdict: Not exactly an original story. Janeway must arrange a prison break, but an astounding guest shot by Joel Grey.

Caylem is a tragic figure, heartbreakingly easy to identify with, and beautifully played. It's easy to forget the rest of the cast when he's on screen. The episode also breaks *Trek*'s golden rule that stories should be about the regulars, and not the guest stars. This rule-breaking works to great effect here, and yet doesn't detract from the regulars – Tuvok, B'Elanna and Janeway herself all come off well. The villains are never more than one-dimensional jackbooted thugs, but overall the episode is moving and powerful, due to Grey's performance. 9/10.

#129: 'Prototype'

by Nick Correa and Ken Biller

Directed by Jonathan Frakes
Music by Dennis McCarthy
US air date 15-01-96

Plot: B'Elanna beams a damaged robot aboard, which was floating in space. When reactivated, it wants her help to create new power units to preserve its people, robots built by the Pralor. When Janeway refuses, claiming this might breach the Prime Directive, unit 3947 abducts B'Elanna and forces her to build a new prototype. As she works, she becomes intrigued by the challenge, and horrified by the discovery that two robot factions are fighting each other after having wiped out the species that created them.

Déjà Vu?: Right. So, there's this race of robotic life forms who wiped out their creator, then split into two factions, one grey and one gold, to fight each other . . . Can we say any Dalek story after 'Resurrection of the Daleks?'

The robot masks are amazingly like the Cybernauts from *The Avengers*.

B'Elanna mentions 'adjusting the flux capacitance'. Flux capacitance derives from a flux capacitor – which was the device that made time travel possible in the *Back to the Future* trilogy.

Behind the Scenes: The Pralor and Cravic ships and costumes are the same ones painted different colours.

As well as playing Riker in *TNG*, Frakes directed *First Contact* and *Insurrection*.

Voyager Database: The robots are 'automated personnel units' designed for dangerous tasks such as asteroid mining.

The robots' built-in weapons give a chromodynamic energy discharge.

B'Elanna's tools include a submicron scanner and phase coil resonator.

All the robots' power sources have a unique energy signature. A standardised unit with universal signature is the solution.

Unit 3947 has been 'alive' for 1,314,807 hours, 33 minutes. Or just over 150 years.

While in the Maquis, B'Elanna once used a holoimager to project the image of a decoy ship.

The Cravic are gold, compared with the Pralor's silver.

(Lack of) Continuity: B'Elanna refers to Data from *TNG*, saying he's the only sentient android in the Federation (apart from Lore, Julianna, the various ones from 'I Mudd', etc.).

Ye Canna Change the Laws o' Physics: Unit 3947's power source is incompatible with the EPS conduits, but plugging it in anyway may buy time! Shouldn't this just . . . well . . . not work? He's powered by tripolymer plasma. Warp plasma is too highly charged, and would burn out his systems in seconds. It also radiates at too high a frequency to modify electrochemically. Modifying a series of anodyne relays to regulate the plasma will increase his capacitance of relays.

Transporter targeting scanners can't penetrate the subspace defence barrier around the Pralor ship. The Pralor ship then fires quantum resonance charges.

Puzzles: Why do the robots need clothes?

Why isn't Tuvok there when 3947 is reactivated – he is the security chief, after all, and this is a potential threat.

Why does Harry have to activate a containment field

manually after a hull breach? Surely this should be done automatically, faster than human response time.

Bloopers: In the scenes in Engineering from 3947's viewpoint, 3947 can't possibly look at itself in the monitor without turning its head, but the image in the monitor shows it has not done so.

You can often see the actors' throats moving under the masks when the robots speak.

Learn Your Lines: Janeway: 'Unfortunately, extinction is often the natural end of evolution.'

Janeway: 'Who are we to swoop in, play God, then continue on our way without the slightest considerations of the long-term effects of our actions?' Starfleet officers, that's who. And she does it often enough later in the series.

Highs: Nicely directed, but the budgetary limitations show.

It's nice to see that Harry and B'Elanna still have a good chemistry. That pair are made for each other, if you ask me . . .

Lows: The robots are cheap-looking.

Some warp plasma appears to be kept in a yellow tartan thermos flask.

Verdict: There's nothing intrinsically annoying about this episode – it's just utterly dull and unmemorable. Nothing of note actually happens, except that there's a nice space battle and B'Elanna spends a lot of time talking to a man in a mask – and it doesn't help that the robots are so hugely derivative either. There's no character advancement, no excitement, no arc development, no learning experience . . . And, sadly, no interest for the viewer. 3/10.

#131: 'Alliances'

by Jeri Taylor

Directed by Les Landau
Music by Dennis McCarthy
US air date 22-01-96

Plot: Stardate 49337.4. Neelix discovers a group of Trabe refugees on a planet. The Trabe originally were slavers of the Kazon, until the Kazon rebelled. All Kazon technology is taken from the Trabe. The Trabe leader, Mabus, convinces Janeway that maybe it's time she, the Trabe and the Kazon all made peace with each other. A venue is arranged on Sobris, where the Kazon-Pomar will host their meeting with the leaders of the main Kazon sects, but betrayal is afoot, and someone intends the meeting to be a trap.

Déjà Vu?: Anthony de Longis himself describes the betrayal scene as reminiscent of the end of *Godfather III*.

Behind the Scenes: In the original script, Culluh dies with the other Majes.

The faint intro melody to the end theme is back.

The memorial service is in the mess hall, with all the furniture removed.

Voyager **Database:** Impedrezene stimulates cardiac function.

Kurt Bendera once saved B'Elanna's life near the Cardassian border. Chakotay met him at a mining colony on Telfas Prime.

Two crew members have been killed in four Kazon attacks over the past fortnight, but they're not named.

All Kazon technology is stolen from the Trabe. The Trabe kept them in slave camps, and encouraged the sects to fight each other, so that they wouldn't unite against their masters. The Trabe were rich scholars and artists, and nobody spoke of the slaves that supported them. Mabus was eight years old when the Kazon did rebel, and now the Kazon won't let the Trabe survivors settle anywhere.

(Lack of) Continuity: Jal Surat was murdered by Culluh (beamed into open space) in 'Maneuvers' but is somehow alive again.

The background to the Kazon–Trabe relationship was set up in 'Initiations' and 'Maneuvers'.

Tuvok is working on an orchid-growing project, grafting a cutting from a South American orchid on to a Vulcan favinit plant to produce a unique hybrid. This hobby was mentioned in 'Tattoo'.

Mabus says the Kazon rebelled 'over thirty years ago' – actually 36, as he was 8 at the time and is now 44. In 'Initiations', this revolt happened 26 years ago.

The Kazon are suddenly a lot more sexist than before, as if to emphasise how bad they are.

Ye Canna Change the Laws o' Physics: Bionutritional supplement deals with the Trabe's malnutrition.

Puzzles: Seska has told both Chakotay and Culluh that the baby is theirs. Which will it be . . .?

Bloopers: Right at the start, as Tom says 'not as bad as they hit', you can see a slight gap between the open hole in the set that is the main viewer, and the starfield backdrop.

Learn Your Lines: Janeway: 'We have to have something stable to rely on, and we do: the principles and ideals of the Federation. As far as I'm concerned, those are the best allies we could have.' None of which stops her dumping them when the occasion suits.

Highs: Janeway's visit to Tuvok's quarters.
   The betrayal.
   When Culluh says Seska has assured him that Janeway is 'sincere', it sounds as if he really wants to say 'desperate' – a nice touch.

Lows: Subtlety in theme – sexist Kazon and white supremacist Trabe – is distinctly lacking.

Verdict: The arc continues, as we hit an episode with an inevitable betrayal. Sadly, the plot doesn't stand up to close inspection – Janeway must have been suspicious, and the Trabe's motives are a bit vague as well. There's also no explanation of why the Kazon-Pomar let the meeting take place on their planet. On the plus side, Neelix is again used in a more serious negotiating/local guide role, and he is a lot more bearable in that than as the comedy relief. Seska and Culluh are used quite well, and De Longis as Jal Culluh is getting ever better with each appearance. It's a shame that Kazon society is suddenly so misogynistic, which it hadn't been before.

The whole thing should perhaps have been a two-parter, and could certainly have done without the ham-fisted lecturing that Janeway delivers and the men who want to keep their women under their thumbs. Nevertheless, a decent effort, with a great ending. 7.5/10.

#132: 'Threshold'

by Brannon Braga
from a story by Michael DeLuca

Directed by Alex Singer
Music by Jay Chattaway
US air date 29-01-96

Plot: Stardate 49373.4. A team of Tom, Harry and B'Elanna develop a means to achieve transwarp, and break the warp-10 barrier. Tom makes the first flight, but, upon his return, begins to evolve into a new reptilian species. Before the process is complete, he abducts Captain Janeway, and flees the ship.

Déjà Vu?: A certain amount of the story is hugely reminiscent of *TNG* episode 'Genesis' in which the *Enterprise* crew de-evolved into more primal life forms, such as lizards and spiders. Bits falling off Tom, especially his tongue, are reminiscent of Cronenberg's version of *The Fly*. Since Tom is supposedly evolving into a possible human future, we can throw in the *Outer Limits* episode 'The Sixth Finger' here too, in which David McCallum evolves into a bald-headed future alien.

Achieving warp 10 is said to leave you occupying every point in the universe simultaneously – a neat description of the infinite-improbability drive in *The Hitch-Hiker's Guide to the Galaxy*.

Behind the Scenes: Robbie McNeill (Tom Paris) particularly enjoyed the chance to wear prosthetics and act crazy rather than doing 'all the usual things'.

***Voyager* Database:** Shuttlebay 2 is the main hangar at the stern of the secondary hull.

Neelix spent two years as an engineer's assistant on a Trabalian freighter.

Tom has an enzyme imbalance in the cerebellum which gives him a 2 per cent chance of cerebral haemorrhage under transwarp stress.

While the shuttle is at transwarp, sensors pick up data on the whole sector – five billion gigaquads of it.

Neelix names a new coffee blend 'Paris Delight'.

Tom doesn't trust people who don't cry – including B'Elanna. He never believed it was the sign of weakness his father claimed. He lost his virginity at seventeen while his parents were away for the weekend.

(Lack of) Continuity: Transwarp was first mentioned in *Star Trek III: The Search for Spock*, in which the *Excelsior* was fitted with transwarp that didn't work. The Borg make use of transwarp conduits to zip around the galaxy from *TNG* episode 'Descent' onwards. In this episode, warp 10 is used as a synonym for *Excelsior*-style transwarp, as the Borg's transwarp conduits merely allow travel twenty times faster than maximum warp.

For *Star Trek: The Next Generation*, the warp-speed scale was designed on an asymptotic curve, with warp 10 as an infinite value. This limit was deliberately exceeded in 'All Good Things', as a hint that it was a future development.

The shuttlecraft *Cochrane* is named after the warp-speed pioneer Zephram Cochrane (TOS – 'Metamorphosis', *Star Trek: First Contact*).

Ye Canna Change the Laws o' Physics: The problem with the warp-10 holodeck simulations is subspace torque in the nacelle pylons, which rip the shuttle from the engines, rather than the other way round.

At transwarp, a tritanium hull depolarises (magnetically, I assume), creating velocity differential. A depolarisation matrix around the hull sorts it out. But wouldn't that imply a matrix to depolarise it, when they want the opposite? (Neelix's reaction to the above is 'I have no idea what they just said.')

The shuttle disappears off sensors when it hits the transwarp threshold. Isn't that to be expected, if it has instantly gone to infinite velocity?

The shuttle returns from transwarp out of a quantum surge from subspace. A surge of what? And the transwarp involving subspace is Borg-style transwarp conduits, which are subspace tunnels, not the warp-10/infinite-velocity transwarp.

Tom has elevated serotonin levels in the hypothalamus. The hypothalamus is a part of the brain that deals with autonomous functions including feeding, sleep and sexual arousal. Serotonin is a neurotransmitter also necessary for sleep.

The Doctor thinks Tom's changing molecular pattern is due to an allergy! His electrolytes are breaking down, and interstitial fluids congealing. Electrolytes are ions required by cells to regulate the flow of moisture through cell membranes – and, since the human body is 80 per cent water, they're therefore very important. The alveoli in his lungs are also congealing, and no longer processing oxygen. (These are sacs in the lungs, full of capillaries, where $oxygen/CO_2$ exchange takes place). Tom ends up breathing 80 per cent nitrogen, 20 per cent acid dichloride. His cellular membranes are breaking down. His lymphatic system breaks down.

Mitosis is cell division.

When Tom evolves, he gains an extra heart after his DNA rewrites itself. There are neuroelectrical and synaptic changes. Three unidentified organs appear, while others atrophy and are absorbed into the body.

The amount of his original DNA that is left can be determined by nucleogenic scan. Highly focused antiproton radiation will destroy the mutant DNA (and the real stuff, I'd wager!).

Warp 10 accelerated Tom's evolution, putting him through millions of years' worth of human evolution – apparently man will evolve into legless salamanders.

Puzzles: Tom wants to hit transwarp, switch off, then turn around and wait for *Voyager*. But, if transwarp really is infinite velocity, then wouldn't he be on the other side of the universe? Worse yet, switching off the engines returns Tom to where he started, which is a bit useless. Or as Arnold Rimmer might put it, 'We haven't budged a smegging inch.' Somehow, after abducting Janeway, he manages to stop at a nearby planet, without being returned to his starting point – and also without going further than a regular shuttle journey.

Learn Your Lines: Tom: 'You know anything about quantum warp theory or multispectral engine design?' Neelix: 'No, but I'm a quick study.'

Doc: 'What did he ingest?' B'Elanna: 'Just a cup of Neelix's coffee.' Doc: 'It's a miracle he's still alive.'

Highs: The Doc waking Tom.
Robbie McNeill is quite good.

Lows: The science, the outrageous inconsistencies from one scene to the next, and the whole lizard-babies thing. It's also fairly inconceivable that Chakotay is so stupid that he needs Tuvok to explain that Captain Janeway must be the female lizard.

Verdict: Frequently voted the worst ever episode, and often the worst *Trek* of all, 'Threshold' isn't quite that bad – but it is pretty dire. Apart from the whole thing being a combination of *Outer Limits* rip-off and *TNG* remake, the script is just so littered with inconsistencies. The concept is stupid, the script blinds us with technobabble (and not even good technobabble), and it has possibly the silliest twist in the tale ever to blemish the screen. That said, McNeill is fun, especially after his tongue falls out (you'll know what I mean when you see it), and almost manages to save the episode. 4/10.

#133: 'Meld'

by Michael Piller
from a story by Michael Sussman

Directed by Cliff Bole
Music by David Bell
US air date 05-02-96

Plot: When a body is found in Engineering, the Doctor quickly determines that it was murder, made to look like an accident. It doesn't take Tuvok long to identify Crewman Lon Suder (Brad Dourif) as the prime suspect. Suder readily confesses, saying he killed the man because he didn't like the way he was looking at him. While Janeway tries to decide on a suitable punishment – not wanting to execute him, and locking him up for the duration of the voyage being impractical – Tuvok tries to help Suder resolve his emotional difficulties by performing a Vulcan mind meld. Unfortunately, although Suder receives some of Tuvok's calm, Tuvok also begins to experience some of Suder's darkness within himself.

Behind the Scenes: Tim Russ has stated that Dourif has been his favourite guest star to work with so far. 'I was a major fan of his from *Dune* and *Exorcist III*.'

Though Tuvok meditates a lot, Russ's equivalent is playing flight-simulator games. ('I fly computer flight simulators on my Macintosh computer. For example FA18 Hornet, A10 Cuba, and occasionally I fly on line.')

The brig set is shared with *DS9*, which used it for the Starbase brig in 'Blaze of Glory'.

Voyager **Database:** Tom begins a gambling ring, to bet replicator rations against the next day's radiogenic-particle count. This is part of the arc leading to 'Investigations'.

Kal Rekk is the Vulcan Day of Atonement. Vulcans used to celebrate it with the Rumari, a pagan festival involving food, drink and nudity, which hasn't been observed for over 1,000 years (pre-Surak?). Unfortunately, the Kal Rekk is celebrated by solitude and silence.

Checking out the holidays of crew members' homeworlds is part of Neelix's duty as morale officer.

Starfleet Directive 101 confers the right to remain silent.

The Doctor has the medical knowledge of every Federation world.

Penuckle is a Cardassian card game.

(Lack of) Continuity: Suder is Betazoid – the same race as Lwaxana Troi – and so has empathic and telepathic abilities.

He complains that he can't even sense his own emotions, let alone other people's.

Ye Canna Change the Laws o' Physics: Suder is not insane, because he shows no sign of bipolar disorder, which would be a schizoid personality, and there are other disorders . . . Targeted neurosynaptic therapy (brain surgery!) didn't work on Suder. Nor did holodeck violence (it just doesn't feel the same).

After the meld, Tuvok has a lack of neuropeptides in the limbic system, and an imbalance in the mesiofrontal cortex, where the Vulcan psychosuppression system is located. This is a result of incompatibility with Betazoid telepathic centres.

Puzzles: How did Suder's DNA get in the wound, when he used a large tool (if you'll pardon the expression) to commit the crime? Did he sneeze in it or something?

Bloopers: Chakotay gives Tuvok a two-fingered salute in the ready room.

During his holo-murder, Ethan Phillips's prosthetic scalp for Neelix is dislodged as he slides down the wall.

Learn Your Lines: Doc: 'All of us have violent instincts. We evolved from predators – well, apart from me, of course: I was programmed by you predators.' Does this mean he has violent impulses too?

Suder: 'If you can't control the violence, the violence will control you.'

Highs: The conversation in the Brig about violence.

Tuvok's holodeck murder of Neelix.

Russ's whole performance – for example the subtle way he uses his hands while talking to Janeway.

The angry Tuvok baiting Janeway about punishments.

Lows: As usual in modern *Trek*, and especially this series, Vulcans are generally put down. They seem to have become whipping boys now Spock has gone.

Verdict: A good one. Though it revolves around a debate over punishment and rehabilitation, this is still one of the best character shows the series has produced. Every scene between Tuvok and Suder is electric, and both actors are superb. It's perhaps typecasting to see Brad Dourif as yet another serial killer, but he and Russ play off each other so well that it doesn't matter. The darker cinematography is used to great effect by the director, and Russ totally changes persona with the most subtle signs – such as when he is clenching his fists very slightly after the first meld. There are complexities in Suder's helping Tuvok, and in whether the 'weak' Janeway really disgusts Tuvok, since they're old, and close, friends. It even succeeds in being thought-provoking, over whom you agree with on the subject of punishment. Marvellous, in spite of the technobabble intrusion at the end. 9/10.

#134: 'Dreadnaught'

**by Gary Holland and Lisa Klink
from a story by Holland**

Directed by LeVar Burton
Music by Dennis McCarthy
US air date 12-02-96

Plot: Stardate 49447. When the sensors pick up energy traces from Cardassian weapons, B'Elanna guiltily realises that something from her past is about to haunt her. In this case, Dreadnaught, an intelligent Cardassian missile which she reprogrammed to destroy a Cardassian fuel dump. While making its way through the Badlands it was dragged to the Delta Quadrant by the Caretaker, and is now heading towards a heavily populated planet which it believes to be the target. B'Elanna must beam aboard and outsmart a computer she programmed, to save the innocent planet Rakosa V.

Déjà Vu?: Kes had an uncle called Elrond! That explains why she's described as elfin – she's related to some Tolkien elves. (In the script it says Elrem, but I don't think it's a glitch in the video: Lien definitely says Elrond.)

Behind the Scenes: Lots of fixtures and Okudagrams from *DS9* stock are used in the 'Dreadnaught' set.

B'Elanna's hair becomes more brown than black halfway through the episode, in the scenes aboard the missile.

Voyager **Database:** The Doctor has checked historical and anthropological databases from over 500 worlds and still hasn't chosen a name.

Dreadnaught has a warhead combing one metric tonne of matter with one metric tonne of antimatter. This is enough to destroy a small moon. Originally the Cardassians sent it to hit a Maquis arms dump on Sakura Prime, but the detonator failed. Two years ago, on Stardate 47592, Chakotay and B'Elanna reprogrammed it to attack a Cardassian fuel depot on Aschelan V, which it would approach through the Badlands to avoid detection. B'Elanna didn't tell Chakotay what she planned until Dreadnaught had launched.

Dreadnaught decoys pursuers with a false sensor image 100,000 kilometres away from its real position – which is given away by a neutrino surge. It is programmed to identify its target by size, radiothermic emissions and atmospheric compounds.

Type-6 torpedoes, like those carried by *Voyager*, weren't in service when Dreadnaught was launched.

B'Elanna's capture and coercion into deactivating Dreadnaught was number seven out of 39 possible threats programmed into it by her. Its computer is adaptive, however, and has spent the last two years thinking up new potential threats and strategies.

(Lack of) Continuity: The Badlands are where both *Voyager* and the Maquis ship were grabbed by the Caretaker.

As part of the story arc, Tom fought (verbally) with Rollins over the helm report. A good trick, considering that Rollins is one of those confirmed killed in 'Caretaker'.

The Kazon have been spreading stories of *Voyager*'s hostility, in the hope of preventing them from making friends.

Dreadnaught mentions the Federation–Cardassian treaty of 2367. In fact it was signed in 2366 (*TNG* – 'The Wounded' and 'Unification').

To keep in line with the other *Trek* starships, we get to hear *Voyager*'s self-destruct instructions: 'Computer: initiate the self-destruct sequence. Authorisation Janeway pi one one zero.'

Ye Canna Change the Laws o' Physics: Dreadnaught masks its warp trial with a randomised EM field – isn't that itself detectable?

Dreadnaught's only possible weakness is its thoron shock emitter. Getting that to fire at full power will destabilise the reactor, and a tachyon beam might overload it. This fails when the missile sends a plasma surge back along the beam. How can it send a slower-than-light surge back up against the flow of faster-than-light particles? It can't.

Puzzles: Isn't putting artificial gravity and life support in a missile a waste of resources?

Bloopers: When life support is terminated, Dreadnaught urges B'Elanna to beam back to *Voyager*, even though it has jammed the transporter lock on her earlier.

Learn Your Lines: Tom: 'When a bomb starts talking about itself in the third person, I get nervous.'

Janeway: 'Doctor, I forgot about you.' Doc: 'How flattering.'

Highs: When everyone else is evacuating the ship, Tuvok stays with Janeway. He claims it's in case she is injured and can't complete the mission, but he's obviously being economical with the truth.

Lows: A bit slow.

Verdict: Like 'Prototype', this is a B'Elanna episode in which not much actually happens, bar Dawson talking to herself a lot. There's never any real tension or excitement, though there are flashes of humour. It's also top heavy with technobabble. 6.5/10.

#130: 'Death Wish'

by Michael Piller
from a story by Shawn Piller

Directed by James L Conway
Music by Jay Chattaway
US air date 19-02-96

Plot: Stardate 49301.2. While trying to draw a sample from a rogue comet, *Voyager* accidentally frees Q2 from his prison. He had been put there by the Continuum to prevent him from committing suicide. Q shows up to take him back, but Q2 demands political asylum in the Federation. Janeway agrees to hold a hearing, with Q representing the Continuum, and Tuvok representing Q2. If Q2 wins, he will be made mortal and allowed to die. Despite Q's attempts to bribe Janeway by suggesting he'd send the ship home if she found in the Continuum's favour, the case is stalemated – until Q2 and Tuvok suggest visiting the Continuum itself.

Behind the Scenes: Kate Mulgrew – a close friend of both John de Lancie (Q) and the director James L Conway – describes shooting as 'eight days of intense creative pleasure for me'.

Riker is the first Starfleet regular from another *Trek* series to appear in *Voyager*.

Voyager Database: Q2 does a little hand spin when using his powers, whereas 'our' Q snaps his fingers.

No other Q has ever tried to commit suicide.

Thaddius Riker – Old Iron Boots – commanded the 102nd New York Infantry under General Sherman in 1864. Q2 once saved his life.

The Q are *not* omnipotent – all else is propaganda!

The 'double effect' of assisted suicides dates from the Bolian Middle Ages, and states, 'An action that has the principal effect of relieving suffering may be ethically justified, even if the same action has the secondary effect of causing death.'

The Continuum we see isn't the literal appearance of it: it's merely how it could be shown in a manner that humans (and Vulcans) might understand. It's a desert road with such oddities as a scarecrow in Starfleet uniform, and a handless clock. The Q play croquet with planets. Tuvok and Janeway are the only non-Q visitors the Continuum has ever had.

One of Q2's suicide attempts started a hundred-year war between Vulcans and Romulans.

Made mortal, Q2 takes the name Quinn, and dies from ingesting Nogatch hemlock, for which there is no cure.

(Lack of) Continuity: The omnipotent Q has been a thorn in Picard's side throughout *TNG*: he put humanity on trial in 'Encounter at Farpoint', made Riker a Q in 'Hide And Q', introduced the Borg in 'Q Who', was stripped of his powers in 'Déjà Q', forced the crew to be Robin Hood's Merry Men in 'QPid', fetched a new Q in 'True Q', gave Picard a second chance at life in 'Tapestry' and bounced Picard through time in 'All Good Things'. He also showed up on *DS9* in 'QLess'. Though he was originally a villain, by 'Q Who' there was a sense that he may not be just an evil adversary, and by 'Déjà Q' he was set to be comic relief for most of his appearances.

Janeway points out Q's one remaining virtue – he has never been a liar.

Ye Canna Change the Laws o' Physics: The double-effect discussions are clearly based on the debate over Jack Kevorkian.

Puzzles: Why does Q2 have a Starfleet uniform?

It seems very odd that Vulcan, with its respect for life under all circumstances, would have a culture of ritual suicide. It's doubly odd that this hasn't shown up before, especially when Sarek is dying from Bendii Syndrome in 'Sarek' and 'Unification'. The Klingons, on the other hand, *do* have such a culture (suicide rather than capture in various episodes, and the Hegh'bat ceremony Worf wants in 'Ethics') and it would seem more suited to them. The impression given is that this story was originally a *TNG* idea, with Worf fulfilling Tuvok's role as Quinn's counsel.

Bloopers: Riker still has a *TNG* combadge, but clearly knows of *Voyager*'s disappearance, so he should have one of the new *Generations/DS9/Voyager* ones.

Why wipe his mind, too, and not let him report to Starfleet? Unlike the other witnesses, he's not from a past era.

Learn Your Lines: Neelix (concerning Welsh rarebit): 'She never told me she liked rarebits. What is a rarebit, anyway?'

   Tuvok: 'I am curious: have the Q always had an absence of manners, or is it the result of some natural evolutionary process that comes with omnipotence?'

Highs: The scene in which Q calls himself as a witness.

Verdict: A brilliantly funny Q episode, which, like 'Meld', manages to be thought-provoking without being annoying. Gerrit Graham is an excellent guest as Q2, and he and de Lancie spark well off each other. De Lancie and Mulgrew also have great chemistry. This is an episode that requires a second or third viewing to pick up all the subtleties and the humour. Add to this some thought-provoking dialogue about execution versus suicide, and a very complex moral mine-field, and this becomes so much more than just another Q comedy hour. Best of all, it manages this without ever becoming lecturing. Simply wonderful, and the best Q episode since 'Tapestry'. 9/10.

#136: 'Lifesigns'

by Ken Biller

Directed by Cliff Bole
Music by Paul Baillargeon
US air date 26-02-96

Plot: Stardate 49504.3. Answering a distress signal, the ship rescues a dying Vidiian woman. The Doctor stabilises her, and then manages to transfer her consciousness into a holo-matrix before her brain stops functioning. He then extrapo-lates her original appearance and gives her a holographic body. She turns out to be a doctor, Denara Pel, and together they work on a way to save her brain functions. This entails a graft of brain tissue from a reluctant B'Elanna. As they work together, however, the Doctor finds himself developing an emotional attraction to Denara.

Déjà Vu?: B'Elanna's dilemma over whether to donate tissues to help an enemy echoes Worf's dilemma over whether to donate blood to a Romulan in *TNG* episode 'The Enemy'. In Worf's case, he refused.

Behind the Scenes: The song is 'I Only Have Eyes For You'.

Voyager **Database:** The Doctor holds 50 million gigaquads of data.

Healthy Vidiians look human apart from a small vertical ridge in the middle of the forehead.

Among Vidiians, congregating in groups is discouraged as a public-health risk.

Denara calls the Doctor 'Shmullus' after her uncle.

The Doc seeks Tom's advice on what to do about his feelings for Denara. Tom's first rejection was from Susan Crabtree at the Academy.

The Doctor makes his first personal log entry.

Grimes takes Paris's place at the helm. Crewman Foster is also named.

(Lack of) Continuity: Tom's misbehaviour continues as part of a bubbling story arc. His being an automobile aficionado, from 'The 37s', is mentioned again.

Denara was treating the Phage on Fina Prime.

The brain operation the Doctor performs was developed by Dr Leonard H McCoy, a.k.a. Bones, in 2253. This would be before he joined the *Enterprise* crew.

The Doctor again says that he was activated on Stardate 48308 rather than shortly after Stardate 48315.6. Unlike the case in 'Projections' there's no malfunction to blame this time. This will be subtly retconned in 'Relativity'.

Seska plans an ambush at Hemikek IV, and instructs her spy on *Voyager* to cause a warp-coil accident by misaligning the magnetic constrictor coils.

Ye Canna Change the Laws o' Physics: Lectrazine stabilises Denara's renal and cardiovascular organs (kidneys, heart and lungs). High dosages of inaprovaline stimulates cell regeneration.

Her parietal lobe has been implanted with a web of

bioneural circuitry and nanofibres. These store synaptic energy and act as a neurocortical stimulator to supplement her higher brain functions. The parietal lobe is a lobe between the frontal and the occipital lobes of the brain.

Denara Pel is a haematologist – a specialist in the study of blood disorders. Her synaptic patterns are stored in the holodeck pattern buffers for a few days.

The Doctor grafts some DNA from B'Elanna's parietal lobe into Denara's cerebral cortex, and must create an axonal pathway from there to the basal ganglia. This would probably be the pons in a human brain.

Puzzles: Since Denara wants to tour the ship, why not use a holodeck version instead of refusing her?

We learn in 'Message in a Bottle' that the Doc has had sex. Presumably it was in this episode, but what I want to know is, was it with the holographic Denara, or with the real one? Or both?

Learn Your Lines: Kes: 'Romance is not a malfunction.'

Doc: 'Mr Paris, I assume you have a great deal of experience at being rejected by women.' (And he means this as a compliment!)

Highs: The 57 Chevy on Mars.

The Doctor and Kes discussing romance. His subsequent choice of time to tell Denara of his feelings.

Lows: The slimy gigolo.

The unsubtle lecture about looks not mattering where love is concerned.

Verdict: The Doctor gets a romance . . . He and the guest star (Susan Diol) don't seem to have that much chemistry, or at least not enough to really make the show work in a naturalistic way. There are some nice humorous moments, but that artificiality, and a preponderance of technobabble in the latter parts, do rather work against it. It's not actually bad, and it does help the Doc develop a little more, but it's just not good enough. 6/10.

#135: 'Investigations'

by Jeri Taylor
from a story by Jeff Schnauffer and Ed Bond

Directed by Les Landau
Music by Jay Chattaway
US air date 11-03-96

Plot: Stardate 49485.2. Neelix, while producing his daily newscast, *A Briefing with Neelix*, discovers that Tom Paris is to leave the ship. Tom's fights with authority have finally driven him to resign his commission and quit. Hardly has Tom left on a Talaxian freighter, than it is attacked and he is abducted by the Kazon-Nistrim. Culluh and Seska have heard from their spy on *Voyager* that he was quitting, and may be open to joining them. Meanwhile, Tuvok and Chakotay use Neelix's nosiness to flush out their prime suspects – Hogan and Jonas. Tom's insubordination over the last few weeks, however, was a ruse cooked up by him and Janeway, and he is really out to discover Seska's plans.

Behind the Scenes: Watch the teaser, and take note of the man in the green uniform, to whom Harry is talking. That is the then Crown Prince, now King, Abdullah of Jordan!

Some comfortable-looking settees and a new console/monitor have appeared in the mess hall set, near the door.

***Voyager* Database:** Neelix serves Hlaka soup and zabee nuts.

Ensign Pablo Baytart juggles for a hobby.

Harry edited the Starfleet Academy newspaper for a year, and reported on the first Maquis actions.

Neelix's old friend Laxeth used to sell Pendrashian cheese, but is now communications officer on a Talaxian convoy.

Hamilton is the name of another crew member.

(Lack of) Continuity: The plasma burst irradiates the warp nacelles, and burns out the lining, made of verterium cortenide. This is a dense composite of polysilicate verterium and monocrystal cortenum – minerals found only at Hemikek IV. The instruction to sabotage the ship for the ambush at

Hemikek IV came in the previous episode.

Neelix mentions signals to Mithren, where his contact in 'Persistence of Vision' was, and Kotati.

Ye Canna Change the Laws o' Physics: Jonas gets second-degree burns. In the real world, burns are classified by degree of depth: first-degree burns, such as severe sunburn, cause redness and pain; second-degree burns cause blistering of the skin; third-degree burns destroy the dermis and epidermis. Incidentally, most burn victims die from infection, as, contrary to popular belief, the destruction of skin tissues by heat leaves it open to attack, rather than cauterising the wound. (It's handy having an uncle who is a retired BP firemaster!)

Puzzles: So, if they couldn't go to Hemikek for the vital minerals, how did they repair the warp coils?

Why doesn't Tom kill Seska? After seeing what failure to do so resulted in after Chakotay's visit to her, you'd think someone would have learned a lesson.

Bloopers: Neelix promises Tom that he made a lot of friends, and everybody will be sad to see him go. Then only Neelix and Harry show up to see him off.

Neelix's stunt double is obvious, and therefore a bit of a throwback to the old days of TOS stuntmen who looked nothing like the people they were doubling. He doesn't have Phillips's build.

Highs: The running gag about the Doctor wanting to do a broadcast on topics such as 'How to keep your nostrils happy' and 'The Klingon glottis, friend or foe'.

Tom's leaving is actually quite moving.

Neelix has quite a neat move to drop the spy into the warp core.

Lows: Neelix's broadcasts, especially the opening one.

Tom's leaving would have been more moving if he had actually left!

Verdict: The arc that has been building for weeks finally gets its first payoff (of two). Using Neelix's sudden desire to run a news service as a framing device, we finally discover what has been motivating Tom, and see them make a play against the Kazon. However, the crew don't actually seem to gain much beyond avoiding one ambush and getting rid of the spy – Seska and Culluh are still out there. Despite this, there are some good twists, and even Neelix isn't too annoying apart from his news broadcasts. Very foolish of Tom not to kill Seska when he had a gun on her, though. And how did he get that shuttle? 7/10.

#137: 'Deadlock'

by Brannon Braga

Directed by David Livingston
Music by Dennis McCarthy
US air date 18-03-96

Plot: Stardate 49548.7. After passing through the spatial anomaly of the week, the ship gets hit by proton bursts. As repair crews work, Harry is killed by explosive decompression, and Kes vanishes. However, an undamaged *Voyager* is also stranded without power. It turns out that the anomaly duplicated the ship and crew, but didn't duplicate the antimatter – and there isn't enough to run both vessels. Both *Voyager*s occupy the same space and time, but slightly out of phase with each other, and Kes made it to the undamaged one, where she explains that their attempts to deal with the problem by proton bursts are damaging her *Voyager*. As the two Janeways team up to find a solution, the undamaged *Voyager* is attacked by Vidiians, who storm the ship.

Déjà Vu?: The crew and ship's duplication is reminiscent of Moonbase Alpha's duplication in the *Space: 1999* episode 'Another Time, Another Place', though the *Voyager* producers resist the urge to have the duplicate ship reach a duplicate Earth.

Worse still, the *Red Dwarf* episode 'Demons and Angels' triplicated their ship, and included the fact that a vital component wasn't triplicated.

Duplication of ships and characters is an old trick in *Star Trek*, from TOS episode 'The Enemy Within' onwards through the Mirror Universe series, Riker in 'Second Chances' and so on.

Killing off the crew isn't new in *Trek* either – almost every regular character in the other three series died at some point, and then came back.

Harry's death is lifted straight from the end of *Aliens*.

Behind the Scenes: The Vidiian ship is new, but will be seen again later.

***Voyager* Database:** The galley's thermal array vaporised an entire pot roast and needs new anodyne relays.

Human/Ktaran babies are common enough for rare problems to be notable.

Three hundred and forty-seven Vidiians invade the ship, though we see only four.

(Lack of) Continuity: Harry previously died in 'Emanations' and here goes spacewalking without a spacesuit when a hatch blows out.

Samantha Wildman's baby is born twice. The surviving *Voyager*'s baby dies after the proton bursts interfere with its osmotic pressure therapy. The lost *Voyager*'s one is brought over by that *Voyager*'s Harry.

Tuvok's wife was in labour for 96 hours with their third child.

The Doctor of the damaged *Voyager* sets up extra facilities in Holodeck 2.

Ye Canna Change the Laws o' Physics: A large plasma drift half the length of the sector is a streamer of interstellar gas. The ship is duplicated by a subspace divergence within it.

The baby has a slight haemocythemic imbalance, for which osmotic pressure therapy should stabilise the cell membranes. This is evidently some kind of problem with the blood-cell membranes.

Proton bursts in the sensors will keep the warp core ticking over. Wouldn't proton bursts in the warp core do it better? On the damaged *Voyager*, magnetising the hull might protect against the proton bursts. I'd hope they'd remember to use a *positive* magnetic field – a negative one would attract them more, as protons are positively charged.

To reverse the duplication, they try recreating the divergence and depolarising it. Reversing the polarity might have more luck, rather than removing it. This entails having both ships emit a resonance pulse – of what? – from the main deflectors.

Kent State University tried this experiment, according to Janeway. This university really exists, but hasn't tried experimenting with subspace divergences . . .

Puzzles: So which *Voyager* was the original, and which was the duplicate? Well, both of them . . .

If the antimatter wasn't duplicated, then how can the surviving *Voyager* be repaired and refuelled?

Bloopers: Although the two *Voyagers* are supposed to be occupying the same space and the same time, out of phase with each other, the only exterior shot we see (when they try to merge the ships) shows them hanging side by side in space.

Learn Your Lines: Janeway to Harry: 'We're Starfleet officers. Weird is part of the job description.'

Highs: Harry's death is cool.
The invasion by Vidiians.

Lows: Silly science, and duplication is unoriginal.

Verdict: A pretty good episode all round, with Harry's best death to date (even if it is cribbed directly from the climax of *Aliens*). Though the science is, as usual, supremely silly, the concept is fun, and the ensemble cast are on top form. Kate Mulgrew proves once again that she is the star, somehow managing to put a subtle difference into the two Janeways even though they're the same person. Not entirely a classic, but damn good fun anyway. 7/10.

#138: 'Innocence'

by Lisa Klink
from a story by Anthony Williams

Directed by James L Conway
Music by Jay Chattaway
US air date 08-04-96

Plot: While searching for mineral deposits on a moon of Drayan II, Tuvok's shuttle crashes, killing his copilot, Bennet, and stranding him. Tuvok soon makes contact with three stranded children, whose ship was knocked down by the same storm, killing the adults on board. They say they were sent here to die, and are afraid of a monster said to live in a nearby cave. Meanwhile, the Drayan authorities are upset by *Voyager*'s trespassing on their sacred moon, and want them to leave.

Déjà Vu?: The monster said to live in the cave is the Morok. This was the name of a group of aliens in the *Doctor Who* story 'The Space Museum'. In this case, though, its cave-dwelling nature suggests it was probably derived from HG Wells's Morlocks, in *The Time Machine*.

Behind the Scenes: Some more grey has crept back into Chakotay's hair.

The jungle is a studio set, of course.

***Voyager* Database:** Chakotay once goofed on a first-contact mission, forgetting that male and female Tarkannans have different sign languages, and accidentally propositioned the ambassador. He doesn't say which sex the ambassador was, or whether his offer was accepted.

The Drayans were once a hi-tech race, but changed their ways after Alcia's grandfather feared that technology was becoming more important than people in their society.

Starfleet emergency rations are concentrated, vitamin-enriched nutritional supplements.

Vulcan children are taught to detach themselves from their emotions by visualising them, and then envisioning their being suitably dealt with. An example given is to visualise fear as a thundercloud, and then 'see' it being blown away by a strong wind. Tuvok claims Vulcans never feel fear.

Tuvok's children all achieved the ability to meditate at the apparent age of these three children.

Once we learn that the Drayans age backwards, Tressa turns out to be 96, and says Tuvok reminds her of her grandson.

The second Drayan moon is Crysata, meaning sacred ground.

Tuvok wouldn't try to protect someone from the *natural* conclusion of life, as Vulcans believe that death is the end of a journey.

(Lack of) Continuity: The ship is still seeking polyferranide deposits, as in 'Tattoo'.

The warp core runs for three years without refuelling, and contains a compositor which recrystallises dilithium.

The Federation has over 150 worlds in it.

Tuvok says that having pointed ears doesn't improve hearing, though this contradicts Spock's abilities in TOS. He also has four children, whom he pointedly describes as 'well behaved'. He says that his attachment to his children goes beyond the emotion of love, as they are a part of him.

As seen in *Star Trek III*, Vulcans believe that the katra, their soul, survives the body's death. Tuvok does not subscribe to this belief.

Ye Canna Change the Laws o' Physics: The shuttle crash was caused by unusually strong and unpredictable atmospheric currents, thanks to a thermal inversion gradient due to electrodynamic turbulence, itself caused by solar flares. This is actually scientifically accurate: it's Tuvok's way of saying there are thunderstorms around.

Drayans age in reverse. So, how are they born? I mean, an adult body could hardly fit in a uterus . . .

Tuvok's Vulcan lute ('Persistence of Vision') is a five-stringed instrument tuned on a diatonic scale – in other words, using the five tones and two semitones familiar in Western music.

A dielectric field protects the shuttles from the turbulence.

This simply means that a field of nonconductivity keeps lightning from knocking them down.

Puzzles: How could Chakotay forget something about a race nobody has met before? If the Tarkannans were known, then it couldn't have been a first-contact situation.

Tuvok would trust a child with a phaser? Bloody hell, I wouldn't!

Learn Your Lines: Tuvok: 'Vulcan parents never shield their children from the truth. Doing so would only hinder their ability to cope with inevitable difficulties.'

Tuvok: 'We often fear what we do not understand. Our best defence is knowledge.'

Highs: Tuvok tries to repair the shuttle, in the vain hope that the three kids will behave themselves.

He has a good singing voice, too.

Lows: The twist is a bit obvious, to say the least.

Alcia is also very annoying.

Verdict: It sounds like a recipe for disaster – strand a character on a dubious jungle set with three kids. Incredibly, it works, mainly thanks to Tim Russ's performance, which subtly proves that Vulcans do get as pissed-off by annoying kids as the rest of us. Even more amazing, the child actors are quite bearable too. The story doesn't really go anywhere, but it does give Tuvok some great dialogue, and some moving scenes. On the downside, the twist is a bit cheesy, and the adult aliens are annoying – though, oddly, that fits, given the nature of the twist! 8.5/10.

#139: 'The Thaw'

by Joe Menosky
from a story by Richard Gadas and Michael Piller

Directed by Marvin Rush
Music by David Bell
US air date 29-04-96

Plot: The ship finds several people frozen under a planet's surface, whose hibernation unit hadn't woken them up after a global disaster had passed. In fact the system has worked, but the sleepers have chosen not to come out. When B'Elanna and Harry plug themselves into the system, they find that the sleepers have a mental world in which they are being terrorised by a sinister clown, and other characters created by the system. The designers had arranged for a computer to generate anything the sleepers' brains wished, but it had also generated their worst fears and dark sides.

Déjà Vu?: This one will probably go down as the *Voyager* episode most notably ripped off, rather than the other way round. The basic concept of people in suspended animation being used to fuel the existence of an artificial intelligence occupying an artificial reality is the one behind the hit movie *The Matrix*. However, the concept is rather older, and the first screen version of a computer-generated mental landscape was another matrix – the APC Net in the *Doctor Who* story 'The Deadly Assassin'.

Michael McKean's performance as the clown is reminiscent of the Joker.

Harry's being aged, then sent to childhood, echoes what happens to Nyssa and Tegan in the *Doctor Who* story 'Mawdryn Undead'.

Behind the Scenes: The opening part of the teaser, with Harry playing the clarinet for Tom, and thus disturbing Baytart in the neighbouring cabin, was actually filmed for 'Death Wish', but cut due to timing constraints. Eventually it ended up here, replacing a straightforward approach to planet shot.

***Voyager* Database:** Fluid conduits in the walls conduct sound too well.

Voyager was built for combat performance first and foremost.

The System is adaptive, reading the sleepers' minds to change the artificial environment, and generating the clown from the sleepers' fear.

Harry visited a radiation-disaster hospital on a colony when he was nine.

(Lack of) Continuity: Harry practises his clarinet for a duet with Lt Susan Nicoletti, whom Tom claims to have been unsuccessfully pursuing for six months.

Galorndon Core, where Chulak of Romulus was defeated, is a planet in the Romulan Neutral Zone, seen in *TNG* episodes 'The Enemy' and 'Unification'.

Ye Canna Change the Laws o' Physics: Solar flares caused the planet to suffer magnetic storms, radiation and glaciers nineteen years ago. In real life, solar flares have sometimes been considered a possible cause of ice ages.

The Doctor says high norepinephrine levels are a sign of high stress. This is accurate.

Learn Your Lines: Janeway: 'The ability to recognise danger, to fight it or run away from it – that's what fear gives us. When fear holds you hostage, how do you make it let go?' Which is the literal point of the episode.

B'Elanna: 'There's no way an artificial intelligence can replace actual brain functions.' Doc: 'I'll choose not to take that personally, Lieutenant.'

Highs: Michael McKean is scary as the clown.

Janeway's final defeat of him is clever, and has some great lines.

Lows: The screaming baby Harry.

Verdict: Another near-classic. Michael McKean's clown really makes the show – he's utterly surreal and scary, in a way that the more famous Joker never has been on screen. Though a low-budget show with stock sets, this still ends up as a highlight of the series, because the theme – the struggle against fear – is both obvious and accessible, yet also handled with subtlety. The dialogue sparkles too, and there's a notable lack of technobabble except for in a few scenes. The final clown/Janeway scene is also stunning, with a neat twist. Marvellous, and up there with the best that *Trek* has to offer. It's a shame that the producers often forget that bigger isn't necessarily better, as *Trek*'s best episodes tend to be low-key ones like this surreal and magnetically attractive one. 8.5/10.

140: 'Tuvix'

by Ken Biller
from a story by Andrew Price and Mark Gaberman

Directed by Cliff Bole
Music by Jay Chattaway
US air date 06-05-96

Plot: Stardate 49655.2. While on an away mission to look for new food plants, Tuvok and Neelix are combined into a single being, Tuvix, by the transporter. The new being has a single personality, but both men's memories. At first he makes a lot of friends, but Kes misses Neelix and finds Tuvix's advances unpleasant. When the Doctor discovers that one of the plant samples is a parasite whose DNA caused the fusion, he realises that the process can be reversed – but Tuvix doesn't want to die.

Behind the Scenes: The original title was 'Symbiogenesis'.

The science lab is a revamp of the isolation part of sickbay, but with a blue background instead of a yellow one.

Voyager **Database:** Tuvix has double the memories, but only one consciousness. For some reason he has more of Neelix's mannerisms than Tuvok's. He is also right-handed, like Neelix, whereas Tuvok is left-handed. He tries naming himself Neevok, before settling on Tuvix.

Trellian crêpes are Kes's favourite food.

Tuvok sent Janeway letters when he was assigned to Jupiter Station, and she has kept them, which suggests some interesting possibilities. When Kes says she loves Neelix, not Tuvix, Janeway says she knows how Kes feels!

Tuvix describes execution as what they used to do to murderers centuries earlier. He views Tuvok and Neelix as his parents, and has both their wills to live.

Sickbay is on Deck 5.

(Lack of) Continuity: Harry plays his clarinet again.

Tuvix takes hours to do things Tuvok thought would take days, by following hunches.

Tuvix still loves Kes (the Neelix part of him) and T'Pel (the Tuvok part). He says Tuvok is devoted to his wife.

Tuvix's cooking is better than Neelix's.

Ye Canna Change the Laws o' Physics: All Tuvok and Neelix's biomatter – proteins, enzymes and DNA – were fused on a molecular level. The orchid material is also fused in, hence the pattern on Tuvix's uniform – an illogical but subtle and attractive stylistic touch.

The orchid contains chloroplasts, cytoplasmic proteins and lysosomal enzymes. In fact all plants have chloroplasts, which perform the act of photosynthesis, while all cells contain cytoplasmic proteins, which are the substance in which the various organs of the cell are suspended.

Tom and B'Elanna experiment with a chrysanthemum and clematis – two real flowers – as well as the alien orchid.

Attaching a radioisotope marker to the orchid DNA strands to beam them out is compared to the barium meal given before X-rays in modern hospitals.

Puzzles: How come Neelix gains a Starfleet uniform when they're separated?

Bloopers: Just after Tom brings the ship down from warp 6 to impulse on Tuvix's orders, Janeway makes her decision in her ready room . . . And the stars visible through the window are still streaking with the warp effect, rather than being the slowly moving backdrop curtain used for shots when the ship is at impulse.

Learn Your Lines: Tuvok: 'Mr Neelix, do you think you could behave a little less like yourself?'

Tuvix: 'A name can have a significant effect upon a person's sense of identity.'

Janeway: 'At what point did he become an individual, and

not a transporter accident?' Or at what point does it become a baby and not a collection of fertilised cells? A (retroactive) debate about abortion.

Highs: The Doctor's verdict on Tuvix's fitness.

The ending is quite stunning in its audacity: Janeway cold-bloodedly murders Tuvix, and nobody says a word against it, other than the Doctor.

Tuvix's uniform is really great. They should all be like that.

Lows: It's a bit slow in places.

Verdict: Once again, the basic premise sounds appallingly silly, but the episode rises way above its concept. This can certainly be attributed to the performance of Tom Wright as Tuvix, since the pacing of the episode is rather slow. He carries it almost single-handedly, and is just excellent. This is by far the most debated episode in fandom, especially on the Internet, over whether Janeway was right or wrong to forcibly separate Tuvok and Neelix, murdering Tuvix in the process. It's impossible to tell whether the shocking ending was planned from the start, or was the outcome of needing a reset for the following week, but either way it worked to provide one of the series' most thought-provoking, and the single most discussed, episode. 8/10.

#141: 'Resolutions'

by Jeri Taylor

Directed by Alex Singer
Music by Dennis McCarthy
US air date 13-05-96

Plot: Stardate 49690.1. Janeway and Chakotay contracted a virus from an insect bite, which will kill them if they leave the planet they were exploring. After being on line for a month solid, the Doctor finally gives up on finding a cure, and returns them to the planet in stasis tubes, along with

supplies, a replicator, a prefab shelter and a Type-9 shuttle.
Janeway leaves Tuvok in command, with orders not to try
contacting a nearby Vidiian colony to ask for their medical
knowledge. On the planet, Janeway befriends a monkey and
dodges storms. Harry persuades Tuvok to disobey instructions and contact the Vidiians, and Denara Pel says she has a
cure, but the rendezvous is a trap. Meanwhile, Janeway and
Chakotay's relationship develops.

Déjà Vu?: Oddly reminiscent of 'The Paradise Syndrome',
TOS episode with Kirk as a Native American.

Behind the Scenes: There's some lively location filming in
the Angeles National Forest (also used for the shanty town in
Star Trek: First Contact), including some attractive night
shooting, which is far more expensive than normal location
shooting.

The Vidiian ship model from 'Deadlock' reappears, with
some new smaller attack vessels.

Voyager **Database:** A Type-9 shuttle has a maximum speed
of warp 4. This would take 700 years to get home.

A bath is Janeway's favourite way of relaxing.

Kes's father died shortly after she turned one year old.

Chakotay's father thought it important that he learn to
build log cabins. Chakotay also used to give his mother neck
rubs, as he was the only one in the family whom she trusted
not to make the pain worse.

Janeway's parents insisted she learn camping and gar-
dening, which is convenient.

(Lack of) Continuity: Denara Pel previously appeared in
'Lifesigns', and still calls the Doctor 'Shmullus'. B'Elanna's
phage-resistant Klingon DNA was mentioned in 'Faces' and
we're told that the Vidiian ship destroyed in 'Deadlock' had
over 300 Vidiians aboard, which means that either there were
647 Vidiians altogether in that episode, or they were
somehow able to put more people on to *Voyager* than they
actually had.

When B'Elanna tells Harry it's 'time to move on' this also
seems to mark the end of the B'Elanna–Harry relationship

(such as it was).

As becomes increasingly common, when the going gets tough, Chakotay wants to give up and settle where they are.

It takes *Voyager* six weeks to travel the 70 light years from the planet to the rendezvous point with the Vidiians. That would equate to 115 years to get home, so the ship must have travelled more slowly than usual.

Chakotay tells Janeway a tribal myth, which turns out to be about how he joined the Maquis and ended up on *Voyager*.

Ye Canna Change the Laws o' Physics: The osteogenic stimulator sets broken bones – by causing them to grow back together, judging by the word.

Puzzles: Why doesn't Tuvok change to a red uniform and captain's pips? Every other character in *Trek* who has been promoted this way (Data, Worf, etc.) has done so.

What about the shuttle Janeway and Chakotay had – was it left behind on the planet?

Bloopers: At one point Tuvok says it has been six weeks since they left the planet. A couple of scenes later, Harry says it has been three weeks.

In spite of now being captain, Tuvok keeps his lieutenant's pips. Anybody would think he knew Janeway would soon be back.

When Chakotay starts pulling the segments of the shelter out of their containers, you can see they're rubber sheets stretched over wooden frames, unlike the more solid finished shelter.

When Janeway goes to bed after Chakotay made her a headboard, there's no sign of it on the bed.

Learn Your Lines: Chakotay: 'I can't sacrifice the present for a future that may never happen.'

Highs: Captain Tuvok, and especially that beautiful Vulcan robe – I want one of those . . .

At least the night-filming is good.

Chakotay admitting that his tribal-myth story is made up.

Lows: Janeway turning into a *Doctor Who* companion.

The homespun costumes are especially hideous.

Verdict: Thoroughly dire. This so utterly and completely destroys any sign of Janeway being a strong female character. She's virtually unrecognisable here: when the monkey appears in the woods she screams for Chakotay; when clouds fill the sky at the beginning of the storm, she asks, 'What happened to the sky?' (Has she never seen a storm before?) She's incapable of running and holding a briefcase at the same time, and while the storm rages she hides – yelling and whimpering – under a table.

Back on the ship, Tuvok as captain is the highlight, though that isn't saying much since he's out of character too, alternating between claiming to suppress emotions and claiming not to have them, and behaving like a bad Hollywood Captain Bligh. And the worst thing is that this is the best part of the show. 1/10.

#142: 'Basics'

by Michael Piller

Directed by Rick Kolbe
Music by Dennis McCarthy
US air date 20-05-96

Plot: The ship rescues a dying Kazon, Tierna, who claims to have brought a message from Seska: Chakotay's baby has been born, and Culluh is set to kill mother and child because it isn't his. Tierna was sent to try to persuade Chakotay to attempt a rescue, but the Kazon gunners shot his shuttle to pieces. On a vision quest, Kolopak tells Chakotay that he must face his responsibilities as a father. The ship is constantly attacked by the Kazon, concentrating on an apparently unimportant area. Tierna then uses a hidden explosive in a suicide that disables the ship. Tom takes a shuttle to seek reinforcements from a Talaxian colony. The ship is stormed by Kazon, and, when Janeway tries the self-destruct, it fails, because that is controlled by the 'unimportant' area the Kazon attacks hit. Culluh and Seska, both still happily allied and proud of their trap, land the ship on a volcanic planet, and dump the crew there. When *Voyager* takes off, it is crewed by the Kazon, and only the Doctor and Suder remain on board.

Behind the Scenes: The extension of the landing struts is from 'The 37s' but the rest of the landing is a new effect.

Voyager **Database:** One of Chakotay's ancestors, Ce Acatl, was the result of an Indian woman raped by a white man.

The trap is sprung at Gema II.

A drug called pulmozine is named.

The Doctor can perform an autonomic-response analysis as a lie detector, but for it to be effective the baseline responses for the species must be known.

The secondary command processors in the starboard ventral section control the autodestruct sequence.

The crew are stranded on Hanon IV.

(Lack of) Continuity: Suder, confined to quarters, has taken up orchid husbandry under Tuvok's guidance. He names his newest creation the Tuvok Orchid, and wants to persuade Janeway to let him help make the airponics section more effective. He is also still taking meditation lessons from Tuvok.

The baby will be trained as a Kazon Iskara. Seska told Culluh that it was a result of Chakotay raping her while she was under his command. Rightly, but surprisingly, this very much offends Culluh.

Ye Canna Change the Laws o' Physics: Amazingly, Harry's idea for the decoy holoships is scientifically sound. Using parabolic mirrors should make it possible to project a holographic picture outwards. Sadly, any points gained for that piece of realism have to be deducted for the (admittedly funny) bit where the Doctor finds himself 'overboard'. Even overlooking his audible yells in vacuum, he should have been projected on to the hull of *Voyager*, and a reflection of him shown in space (and the size of a Talaxian ship too).

Polycythemia is an abnormal increase in red blood cells, according to the Doctor (and it sounds right).

Nitrogen-tetroxide fumes fill Tierna's shuttle. No such gas exists in reality, but such a compound could be made and would be suitably unbreathable.

Chakotay compares Hanon IV to Earth's Pliocene age millions of years ago. Actually 5 million to 1.6 million years ago, a time of great tectonic upheaval, so Chakotay is quite right.

Puzzles: OK, you have a projector to send out false images of ships to make your enemies think reinforcements are with you, and you project . . . Talaxians?! Wouldn't you get better results by projecting the image of a few Borg cubes?

Ce Acatl is an Aztec type of name if ever I heard one.

Bloopers: Tierna starts to cross himself before his suicide bomb.

Hanon IV is pure volcanic lava from the air, but plain old Californian desert on location.

Learn Your Lines: Chakotay: 'How do you take a child into your heart, who was forced upon you by a mother's deception?' That would have made a good theme for the episode, had it been followed up on.

Highs: The Doctor overboard.

Brad Dourif again, as Suder.

Lows: It's all just a setup for the next episode.

There are only about two dozen extras representing the whole crew, and the angle is wide enough to show that there aren't any more.

Verdict: It's a definite plus to see Suder again, and to see Chakotay having a last fling at being a hard man. Sadly, the episode does drag a bit, and there's never any real doubt that the Kazon is lying. Nevertheless, there is an impending air of disaster over the episode, and you just know our heroes are going to get their arses kicked. It's unfortunate, though, that in the end the Kazon settle for stranding the crew rather than killing them, as would have been in character. The cliffhanger should have been stunning, with the crew stranded and the ship gone, but somehow it isn't. The usual desert location and bumpy-headed cavemen inspire only groans. 6.5/10.

Interlude

After Season Two, the series' co-creator Michael Piller retired from the day-to-day grind of producing *Voyager*, leaving Jeri Taylor and Rick Berman in charge. Ken Biller also moved up from story editor to producer, while Brannon Braga moved from producer to executive producer.

With Jeri Taylor having more freedom, this led to a shift in emphasis for the series – the regular aliens such as Kazon and Vidiians would be left behind, as would the lingering tensions between Starfleet and Maquis crews. The ship would encounter more new races, in a pacier and more exciting style.

During the hiatus, *Star Trek: First Contact* was filmed, with Bob Picardo taking the role of the *Enterprise-E*'s EMH, in a scene where Beverly Crusher instructs him to distract some Borg who are trying to break into sickbay. The sickbay set and Jeffries tubes are those from the *Voyager* set. Martha Hackett (Seska) and Ethan Phillips (Neelix) also make cameo appearances, as an *Enterprise* crew member and the holographic maître d' respectively.

Once again, the last three episodes of Season Two were held back, and aired as part of Season Three. This time, however, they were dubbed with third-season stardates, and released to foreign markets in the same order as they aired in the US.

Third Season

Regular cast:
As Season One, but Roxann Biggs-Dawson
now credited as Roxann Dawson

Recurring cast:
Alexander Enberg as Vorik

#146: 'Basics' Part II

by Michael Piller

Directed by Rick Kolbe
Music by Dennis McCarthy
US air date 04-09-96

Plot: Stardate 50032.7. The crew are stranded on Hanon IV, while Tom is in a shuttle seeking help from the Talaxians, and *Voyager* is under Kazon control. While most of the crew dodge man-eating land eels and fight with cavemen on the planet, Suder contacts the Doctor in sickbay. Under the Doctor's instructions, Suder sabotages the ship, so that Tom and the Talaxians will be victorious when they arrive. Meanwhile, Seska discovers that the father of her baby is really Culluh.

Déjà Vu?: Cavemen on a deserted planet always make me think of *Blake's 7* for some reason.

Behind the Scenes: Jeri Taylor says they decided to kill Suder off because they couldn't see how he could really be redeemed, and that he was just too difficult to integrate with the other characters believably and well.

***Voyager* Database:** Tuvok taught archery science at the Vulcan Institute of Defensive Arts for 'several years'. B'Elanna was on the decathlon team before quitting Starfleet Academy.

There are giant cucumbers and eggs on Hanon IV, though there's no sign of what laid the latter. Neelix makes beetle stew, and Janeway eats some grubs.

(Lack of) Continuity: The Kazon fighter type of ship is now called a Kazon Patrol Vessel. There are still only a couple of dozen extras standing in for the whole *Voyager* crew. Hogan is eaten by a land eel very early on, leaving only a scrap of uniform. Eighty-nine Kazon have boarded the ship and manage to run it. This contradicts Chakotay's statement in 'The 37s' that the ship couldn't be run by fewer than 100 people. Wildman's baby still isn't named.

Ye Canna Change the Laws o' Physics: A thoron generator treats radiation burns. Why would radiation from decaying thorium (this is what thorons really are) heal radiation burns? Thoron particles also neutralise tricorder sensors, as an old Maquis trick to hide from searchers. Chakotay intends to make a solar still out of Hogan's uniform. What exactly does he intend to distil? He's not likely to get water out of it on a desert planet.

Puzzles: Why does Wildman's baby still not have a name? Did she ask the Doctor to pick one, or what?

What exactly does Seska die of? She recovers from the phaser overload like everybody else, goes into the ready room to collect her baby, and keels over for no apparent reason.

Once again, it would take the Doc too long to learn something from texts – in this case guerrilla warfare from the tactical database – which he should be able to simply have downloaded into his memory.

Why doesn't the Universal Translator work on the cavemen? Oh, right, the crew have no combadges . . . So how come the different races in the crew still understand each other?

Bloopers: The lip-synch on Tom's line in the recap is way off. The CGI for the land eel is different from that in Part I. There, it was a wyrm with a row of spines down its back, but now it's more detailed, with two vestigial arms in place of the spines.

The bridge rail wobbles and nearly falls off when Culluh

uses it to lever himself up after the phaser overload.

When Suder is killed, he's hit by a yellow phaser beam, despite being shot by a Kazon weapon – which have blue beams in every other shot they've ever had.

Learn Your Lines: Doc (psyching himself up): 'You're not just a hologram: you're a Starfleet hologram!'

Tuvok: 'You may find nobility in a savage, Commander, but he is only interested in killing you.'

Doc: 'Sticks and stones won't break my bones, so you can imagine how I feel about being called names.'

Highs: All the shipboard Doctor/Suder stuff, and the Doctor's bluffing of Seska.

There's a rousing, spine-tingling version of the theme when *Voyager*, now under the control of Tom and the Talaxians, arrives back at Hanon IV.

Lows: The cavemen.

Hogan's early and meaningless death.

Verdict: The shipboard scenes with the Doctor and Suder being the only opposition to Seska and Culluh are by far the best bits. All the events on the planet, to be honest, come over as nothing more than padding.

Getting back to the good points, Picardo and Dourif are both excellent, and it's extremely disappointing that Suder gets killed. There's also a real slash moment as the Doctor lays his hand on the curled-up Suder's back as the latter gets over the emotional distress of having killed again. Half the episode is good, even if it's just the shipboard half. 7/10.

#145: 'Flashback'

by Brannon Braga

Directed by David Livingston
Music by David Bell
US air date 11-09-96

Plot: Stardate 50126.4. While the ship seeks minerals in a nebula, Tuvok collapses, hallucinating that he is either a child failing to save a little girl from falling off a cliff, or back on the USS *Excelsior*, on which he served at the time of the Khitomer Accords. Believing the cause to be a repressed memory, the Doctor agrees to let Janeway mind-meld with Tuvok, and try to find out what the Vulcan's subconscious is trying to tell him. This they do, and both officers find themselves on the USS *Excelsior* at the time of the destruction of Praxis, Stardate 9521.

Déjà Vu?: It revisits some of the events around *Star Trek VI: The Undiscovered Country*.

Behind the Scenes: This episode was held over from Season Two, and is the 30th-anniversary episode. George Takei (guesting as Captain Sulu) was delighted that the script didn't use the hackneyed and 'cornball' idea of time travel to unite the two captains, but found a cleverer way of doing it. He also considers his entrance in the episode to be impressive (and he's right).

The bridge set is a revamp of the *Enterprise-B* set from *Star Trek: Generations*, and the exterior shots of the ship being hit by the Praxis wave are stock footage from *Star Trek VI*.

The Klingon cruiser is a new use of the model built for that movie. Kang's bridge interior is the bridge set for Martok's Bird of Prey in *DS9*.

The isolation section of the sickbay has two chairs fitted in place of the diagnostic bed.

As well as Sulu, Janice Rand and Kang return from *TOS*.

***Voyager* Database:** Bolian tongues have a cartilaginous lining to protect against most corrosive acids – such as Neelix's orange juice with papalla-seed extract. It's a Talaxian tradition to share the history of a meal, to enhance the culinary experience.

Storage Bay 3 is Neelix's pantry.

Vulcans have a psychocognitive branch of medicine. The mind meld to explore a repressed memory usually requires a member of the victim's family to guide him as the pyllora, and help process the memories he encounters. Tuvok's father was an officer aboard the USS *Yorktown*.

Sulu looks nothing like his portrait at Starfleet head-quarters, according to Janeway, because holo-imaging resolution was less accurate in the twenty-third century. Sulu takes a course to Qo'noS (the Klingon homeworld) through the Azure nebula. The two nebulae are different in composition, but look similar and contain cyrillium. The Azure nebula is a Class 2, while the one in the Delta Quadrant is a Class 17. Sulu never recorded his confrontation with Kang in the nebula.

The Klingons fire concussive charges into the Azure nebula to flush out the *Excelsior*.

Tuvok's repressed memory isn't a memory at all – it's a telepathic virus, which masquerades as a memory engram in the way that some normal viruses disguise themselves as blood factors to hide from antibodies. In this case the virus creates a memory so traumatic that the mind would bury it, so evading detection. The virus then feeds on neuropeptides in the brain. Tuvok contracted it when Valtane died, and Tuvok was the last person to touch him.

(Lack of) Continuity: In *Star Trek VI: The Undiscovered Country*, the *Excelsior* was cataloguing these gaseous anomalies in the Beta Quadrant. This journey, eighty years ago, was Ensign Tuvok's first deep-space mission, and he was two months out of the Academy (though Rand says one month). He was one of several junior science officers, but none of this shows up on his official service record, which says his first mission was on the USS *Wyoming*.

Tuvok was 29 aboard the *Excelsior*, and so is 109 in the current season. Raising his own children made Tuvok realise why his parents had sent him to Starfleet, and that he could learn a lot from humans and other races. Therefore he rejoined thirty years ago.

A tachyon sweep of the nebula would reveal cloaked ships. This tactic was first used in *TNG* episode 'Redemption' Part II.

Tuvok was secluded in the Kolinahr (discipline of total

logic from *Star Trek: The Motion Picture*) for six years, but
then underwent pon farr and had to return home to marry
T'Pel. Tuvok trusts Janeway more than anyone else on the
ship. There are other Vulcans on the ship.

It took Janice Rand three years to make it from Yeoman to
Ensign.

Janeway refers to the Federation–Klingon Alliance that
followed the Khitomer Accords.

The Doctor gives Tuvok cordrazine ('City on the Edge of
Forever').

Janeway says that Kirk, Sulu and McCoy belonged to a
different breed of Starfleet officer, who would be booted out
of the service nowadays. She also says there were no
plasma weapons in the twenty-third century, forgetting the
weapon used by the Romulans in TOS episode 'Balance of
Terror'.

Ye Canna Change the Laws o' Physics: The cyrillium can
be collected by the Bussard collectors. These are a part of the
engine that draw in interstellar dust and gas, based on a real-
life idea for spacecraft propulsion – usually called a Bussard
ramscoop. Memory engrams are stored in the hippocampus,
according to the Doctor. In fact long-term memory is scattered
throughout the brain, and mainly operates under co-operation
between the cortices, midbrain and medial temporal lobe.
The surrounding tissue is being damaged through disruption
of the hippocampus, a condition the Vulcans call T'lokan
Schism. This is a form of repressed memory in which Vulcan
minds can essentially lobotomise themselves. Sight, sound,
taste or smell can unexpectedly trigger a repressed memory.
Bombarding Tuvok's telepathic cortex with thoron radiation
should break the meld. I'd say bombarding anybody's brain
with radiation would break a lot of things in there . . .

Puzzles: They want to store volatile mineral in the pantry?
Next to the kitchen and mess hall? Isn't this just a teensy bit
unsafe? And, if Neelix can move his stuff out of the pantry,
then there must be space elsewhere anyway for him to put it
in. So why not just store the cyrillium there?

Bloopers: Tuvok says he's wearing the neurocortical monitor on the parietal bone, but actually it's on the occipital bone.

Learn Your Lines: Tuvok: 'Mr Neelix, I would prefer not to hear the life history of my breakfast.'

Chakotay: 'I've often found that when you don't think about a problem, a solution presents itself.'

Highs: Just about every scene Tuvok has, and every scene Sulu has.

Russ and Mulgrew have a great rapport.

Sulu's speech about loyalty.

It's nice to hear all those old sound effects again.

Lows: The building blocks Tuvok plays with as a meditation aid are a bit silly, though the speech he gives about reflecting the builder's state of mind is interesting.

Verdict: A pretty good episode, that improves – and is more comprehensible – with repeated viewing. Tim Russ and Kate Mulgrew are excellent, of course, and Takei is fun as always. The revelations about Tuvok's bigotry are interesting, and it's very nice to see some familiar faces again. That said, it's nowhere near as funny an anniversary story as *DS9*'s 'Trials and Tribbleations', but it is very good all the same. The plot is quite clever, the characters – at least Tuvok – are developed further, the acting is good, and the dialogue is fine. You can't really ask for more than that, can you? 8/10.

#147: 'The Chute'

by Ken Biller

Directed by Les Landau
Music by Jay Chattaway
US air date 18-09-95

Plot: Stardate 50156.2. Tom and Harry find themselves in a brutal oubliette which the prisoners believe to be hundreds of metres underground. They've been accused of a terrorist bombing. Fighting to survive, Tom is stabbed, and Harry determines to escape, but the only way in or out is through the chute that delivers both food and new prisoners. While *Voyager* catches up with the real bombers, Harry climbs the chute, only to discover that the prison is even more inaccessible than merely being underground.

Déjà Vu?: Any prison movie you care to name.

Piri was the name of the female assassin nicknamed Cancer in the *Blake's 7* episode 'Assassin'.

The long pullback from the space station's hatch is very like the original *Red Dwarf* opening titles.

The serried ridges on the Akritirian prisoners' foreheads are like those on the Klingons in *Star Trek V: The Final Frontier*.

Behind the Scenes: The sets are from stock, and dimly lit to disguise their origins. Neelix's ship is seen again, having been in the shuttlebay all along. The interior set is different from that in 'Caretaker' though, again being quickly assembled from stock pieces.

***Voyager* Database:** The prison is for the planet Akritiri. The inhabitants think it's 300 metres underground, but actually it's a space station. There are close to fifty prisoners aboard. Prisoners are implanted with a 'clamp' – a synaptic stimulator which keeps them on edge and makes them fight each other rather than try to unite and escape. Attempted removal kills the wearer.

The real bombers are the Open Skies terrorist group. Paralithium is fuel for an ion drive, and can also be converted into trilithium.

The Akritirians use pulse guns.

(Lack of) Continuity: The other Delaney sister (we already know one is called Jenny) is Megan. Tom fantasises about her all day.

The bomb in the Laktivia recreational facility which killed 47 Patrollers was a trilithium-based explosive. Dilithium is convertible to trilithium. In *TNG* episode 'Starship Mine' trilithium was the toxic waste of used dilithium, and terrorists wished to steal it for use in bombs. Trilithium was also used by Dr Soran in *Star Trek: Generations*.

Ye Canna Change the Laws o' Physics: The Doctor's analysis says the clamp stimulates the production of acetylcholine in the hypothalamus, stimulating aggression. Actually acetylcholine is a neurotransmitter that controls muscular contractions.

Puzzles: What right or jurisdiction does Janeway have to board the freighter, or tell the Akritirian leader his policies are outrageous? Isn't there supposed to be a Prime Directive about these things? Well, yes, but Starfleet captains – and especially Janeway – break it so often that it's now known in fandom, and among the staff, as the Prime Suggestion.

Bloopers: The chute bends and wobbles when Harry and Zio climb it.

When Harry is brought to sickbay for treatment, he's wearing his uniform instead of the prison clothes. Did he stop and change before being healed?

Learn Your Lines: Tom: 'Trust me, you don't want anybody in here thinking you're soft.'

Highs: Harry futilely trying to urge the other prisoners to cooperate, then finding that Tom has wrecked his escape device, and being urged by Zio to kill Tom.

Lots of amusing slash moments, such as Tom holding Harry as they discuss the food at Sandrine's. When Tom tells Harry to look after himself first and foremost, it looks as if they're about to kiss. Don McManus as Zio. Janeway storming the prison.

Lows: The young terrorists caught by *Voyager* are exceedingly unconvincing.

Verdict: Mind-boggling. It's as if someone decided to see if they could get away with doing a slash story on screen and in canon. Not only do they get away with it, but it works well too. McNeill and Wang make a great pair as Tom and Harry, and both give their best performances to this point. It's also a very strong and grim episode – complete with full-frontal stabbing and throat-slitting – and it's amazing that it got through the BBFC uncut with a 12 rating, when they were taking the scissors to *DS9* tapes. Les Landau is one of the best directors – watch the positioning of the chute in relation to Zio when he reveals his manifesto, giving him a messianic halo, but in a dangerous red . . .

It does suffer from a bit of a reset button, but, for a cheap episode using stock sets and costumes, this is a bold and successful experiment. 8/10.

#149: 'The Swarm'

by Mike Sussman

Directed by Alex Singer
Music by Dennis McCarthy
US air date 25-09-96

Plot: Stardate 50252.3. A shuttle carrying Tom and B'Elanna is attacked by an alien. *Voyager* soon discovers that these aliens have a fleet of small ships, and jealously protect their space. Janeway must decide whether to go through in four days, or take fifteen months to go around. Meanwhile, the strain of having been active for so long is finally taking its toll on the Doctor – his memory is beginning to fail, too, and his technical support – a hologram of the real Lewis Zimmerman – must be consulted.

Déjà Vu?: Later in 1996, Grace Holloway would also operate to Puccini in the *Doctor Who* TV movie.

Behind the Scenes: Bob Picardo, in addition to the obvious acting and comedic talents, is also a trained opera singer. Here he sings 'O Soave Fanciulla' from Puccini's *La Bohème*.

Voyager Database: The Swarm use neuroelectric weapons. Neelix hasn't met them but knows they're a mystery race who kill anyone who trespasses in their space. The Swarm's language is so alien that the Universal Translator can't handle it.

The Doctor's database is suffering a cascade overload. Reinitialising him would lose all the experiences and traits he's developed over time. The EMH was designed for 1,500 hours of use at most, though B'Elanna had set up compression buffers to extend that life span. The Doctor's personality matrix has grown to 15 million gigaquads.

The injured alien, Chardis, is from Mislen, and explains that the Swarm are so called because the attack in thousands of small ships. They drain energy from targets, and mark victim ships with a polaron burst that makes their shields rotate at 92 gigahertz.

Grafting Zimmerman's heuristic matrix on to the Doctor's primary circuits gives the Doctor the life he needs, but deletes Zimmerman.

(Lack of) Continuity: Lewis Zimmerman appeared in the flesh in the *DS9* episode 'Doctor Bashir, I Presume', though the Doctor previously believed himself to be Zimmerman in 'Projections'.

Earth station McKinley was where we saw the *Enterprise-D* docked in *TNG* episode 'Family'.

A tachyon field disrupts the shuttle's sensors, contradicting the previous episode, in which such a field illuminates a vessel to sensors.

The Swarm's border sensors are the sort of interlaced tachyon grid used in *TNG* episode 'Redemption' Part II.

The Doctor refers to his activation in 'Caretaker', and massaging Kes's feet in 'Elogium'. The Zimmerman hologram is set in a hologram of his office at Jupiter Station ('Projections').

Ye Canna Change the Laws o' Physics: Give me technobabble any day – the Doc's opera terminology is even more of a mystery to me. His lines about axonal connections and preganglionic fibres are accurate. Modifying the shields to refract the detection beams is a sound scientific concept for stealth.

The Doctor's emotional responses are a series of algorithms designed to make him easier to interact with. Aren't ours?

Puzzles: Janeway decides to go through Swarm space because she won't take an extra fifteen months on account of a bunch of bullies. Is she forgetting or just ignoring the fact that they're hostile only to people who trespass in their space first?

Who answered Kes's call to sickbay before she visits the Zimmerman hologram?

The Swarm themselves are still a puzzle. It's a shame they weren't explored more fully.

Bloopers: Kes mumbles her line about applying a (something) impulse to check Tom's motor neurons. From the stardate, this episode happens just before 'Future's End'.

Learn Your Lines: Doc (on Soprani): 'These women are arrogant, superior, condescending . . . I can't imagine anyone behaving that way.'

Highs: The first scene with the two Picardos.

The scene in which Kes forces the Zimmerman hologram to help.

B'Elanna and Kes pace like anxious fathers in a maternity ward while waiting to see if the graft has worked.

Lows: The technobabble-orientated ease with which our heroes escape the Swarm.

There's an annoying soap-opera expression on Picardo's face in the fade-out after he forgets how to perform the operation he's doing.

Verdict: Strangely disappointing, mostly because the aliens of the title appear only in the teaser. The main focus of the episode, the Doctor's memory problems, is interesting, and the scenes involving two Picardos are fun. But in the long run it really goes nowhere, as we already know that the Doc will be OK by the following episode. Picardo and Dawson are on form, and Kes gets some good scenes, but this is eminently forgettable. 5/10.

#144: 'False Profits'

by Joe Menosky and Ken Biller
from a story by George A Brozak

Directed by Cliff Bole
Music by Dennis McCarthy
US air date 02-10-96

Plot: Stardate 50074.3. Finding signs of a wormhole, *Voyager* soon discovers that a nearby planet shows signs of Alpha Quadrant technology that is anachronistic to the planet's level of development. Chakotay and Tom investigate in native garb, and discover that two Ferengi are posing as the godlike 'Sages' of the planet's mythology. Janeway abducts the pair, and discovers they are Arridor and Kol, two Ferengi lost in the negotiations for the Barzan wormhole seven years earlier. With no jurisdiction over them, Janeway is forced to return them to the planet. The pair's joy is short lived, when they are then visited by the Nagus's Grand Proxy, demanding that the Nagus be given a share in their profits.

Déjà Vu?: A direct sequel to *TNG* episode 'The Price', in which a pair of Ferengi got trapped in the Delta Quadrant when a wormhole collapsed after they went through.

Behind the Scenes: The village is a studio set. Most of the Ferengi props are stock items from *DS9*, and their shuttle is the original model from *TNG*.

Voyager Database: The Ferengi have instituted fetishism on the planet, with artificial ears as talismans. There are fines and arrests for not wearing fetish ears, especially in the temple (actually the Ferengi treasury).

(Lack of) Continuity: Several Rules of Acquisition from *DS9* episodes are quoted. Altogether there are 285. Kol has the native women perform Oo-mox (i.e. rub his ears), which are also erogenous zones in the Ferengi.

Ye Canna Change the Laws o' Physics: Residual neutrino emissions are signs of a wormhole, and a phase profile of

them determines that the wormhole's far end is in the Alpha
Quadrant. It's an unfixed wormhole but bombarding a subspace instability with verteron particles will amplify and
polarise them, and draw the wormhole to it.

'Fetish' here is used in the anthropological rather than psychological sense. It's an object of devotion used in religious
or cultural practices as an amulet or talisman, and sometimes
used in magical rituals.

A Ferengi high-energy graviton pulse collapses the wormhole so that it won't return.

Puzzles: Why doesn't Neelix have a headpiece as the Grand
Proxy?

Bloopers: Watch for Rob LaBelle trying with variable success to keep his face straight during scenes set in the treasury.

According to the stardate, this story takes place before
'Flashback'.

Learn Your Lines: Rule of Acquisition 22: 'A wise man can
hear profit in the wind.'

Kol: 'Exploitation begins at home.'

Grand Proxy (Neelix): 'Rule of Acquisition 299: When-
ever you exploit someone, it never hurts to thank them.'

Highs: Neelix's impersonation of the Grand Proxy.

The Song of the Sages is quite funny – and an important
McGuffin to boot, as the mean Ferengi never paid to hear the
rest of it!

Lows: An unconvincing way to prevent *Voyager* from using
the wormhole to get home.

Verdict: Probably the funniest episode of *Voyager*'s first
three seasons. Though a lot of fans got fed up with the
Ferengi arc on *DS9*, this is a fine stand-alone Ferengi
episode. Ethan Phillips makes a much better Ferengi than
Talaxian, which is odd since the Grand Proxy is Neelix in
disguise. Of course, Phillips previously played a Ferengi in
TNG, but not as well as here. Arridor and Kol are much better
here than in their original appearance.

The whole episode is cleverly thought out, well acted and very funny. Definitely worth seeing. 8/10.

#148: 'Remember'

by Lisa Klink
from a story by Brannon Braga and Joe Menosky

Directed by Winrich Kolbe
Music by David Bell
US air date 09-10-96

Plot: Stardate 50203.1. While the ship transports a handful of telepaths to their home, B'Elanna dreams of a youthful romance in another life. As the dreams become more disturbing, and begin to happen while she's awake, it becomes clear that someone is deliberately placing them in her mind for some purpose of their own.

Déjà Vu?: Damn right. The exact same theme of aliens forcing memories on people has already been done at least six times in modern *Trek* alone: *TNG* – 'Violations' and 'The Inner Light'; *DS9* – 'Hard Time'; *Voyager* – 'Ex Post Facto', 'Persistence of Vision' and 'Flashback'.

Seeing B'Elanna in Korenna's place is also straight out of *Quantum Leap*, though they resist the urge to do the mirror gag. Which is just as well, or she'd have seen who was doing it right from the start!

The Regressives tell stories of how transport ships kill them partway to their new home and dump the bodies. This is the same rumour Vila quotes about Federation prison ships in the *Blake's 7* episode 'Space Fall'. The handling of the revelation that the Enarans are responsible for genocide is similar to that in the *Babylon 5* episode 'Secrets of the Soul', though that was made after this one.

Behind the Scenes: At the time this episode was made, there was a major scandal in real life about a historian who had written a book claiming the Holocaust never happened.

Korenna has a great blue leather jacket, unlike the rest of the Enarans' usual *Trek*-style civilian sackcloth.

***Voyager* Database:** Enara Prime has molten seas as a tourist attraction.

Neelix redecorates the mess hall in Enaran style for a reception. They have cushions and beanbags instead of more rigid furniture.

Enarans can share their past experiences through a telepathic link – which is a bit of a giveaway to the truth behind B'Elanna's bad dreams.

B'Elanna is remembering life as Korenna, and her lover is Dathan.

(Lack of) Continuity: Enara Prime has a colony in the Fima system, which was a Vidiian colony in 'Lifesigns'.

Chakotay now has an office with a medicine wheel on the wall, which isn't the one from 'Cathexis'.

The Regressives want to put technology aside, as the Drayans did in 'Innocence'. From the performances, they seem to be equated with New Age travellers, or possibly Amish.

Ye Canna Change the Laws o' Physics: Evidence of telepathy in the frontal lobe is a sign of implanted memories, according to the Doctor. The synaptic patterns are incompatible with B'Elanna's own and are causing damage. These memories were implanted in the subconscious to make them appear during dreams. The Doctor says a theta-wave inhibitor will stop them. In reality theta waves enable hypnagogic and hypnopompic activity, and dreaming. Such a device would prevent B'Elanna from dreaming at all and that would eventually cause massive psychological damage.

Puzzles: How believable is it that not only would Chakotay ask B'Elanna about her wet dreams, but that she would discuss them?

Bloopers: At one point, B'Elanna starts having a vision just before reaching Engineering. Kes finds her unconscious inside Engineering (you can see the warp core in the background) but then says she found her outside . . .

Learn Your Lines: Janeway: 'If they've chosen to conceal part of their history from their own descendants, that's their own decision, whether we approve of it or not.'

Highs: Dawson's performance.

Lows: Lack of either originality or subtlety.

Korenna's boyfriend is no more than a cliché student radical, and not even a very good one.

Verdict: A nice showcase for Dawson, who varies her performance beautifully, according to which character she's playing. Her performance alone makes this show worthwhile, for the actual plot has been done several times in recent *Treks*, and the theme of the danger of shunting minorities into first blame, then camps, then graves, is somewhat clumsily handled. All the same, kudos to Dawson for what is probably her best performance in the series to date. This is also probably the last fling for her and Janeway's mother–daughter analogy, as she will be replaced in that theme by Seven of Nine. 6/10.

#143: 'Sacred Ground'

by Lisa Klink
from a story by Geo Cameron

Directed by Robert Duncan McNeill
Music by Jay Chattaway
US air date 30-10-96

Plot: Stardate 50063.2. While exploring caves occupied by Nechani monks, Kes stumbles into a force field in their inner sanctum, and goes into neuroleptic shock. The Doctor can do nothing, and she will surely die. In order to save her, Janeway must make a spiritual journey that the monks make, to contact the ancestral spirits and ask their help to save Kes.

Déjà Vu?: The tone of the story reminds me of the *Babylon 5* episode 'Atonement'.

The secular split between government and religion on Nechani is identical to that on Bajor in *DS9*.

Behind the Scenes: This is Kate Mulgrew's favourite episode (at the time of writing, anyway).

Voyager **Database:** The Nechisti Order devote their lives to serving the ancestral spirits on Nechani.

The shamans of the Karis tribe on Delios VII have a ritual to increase the electrical resistance of the skin by biofeedback or autosuggestion, which protects them from plasma discharges in their sacred caves.

The Federation cultural database shows that most rituals are ordeals to make the spirit overrule the flesh to survive, by inducing biochemical changes. High neuropeptide levels block the effects of a biogenic field.

(Lack of) Continuity: Chakotay's mother taught him the science behind the vision quest, and it disappointed him that the mystery was gone.

It is standard procedure to carry arms on away missions ('Tattoo').

Ye Canna Change the Laws o' Physics: The Doctor tells us neuroleptic shock is like a coma, but with none of the usual biological markers.

Since plasma is hot gas, the Karis shamans would still get roasted, no matter how electrically resistant they were.

The Doctor says the increase in lactic acids is a sign of light strain. In reality it causes muscle fatigue and cramps.

Adenosine triphosphate exists in all living cells and is their main source of energy. The Doctor incorrectly states that rising levels of this substance indicate a gruelling experience, when in fact it would be getting used up in such a case, to release the energy.

Puzzles: I'm going to leave you a puzzle – what exactly is the key to the ritual? Explaining it would rob the episode of its power and ingenuity.

Learn Your Lines: Janeway: 'I have a feeling that if we scratch deep enough we'd find a scientific basis for most religious doctrines.'

Janeway: 'There's a difference between respecting the spiritual beliefs of other cultures and embracing them myself.' Old man: 'Even when her science fails her, she still believes in it. Now that's a leap of faith!'

Highs: The feeling of superiority one gets, having worked things out before Janeway. The sheer ingenuity of it all.

Lows: Though good and well performed by Mulgrew, the story does demand some stupidity on Janeway's part.

Verdict: Like 'Flashback', this actually improves on second viewing. At first glance it's slow and dull, with an incomprehensible ending; however, with proper attention paid to it, it actually turns out to be subtle and clever, with a much more philosophical and intellectual slant than most episodes have. Some viewers may find that too much work for a lowly couch potato, but the effort is well rewarded. 7/10.

#150: 'Future's End'

by Brannon Braga and Joe Menosky

Directed by Cliff Bole
Music by Jay Chattaway
US air date 06-11-96

Plot: Stardate 50312.5. *Voyager* is attacked by the Federation timeship *Aeon*, from the twenty-ninth century, whose captain explains that *Voyager* will be responsible for the destruction of Earth in his era. The ship escapes, but both vessels are pulled into a time rift that deposits *Voyager* in Earth orbit in 1996. An away team of Janeway, Chakotay, Tuvok and Tom discover that Captain Braxton of the *Aeon* is now an old tramp, having landed in 1967. It turns out that Henry Starling, a computer industrialist, found the timeship and used it to start the microchip revolution. When one of his employees, Rain Robinson, detects *Voyager*, he has his henchman try to destroy her and steal her data. Janeway and Chakotay try to force Starling to hand over the timeship, but he gains the upper hand. The pair are beamed out at the last minute, but Starling uses twenty-ninth century technology to download the computer core, including the Doctor.

Déjà Vu?: *Voyager* is seen from twentieth-century Earth as a UFO, as TOS *Enterprise* was in 'Tomorrow Is Yesterday'.

The whole culture-clash element is reminiscent of *Star Trek IV: The Voyage Home*.

The twenty-ninth-century phaser resembles the Eminian/Klingon weapons from TOS.

Janeway's reference to a computer keyboard as being like 'stone knives and bearskins' is a homage to Spock's use of that line in relation to 1930s radio equipment in TOS episode 'City on the Edge of Forever'.

Behind the Scenes: This two-parter is Tim Russ's favourite episode to date – 'because we were on location in the city of Los Angeles with beautiful weather and I was able to wear casual clothes. And, because I wore a cap, I didn't have to put the ears on. Which took less time in the make-up chair in the morning. It was a lot of fun.' Wearing a knitted cap is in itself a homage to the way Spock used to hide his Vulcan features in TOS episodes, most notably 'City on the Edge of Forever'.

Ed Begley Jr is a noted environmentalist campaigner in Hollywood, and the producers felt that casting him as the ruthless industrialist was a suitable irony. The timeship is built round a shuttlecraft model and life-size prop.

Voyager Database: Janeway played tennis nineteen years ago and now wants to take it up again, but is beaten in straight sets in the holodeck novices' tournament. Tuvok knows tennis, describing it as simple physics.

A graviton matrix in a space-time distortion proves it's artificial.

The timeship *Aeon* is six metres long, with one pilot, and fires a subatomic disruptor, which causes *Voyager*'s molecular structure to . . . well, be disrupted. A Polaron burst from the main deflector can disable this weapon.

(Lack of) Continuity: Tom is an aficionado of twentieth-century America, not just automobiles.

One of Chakotay's 1996 ancestors is an Arizona school-teacher. Janeway has no idea about her ancestor of this era – which will be contradicted by '11:59'.

Braxton describes the LAPD as 'quasi-Cardassian totalitarians'.

Tuvok explains his ears as 'a family trait'.

Ye Canna Change the Laws o' Physics: SETI is the Search for Extraterrestrial Intelligence, which uses radio telescopes to listen for radio signals from space that may be artificial in origin. Griffith Park Observatory has never been used for it as far as I know. Gamma radiation emissions detected by Rain are *Voyager*'s warp emissions. The ship is 20,000 kilometres high for geostationary orbit. Unfortunately someone used the wrong scale, and it should be 22,000 *miles*.

Puzzles: Why aren't the away team wearing their combadges?

Why does Starling get Dunbar to use the twenty-ninth-century phaser, which is rather conspicuous when it vaporises a van?

Bloopers: When the timeship crashes in 1967, you can see one of the studio lights used to shine on Begley's face.

Learn Your Lines: Tom describes what they'll need to pass as 1996 US natives: 'Nice clothes, fast cars and lots of money.'

Janeway: 'Time travel. Since my first day as a starship captain I swore I'd never let myself get caught in one of these godforsaken paradoxes. The future is the past, the past is the future . . . It all gives me a headache.'

Highs: Tom's and Tuvok's exploits.

Starling seems to think he's a Bond villain – and there's nothing wrong with that.

Lows: Begley's hippie make-up in the teaser.

Verdict: The first of what has become an annual fixture – Brannon Braga and Joe Menosky's mid-season two-part epic. Actually, it's pretty good, even though the temporal mechanics don't make that much sense. Most importantly, the characters are all well played, and in particular Tom and Tuvok get to have all the fun. Of course, no opportunity is lost for some culture-clash comedy, and most of the jokes hit the mark. This may not be good science, but it is an amusing adventure. 8/10.

#151: 'Future's End' Part II

by Brannon Braga and Joe Menosky

Directed by Cliff Bole
Music by Jay Chattaway
US air date 13-11-96

Plot: The year 1996. Starling tries to lure Rain Robinson into a trap, but the Doctor saves her, now with a mobile emitter. It emerges that Starling intends to use the timeship to visit the twenty-ninth century and plunder it for more technology. However, because he doesn't fully understand all its complexities, it will explode when it gets there, causing the disaster that Braxton blamed *Voyager* for. Chakotay and B'Elanna take a shuttle to try to snatch the timeship, but crash and are captured by militant survivalists. Meanwhile, Tuvok, Tom, Rain and the Doctor, with only a battered 1971 VW van, try to prevent the timeship from being launched.

Déjà Vu?: The mobile emitter is obviously related to Rimmer's hard-light drive in *Red Dwarf*.

Behind the Scenes: Starling's office includes the light fittings from the Banean house in 'Ex Post Facto', and the timeship is housed in an unused corner of a sound stage.

Bob Picardo had suggested the previous year that the Doctor ought to be modified for use in away missions in stages, so that, for a while, someone would have to carry his head around!

The desert road is out by Victorville. *Star Trek: First Contact* opened in the US a couple of days before this episode aired, and includes the Borg Queen's line 'Watch your future's end!'

Voyager Database: Rain became an astronomer because her brother had a little refractor telescope which fascinated her.

The Doctor's tactile response sensors can be programmed to make him feel pain.

Chakotay learned piloting in North America in his first year at the Academy, then spent two months dodging storms on Venus, and a semester in the asteroid belt. None of which stop him from crashing just about every shuttle he flies in the series, so the Academy's training can't be that great.

The Doctor's new mobile emitter is an Autonomous Self-Sustaining Holo-Emitter. Note the interesting acronym!

The survivalists are so dumb that they think Starfleet uniforms are US military uniforms.

Rain rates Tuvok as a 'freakasaurus', Tom as 'sexy in a howdy-doody sort of way' and the Doctor as 'the guy with the worst taste in clothing I've ever seen.' (She thinks his uniform is some kind of jogging suit.)

The *Aeon* travels by temporal inversion.

The twenty-ninth-century Federation has a Temporal Integrity Committee which says the Temporal Prime Directive insists that *Voyager* be returned to the Delta Quadrant at Stardate 50312.5.

(Lack of) Continuity: Vulcans were vegetarian in Spock's time, but Tuvok tucks into a burrito here.

The Doctor refers to a recent program failure that has left him still trying to recover some of his memories ('The Swarm').

Ye Canna Change the Laws o' Physics: Interferometric dispersion (whatever that is) makes the shuttle invisible to radar.

The Doctor suspects Starling of having a paranoid bipolar complex – in other words, of being a paranoid schizophrenic.

'What's good for Chronowerx is good for humanity' is a play on a 1980s IBM slogan.

Puzzles: Why do Tom and Tuvok have to modify Earth technology to contact the ship? Nothing is wrong with communications, and, even if it were, *Voyager* is monitoring Earth's broadcasts.

Starling pulls the combadge off the Doctor – is it replicated when he's activated, rather than holographic?

Learn Your Lines: The Doctor, on his new mobile emitter: 'In short, I am footloose and fancy free.'

Rain: 'I've seen every episode of *Mission Impossible*, and you are not secret agents!'

Highs: Tom and Tuvok's exploits again; the Doctor's rescue of Chakotay and B'Elanna. It's a definite yippee-ki-ay moment when Starling sees the torpedo about to hit him.

Lows: Rain's fawning over Tom.

The crude exposition of the previous episode in the briefing room.

Verdict: It has become tradition in *Star Trek* for the second half of two-parters not to live up to the first. This one makes a brave, if not entirely successful, attempt. All the comments I made in the entry on Part I still apply here, and there is a suitably exciting and tense climax, but this episode is let down a little by Rain Robinson's stilted fawning over Tom, and by the fact that Chakotay and B'Elanna's capture by survivalists is clearly padding that has no impact on the main plot. However, this capture does at least afford a Doctor scene that's a highlight of the show. It would have been better, perhaps, to do a separate episode about paranoid survivalists, and make them really scary. Still, the regulars are good, Starling is an excellent villain, and there's plenty of fun to be had. Highly recommended. 8/10.

#152: 'Warlord'

by Ken Biller

Directed by David Livingston
Music by David Bell
US air date 20-11-96

Plot: Stardate 50348.1. The ship rescues the crew of a damaged vessel, one of whom dies. Soon, Kes begins acting strangely, and leads the other rescued aliens to take over his home planet. The Doctor discovers that the dead man had an implant that enabled him to infect Kes with his consciousness at the moment of death. Tuvok attempts a rescue, but Kes, possessed by the warlord who first ruled the planet, has now taken over, and he is captured.

Déjà Vu?: Tieran's means of surviving death is identical to that used by Rao Vantika to take over Dr Bashir in the *DS9* episode 'The Passenger'.

Harry's claims about Sports Program Theta 2 echo Lister's attempted explanation about his Wimbledon program in the *Red Dwarf* episode 'Gunmen of the Apocalypse'.

Using Kes's mental abilities, Tieran does a Vader (uses the Force Grip) on one of the subordinates, throttling him without touching him.

The question of whether Tieran would keep his wife now that he's female echoes the *DS9* episode 'Rejoined' but without resorting to silly extremes to make the point.

Behind the Scenes: The guards in the Ilari Imperial hall are armed with Jem'Hadar rifle props from *DS9*.

Tieran/Kes has a pistol from Kirk's fireplace in *Star Trek: Generations*, which was also used by the Hyachs in the *Babylon 5* episode 'Secrets of the Soul'.

The damaged ship is the one seen in *TNG* episodes 'The Survivors' and 'Unification'.

The dungeon force-field generators are from the cell in 'Resistance'.

***Voyager* Database:** Sandrine's is replaced as the social holo-program by the Paxor Resort from Talax, which Tom and Harry spice up with some Polynesian guys and girls in a crude attempt to sex up the show in post-*Baywatch* style.

Harry has three holographic girls in Sports Program Theta 2, which he claims is volleyball.

While possessed, Kes breaks up with Neelix. She never reverses the decision, once freed of Tieran's influence.

Neelix has been participating in *Voyager*'s tactical drills every month.

(Lack of) Continuity: Reference is made to Tuvok tutoring Kes in mental disciplines.

Ye Canna Change the Laws o' Physics: A shuttle's plasma injectors can be modified to suppress its warp trail.

Tieran uses a cortical implant to enhance his neural patterns, and send it along peripheral nerves to bioelectric microfibres in the hand, which then send it into the victim's nerves and brain. A synaptic stimulator should drain him out through the new implant in Kes.

Bloopers: Jennifer Lien mispronounces 'Castellan'.

Learn Your Lines: Tuvok: 'This experience will force you to adapt. You are no longer the same person, and the course of your life will change as a result. Where that new course leads is up to you.'

Highs: Kes/Tieran's telepathic seduction of Tuvok.

Kes's mental confrontation with Tieran.

A nice shot from the rear of the transporter stage.

The moment when Kes/Tieran suggests that s/he, Nori and Ameron be very good friends is loaded with innuendo.

Lows: All done too quickly – there's so much going on here that it should have been a two-parter.

Verdict: Jennifer Lien's performance as her character's evil double is excellent, in contrast to many actors who are unconvincing when called upon to do this. She hops about, full of energy, clearly enjoying herself immensely. Though the story premise isn't very original, the script has tons of stuff that there simply isn't time to address – such as whether Tuvok did fancy Kes, the whole issue of gender swapping and sexuality. The script overflows with things to pick up on, there's a great scene for Tuvok, and some good action. What more could one ask for? 8/10.

#153: 'The Q and the Grey'

by Ken Biller
from a story by Shawn Piller

Directed by Cliff Bole
Music by Dennis McCarthy
US air date 27-11-96

Plot: Stardate 50384.2. While *Voyager* is observing a supernova explosion, Q arrives planning to seduce Janeway into having a child with him. Naturally she isn't impressed by his efforts, and is even less impressed when Q's girlfriend of four billion years arrives as well. Further supernovae damage the ship, and Q abducts Janeway to the Continuum, where she discovers that the suicide of Quinn has led to a civil war.

Déjà Vu?: Lots of Civil War imagery, lifted straight from *Gone With the Wind*.

Behind the Scenes: The female Q, though listed in the script as 'Q Female', is known to crew and fans as Suzy Q after actress Suzy Plakson from *TNG*.

The manor-house interior is a revamp of Lord Burleigh's mansion from Janeway's holonovel.

***Voyager* Database:** Only two other crews in history have witnessed a supernova explosion, but neither was as close as ten billion kilometres.

Q refers to Chakotay as Chuckles, a nickname that has stuck among fans and pros. Q also addresses Neelix as 'bar rodent', which hasn't stuck.

The two Qs have sex by touching fingertips for a moment.

(Lack of) Continuity: It's said that human DNA introduced into the Continuum would be a new thing, but there was a human Q in *TNG* episode 'True Q'.

Again, the Civil War imagery is not literally what the Continuum looks like, but just a frame of reference Janeway can understand. The Civil War came about because Quinn's demise in 'Death Wish' forced the Continuum to examine their freedoms.

Ye Canna Change the Laws o' Physics: A supernova occurs once every century, according to Janeway.

Puzzles: Isn't deciding the outcome of the Q Civil War a violation of the Prime Directive?

Learn Your Lines: Q: 'War can be an engine of change. War can transform a society for the better.'

Tuvok: 'May I remind you, madame, that this rickety barge and its half-witted crew are your only hope at the moment.'

Highs: The female Q.

Q's dressing gown – I want one of those.

Lows: The baby Q, promising a Junior Q story in future. Thankfully this hasn't happened yet.

Verdict: Not as thought-provoking as last year's 'Death Wish', but almost as funny, so I guess one out of two is better than nothing. Mulgrew and John de Lancie (Q) continue to have an excellent rapport, and Suzie Plakson (female Q) makes a fine addition to the Q Continuum. The Q Civil War, however, isn't handled that well, and it seems rather easy for the *Voyager* crew to join in at the end.

This episode probably gets the record for the most sexual innuendo in any *Trek* episode, but behind that is a neat religious reversal, with Q wanting the son of man to be the saviour of the gods. This idea is almost totally buried beneath the surface clutter, but, if you can spot it, it does at least make the episode more than just an amusing time-waster. 7/10.

#154: 'Macrocosm'

by Brannon Braga

Directed by Alex Singer
Music by Dennis McCarthy
US air date 11-12-96

Plot: Stardate 50425.1. Janeway and Neelix return in a shuttle from visiting the Tak-Tak, whose communication includes complex body language. They find the ship empty of crew (who are holed up in the mess hall) and are attacked by a strange creature, which injures Neelix. Now alone, Janeway contacts the Doctor, who tells her that the ship answered a distress signal from a Garan mining colony that had a viral infection. The Doctor accidentally brought the virus aboard, but before he could cure it it expanded to the macroscopic world. Now he has a cure, but his mobile emitter is damaged, so he can't go out and administer it. Janeway gets tooled up to do the job for him.

Déjà Vu?: A partial remake of *TNG* episode 'Genesis', in which Picard and Data returned to the ship in a shuttle to find that a retrovirus had de-evolved the crew into monsters.

Many scenes are also reminiscent of the tone of *Aliens*, and the macroviruses leave yellow ooze at the edges of holes they make in walls or floor, just like the eponymous aliens.

A virus escaping into the macroscopic world was first seen in the *Doctor Who* story 'The Invisible Enemy'. Likewise, a parasitic life form hatching from a living host is seen both in the *Alien* movies and the *Doctor Who* story 'The Ark In Space'.

A viral infection in the bioneural gel packs leads to trouble with the kitchen heating – as in 'Learning Curve' – which incinerates a whole pot roast. This is lifted whole from 'Deadlock'. Again as in *Aliens*, the macroviruses are driven by instinct to gather their hosts together in a nest. The holodeck's separate power supply is put to use acting as a lure to perform a Pied Piper on the macroviruses.

Behind the Scenes: The new compression rifles from *Star Trek: First Contact* make their TV debut.

The macroviruses are Foundation Imaging's redress of the Nakaleen Feeder CGI model from the *Babylon 5* episode 'Grail'.

***Voyager* Database:** Janeway studied American Sign Language, chromolinguistics and the gestural idioms of the Leyron.

Janeway suggests promoting Neelix from morale officer to ambassador.

(Lack of) Continuity: When Janeway mentions Neelix's lungs, he corrects her to 'lung', as he has only one after 'Phage'.

Janeway gets a *Star Trek: First Contact* style of compression rifle from the supply box in Engineering – where did that come from? That model of weapon wasn't issued until after *Voyager* left the Alpha Quadrant.

Klingons don't get nausea because of a redundant stomach – though zero-gravity training made Worf sick to his stomach (singular), according to *Star Trek: First Contact*.

Ye Canna Change the Laws o' Physics: The macroscopic world, quite simply, is the opposite of the microscopic one.

When the environmental controls fail, the ship heats up because the warp plasma conduits can't be vented. Shouldn't they instead cool to the ambient temperature of space?

A parasite that hatches from a living host isn't unknown in real life – the ichneumon wasp is one example, though thankfully it preys only on caterpillars. Here the macrovirus absorbs the growth structure of the victim and uses the glandular tissue from which to launch the flies.

Puzzles: Wouldn't the macrovirus's spike just kill its victim rather than inject them? It's big enough to nail someone to the wall.

Bloopers: Janeway says a communications signal is coming from ten metres away, but, when she and Neelix reach Wildman's quarters, it's more like ten feet.

Learn Your Lines: Janeway: 'I may never put my hands on my hips again.'

Doc: 'One down, ten billion to go.'

Highs: Janeway's fight with the macroviruses in her Ripley/Sarah Connor get-up. A lovely sequence from the virus's point of view on the bridge is an example of some fine direction.

Lows: Easily this season's most blatant rip-off of another show/movie. But at least it was a good choice to rip off, so what the hell!

Verdict: The opening sections of this episode are cribbed directly from Braga's seventh-season *TNG* episode 'Genesis', but it isn't long before Janeway is stripped down to a Linda Hamilton style of vest to do battle with monsters overrunning the ship. It's *Aliens*, pure and simple – even the music when Janeway reaches the bridge is a homage to that movie's score.

The Tak-Tak's body language is silly in the extreme, but you can't fault the producers for actually taking such a thing into account for a change. The direction is great, and the hand-to-hand fight between Janeway and a CG macrovirus is well done. Janeway has a dodgy taste in jazz muzak, unfortunately.

This episode is quite entertaining: there's something about a sweaty Janeway kicking ass all over the ship that's just so much more interesting than the average episode, however dull the actual story may be. 7/10.

#156: 'Fair Trade'

by André Bormanis
from a story by Ronald Wilkerson and
Jean Louise Matthias

Directed by Jesus Trevino
Music by David Bell
US air date 08-01-97

Plot: *Voyager* stops for supplies at a trading station on the edge of the Nekrid Expanse, a huge uncharted area. Neelix has been acting oddly of late, getting in everybody's way. Aboard the station, he meets an old Talaxian friend, Wix Aban. Aban wants Neelix's help to do a black-market deal involving 'medical supplies' – which turn out to be narcotics. When the buyer tries to double-cross them, Wix is forced to shoot him with a stolen phaser, and Tom and Chakotay are accused of the murder.

Déjà Vu?: Punishment by being put into stasis is what happened to Dave Lister in the first episode of *Red Dwarf*.

Behind the Scenes: The station set is actually a redress of the prison from 'The Chute'.

The Kolaati weapons are all stock *DS9* weapons.

***Voyager* Database:** This side of the Nekrid Expanse is the limit of Neelix's knowledge. Beyond this point, everything is as new to him as it is to the rest of the crew. He has been studying Starfleet security protocols and Federation warp propulsion in the hope of being useful in some other way.

Neelix used to be a smuggler. He has been involved in crime with Wix before, but now has second thoughts. Wix served time in jail for something they both did, when Neelix got away. Kolaati traders are the local mafia.

Neelix is sentenced to two weeks' deuterium maintenance, scrubbing the exhaust manifolds.

Vorick debuts.

(Lack of) Continuity: The ship needs pergium to regenerate the filters in the environmental controls, which were damaged in the previous episode.

Neelix describes himself as 'cook, captain's adviser and possibly unofficial ambassador' (as mentioned in the previous episode).

Biomemetic gel was first mentioned in the *DS9* episode 'In the Cards'.

Tom refers to having been jailed for lying – because he tried to cover up the accident that killed some of his fellows ('Caretaker').

Ye Canna Change the Laws o' Physics: The space station is of a contemporary realistic design – modular, so that extra usable space can be added as and when necessary.

The inferior warp plasma is contaminated with 20 parts per million iso-nucleic residue. Warp plasma is highly volatile.

Puzzles: Despite being a Neelix episode in which he's clearly troubled, it doesn't feature Kes.

How wilfully blind is Neelix not to notice that Wix's scheme screams 'criminal deal' from the rooftops?

Janeway won't let Neelix leave – is that punishment or reward?

Learn Your Lines: Janeway: 'I'd have thought you'd have learned by now that the first duty of a Starfleet officer is to the truth' (which is the point of *TNG* episode 'The First Duty'). Neelix isn't a Starfleet officer, though.

Highs: Neelix goading the Kolaati into firing in the vicinity of a leaky warp-plasma canister.

Lows: Well, this is a Neelix episode . . . However, Vorik is also an annoying character – apparently, he's known as 'Vomit' in the ranks of fandom.

Verdict: Urgh! The main problem with this episode is it's just such an unsubtle and heavy-handed lecture. And Neelix is a born survivor – he would know when to tell Janeway that he didn't know any more, and find some way to make his other skills more important. 2/10.

#155: 'Alter Ego'

by Joe Menosky

Directed by Robert Picardo
Music by Paul Baillargeon
US air date 15-01-97

Plot: Stardate 50460.3. While the ship is studying an inversion nebula, Harry seeks Tuvok's advice on how to control his emotions. He has fallen in love with a holographic character in the Paxor resort program, and realises that this is a pretty pathetic love life. Tuvok tries to advise him, but the Marayna holocharacter then takes an interest in him. As Harry's jealousy builds, Tuvok is stalked by Marayna, who is more than she appears to be.

Déjà Vu?: Riker fell in love with the holocharacter Minuet in *TNG* episode '100101', though that was deliberately programmed by the Bynars to keep him in the holodeck.

Behind the Scenes: This episode was originally written as a Tom/Harry two-hander, which explains why Tuvok is suddenly Harry's friend and confidant.

***Voyager* Database:** This features the first in a running series of unattainable women that Harry falls in love with.

The t'aan s'at is the Vulcan technique for deconstruction of an emotional complex.

Tuvok thinks that Harry's loving a computer subroutine is 'interesting'. This is probably the Vulcan term for 'get a life, you loser'.

Vulcans call love at first sight 'shon-ha'lok', the Engulfment. It is the most psychologically dangerous form of love. The k'oh-nar is the feeling of being completely emotionally exposed.

Marayna is actually an alien in a space station within the nebula. She generates the cascade reactions that stabilise it, to preserve its beauty for her people to look at.

(Lack of) Continuity: Harry admires and respects Tuvok, or so we're told. It has never shown.

He studied the Moriarty hologram from *TNG* episodes 'Elementary, My Dear Data' and 'Ship In a Bottle' at the Academy.

Ye Canna Change the Laws o' Physics: Neelix says the lei symbolises the flowering of love. It's a traditional garland given to visitors arriving in Hawaii.

The nebula's plasma strands, which should burn and collapse it, suffer mysterious subatomic cascade reactions, which stabilise it.

Puzzles: Tuvok apologises to Harry. Why? It was Marayna who fell for him, and Harry was the one out of line.

Why not give some holodeck technology to Marayna to help her pass the time? It would be a lot less harmful than giving it to the Hirogen in 'The Killing Game' Part II.

Learn Your Lines: Janeway: 'Beauty and mystery, a tantalising combination.'

Harry: 'Hi, my name's Harry read-me-like-a-book Kim.'

Highs: Tim Russ, and especially Tuvok's amusing definition of love.

There's a nice Moorish wall-hanging in Tuvok's quarters – another thing for the 'I want one' list.

The holographic girl who tries to garotte B'Elanna is very creepy, as she looks extremely gleeful about what she's doing.

Lows: Vorik.

Tom negating Tuvok's sound advice.

Harry's jealousy is even more crazy than Neelix's in Seasons One and Two.

Verdict: Harry and Tuvok fight over a woman? Bizarre. Russ is good as always, but Harry's jealousy is ludicrous, like the worst extremes of Neelix back in Season One. The new holodeck program isn't great either, turning the padding scenes into Baywatch. The plot does eventually make some sense, at least as far as Marayna is concerned, but by that time it's way too late. 3/10.

#158: 'Coda'

by Jeri Taylor

Directed by Les Landau
Music by Dennis McCarthy
US air date 29-01-97

Plot: Stardate 50518.6. Janeway and Chakotay take a shuttle trip, but are forced by storms to crash-land on a planet.

Chakotay tries to revive Janeway, but she dies – and finds herself back in the shuttle, approaching a temporal anomaly. This time the shuttle is shot down by Vidiians, and she is killed again, before finding herself back in the shuttle. They turn around and return to *Voyager*, where Chakotay forgets all that happened, and Janeway dies of the Phage. Eventually time stabilises, and she finds that she was dead all along – the whole thing is an after-death experience, and her late father has come to guide her to the afterlife.

Déjà Vu?: Yes, literally, and for the characters too! But, apart from that, the first half of the episode is very like *Groundhog Day*, with Janeway going through the same day several times, but in different ways.

The revelation of the entity that seeks souls after death reminds me of the Soul Hunters in *Babylon 5*, though here it's much cruder. The time loop is also reminiscent of the far superior *TNG* episode 'Cause and Effect'. Janeway becomes an insubstantial ghost on the ship, much like Geordi and Ro did in *TNG* episode 'The Next Phase'.

Behind the Scenes: This episode was written largely to tie into Jeri Taylor's biography of Janeway, 'Mosaic'. This book, along with its sequel, 'Pathways', is the only novel intended to be regarded as canon along with the episodes. Unfortunately both books contradict some episodes, and are later contradicted, so it's unlikely that they're still considered canon.

***Voyager* Database:** At the talent night, Janeway danced the Dying Swan for the first time since she was six.

Janeway's deaths, in order, are: attacked by a Vidiian, blown up in an exploding shuttle, put to sleep by the Doctor, massive cerebrovascular collapse.

Janeway's father, a Starfleet admiral, drowned under the polar ice cap on Tau Ceti Prime fifteen years ago. Kathryn stayed in bed for months afterwards, moping.

The cause of Janeway's troubles is an alien parasite in her cerebral cortex.

(Lack of) Continuity: Concomitant stress in the thalamus is one of the early signs of the Phage. The disease then produces hallucinations, dementia and insanity. Klingon DNA has Phage antibodies and can provide a vaccine but not a cure ('Faces' and 'Lifesigns'). Note that these points may not be true, but may be figments of Janeway's imagination.

Kes has detected discarnate presences before, in 'Cathexis'.

B'Elanna suggests that Janeway may be phase-shifted, like Geordi and Ro in *TNG* episode 'The Next Phase'.

Ye Canna Change the Laws o' Physics: Cerebrovascular collapse means the blood supply to the brain is no longer functioning.

A tachyon burst apparently might disrupt a temporal field. Well, since tachyons are faster-than-light particles, I suppose they might have some effect, if such a thing as a temporal field could actually exist.

Puzzles: Why is Janeway surprised that Kes doesn't sense her in Tuvok's quarters? She originally sensed Janeway only when she walked through her, and they don't even touch in the later scene.

It's not made clear whether the shuttle is recovered, but we'll give them the benefit of the doubt.

Bloopers: When Janeway recommends taking cover from the Vidiians on the planet, a 'lightning strike' illuminates the sound-stage wall in the background.

Learn Your Lines: Janeway: 'Come on, Chakotay, there must be some talent you have that people would enjoy.' Chakotay: 'Me, get up in front of people and perform? I don't think so.'

Highs: One chilling moment when the Doctor performs euthanasia on Janeway to spare her from suffering the full effects of the Phage. The fact that Picardo isn't playing it as an 'evil' version of the Doc makes it impressive.

Tuvok's goodbye log entry is good too, and the music that accompanies it harks back to Gerald Fried's bass guitar theme for Spock in TOS.

Janeway trying not to cry at her memorial service.

Lows: More Vulcan/Tuvok bashing, this time over poetry readings at Talent Night.

Janeway's father being a cheesy devil-entity rather than the part of her mind that was tired of her life. The 'Get back to Hell' is really laying it on thick.

Verdict: If this had been a straightforward tale of Janeway facing her own mortality in a near-death experience it would have been a fascinating exploration of a surprisingly common yet mysterious phenomenon. Unfortunately the shoehorning in of an alien entity who then turns out to be a possible devil kills it stone-dead. It's not entirely a bad episode, but that twist is just so disappointing. A wasted opportunity that really could have been so much more. 5/10.

#157: 'Blood Fever'

by Lisa Klink
from a story by Jeri Taylor (uncredited)

Directed by Andrew Robinson
Music by Dennis McCarthy
US air date 05-02-97

Plot: Stardate 50537.2 (Valentine's Day, incidentally). Vorik tries to mentally rape B'Elanna. While the Doctor then tries to find a way to let him handle his pon farr without any Vulcan females on board, B'Elanna leads Tom and Neelix to some caves on a planet, looking for minerals. B'Elanna soon becomes irrational, flinging herself at Tom, as she suffers the pon farr for herself.

Déjà Vu?: 'Amok Time' from TOS. As in that episode, this features a young Vulcan undergoing his first pon farr, who tries to hide it from his shipmates, but the ship's doctor deduces it, and ends up getting into a punch-up to shake it off.

The Sikari resemble the Enarans from 'Remember'. Since they say their planet is a colony and not a homeworld, perhaps they're an Enaran offshoot.

Behind the Scenes: The director Andrew Robinson (better known as Garak in *DS9* – or Scorpio in *Dirty Harry*) says this was a great script with a good story, though he feels there's unrealism in the supposedly roguish Tom Paris not giving in to B'Elanna's demands for sex.

Robinson used a hand-held camera in the main scene between McNeill and Dawson in the cave, because he felt it gave an intimacy to the scene.

Dawson praises McNeill for this episode, describing him as a 'real trouper'. She says the pair had a lot of fun shooting it. She also highly praises Lisa Klink for writing such a multilayered script.

Voyager **Database:** Gallicite is needed to refit the warp coils.

Neelix once worked in a mining colony.

Vorik enjoys climbing, especially in the Osonic caves (climbing inside caves?), and Tom also has considerable rock-climbing experience.

The koon-ut so'lik is the Vulcan marriage proposal.

Tuvok had his right elbow-joint replaced after an injury in combat training. Is this why he's left-handed, or was he always that way?

The Sikari colony was destroyed by invaders in less than an hour. At the end of the episode, the attackers are revealed to be the Borg.

From here on, Tom and B'Elanna develop a relationship that is still going strong, though it's just flirting until 'Day of Honor'.

(Lack of) Continuity: The natives of the planet are the Sikari, not to be confused with the Sikarians in 'Prime Factors'.

Vorik assumes his arranged mate has given him up for dead – that Vulcan marriages are arranged was established in 'Amok Time'.

There are 73 males on the ship, probably not counting the Doctor.

Vorik says all Vulcans get pon farr, when every previous mention of it in *Trek* has said it applies only to the men. There is virtually nothing about pon farr in the medical database, as Vulcans won't talk about it. That seems illogical and life-threatening. Conversely, there is copious data about Klingon mating rituals. A holographic mate doesn't work to ease pon farr, as there is no telepathic bond. Vorik says how one deals with pon farr is a test of a Vulcan's character. (He's not doing well, starting with rape even before the neurological imbalance takes hold . . .) Tom refers to Klingon females throwing heavy objects as part of their mating rituals, which Worf told Wesley in *TNG* episode 'The Dauphin'.

Learn Your Lines: Doc: 'For such an intellectually enlightened race, Vulcans have a remarkably Victorian attitude about sex. I fail to see the logic in perpetuating ignorance about a basic biological need.'

Highs: Roxann Dawson is excellent. The direction is also good, especially the hand-held-camera work. The sound effects in the caves work really well, making them feel more real and claustrophobic to the viewer than any other caves in the series before or since.

Lows: The Doctor pimps for holographic women. Would he supply inflatable dolls to human patients? The continuity is abysmal, and the tone grossly offensive.

Verdict: The most offensive episode ever. You've got a married Vulcan – surely that could only result in a story looking at the choice pon farr offers between being unfaithful or death. This 'married Vulcan' story is rejected presumably because it would be too similar to 'Amok Time'. Furthermore, a Klingon female is humiliated by having to beg Tom for sex. As if that weren't bad enough, nothing is made of the fact that Vorik did the Vulcan equivalent of starting to rape B'Elanna (and he tries the human version later) with no comebacks whatsoever. The verdict seems to be that in the twenty-fourth century it's OK to rape someone who turns you down, and try to beat her to death if you're just too horny to control yourself! Despite good direction from Andrew Robinson, and a great performance from Dawson, this is simply rubbish. It's misogynistic, continuity-breaking and badly written.

At least the camera work and sound effects in the caves are good. I could go on, but had better spare you. 0/10.

#159: 'Unity'

by Ken Biller

Directed by Robert Duncan McNeill
Music by David Bell
US air date 12-02-97

Plot: Stardate 50614.2. Chakotay and Ensign Kaplan take a shuttle to investigate a Starfleet distress signal coming from a nearby planet. They are ambushed upon landing, and Kaplan dies. Chakotay is knocked out but wakes up to find himself in a commune built by a disparate group who claim to have been abducted from the Alpha Quadrant. Meanwhile, when *Voyager* comes looking for the shuttle, they encounter a Borg cube.

Déjà Vu?: The Romulan ex-Borg, Orum, shares his name with a character in the *Doctor Who* story 'Carnival of Monsters'.

Behind the Scenes: The Borg cube is the new one built for *Star Trek: First Contact*, and will be the standard model for Borg ships in *Voyager*. The costumes, likewise, are from *First Contact*.

The colony set is largely a redress of the prison from 'The Chute' again.

When Chakotay is first connected to the neural transceiver, there are several flashback clips, including the battle at Wolf 359 (clip from *DS9* – 'The Emissary'), exploding Klingon ships (clip from *DS9* – 'Way of the Warrior'), a field of blue bonnets (Riley's favourite flower), Riley's grandfather, Orum as a full Borg, a Borg cube at warp (clip from *TNG* – 'Best of Both Worlds') and some stock cityscape matt paintings.

***Voyager* Database:** This is the first annual Chakotay-has-a-doomed-romance episode.

The planet has a population of 80,000 ex-Borg.

Riley Frazier worked on a ship in the Bolian sector seven years ago. Her ancestors were Texas homesteaders. There are four humans in Riley's camp, along with Klingons, Cardassians, Romulans and others.

The planet is chaotic, with lots of factional fighting. The Klingons started it by attacking the Cardassians, then the Farn attacked the Parein and it all snowballed. Riley and Orum want to bring peace.

The Borg have been known to retrieve damaged technology.

Chakotay is vegetarian, unless he's just saying so to please Riley.

The Borg ship 'died' five years ago, after being hit by an electrokinetic storm, and 1,100 dead Borg are aboard. Its main power conduits were overloaded by a massive electromechanical discharge.

(Lack of) Continuity: The Borg debuted in the second season *TNG* episode 'Q Who', though in that episode it is also stated that the destruction of both Federation and Romulan outposts in the Neutral Zone (and in the episode 'The Neutral Zone') was their work.

Riley Frazier claims to have been assimilated from one of the Starfleet ships at the Battle of Wolf 359, which was seen in *TNG* episode 'Best of Both Worlds' Part II and the *DS9* pilot, 'Emissary'. Riley Frazier can't have been assimilated at Wolf 359: that cube was destroyed shortly thereafter, so couldn't have returned to the Delta Quadrant. Since there's a Romulan Borg here too, it would make more sense to assume that both were assimilated from outposts along the Neutral Zone, which we know the Borg attacked in *TNG* Season One.

It was established in *TNG* episode 'Descent' Part II that, when Borg ship's crew become individuals cut off from the Collective, they all go crazy.

The shuttle is dismantled, leaving *Voyager* with only two.

Although the dead Borg has damage from vacuum, *Star Trek: First Contact* shows that the Borg can function in vacuum, at least for a while.

Ye Canna Change the Laws o' Physics: The dead Borg has

alveolar damage, and swelling to the pulmonary system – consistent with exposure to space. This is quite accurate. He also has signs of severe cardiac depolarisation (electrocution). It comes back to life when the Doctor accidentally triggers a backup neuroelectric power cell, but this only produces a programmed autonomic response. Borg neural transceivers have a medical application – a subspace transfusion of a neuroelectric field that regenerates injured components. The ex-Borg can make a small Collective via a portable neurotransponder to repair neural tissue.

A residual mindlink remains for an hour or two, and Riley has sex with Chakotay while this is the case (does this mean Orum and the others are feeling it too?).

Puzzles: Why does Riley have a wig? It's not as if she needed one on the planet of ex-Borg, and therefore its only purpose can be to delay both Chakotay and the viewer finding out she was a Borg.

The Borg use Earth numerals and notation for their consoles?

Learn Your Lines: B'Elanna: 'I'm not being apprehensive, Tuvok: I'm just nervous as hell.'

Highs: The autopsy of the dead Borg.
   Chakotay's reactivation of the cube.

Lows: Chakotay and Riley's relationship lacks chemistry.

Verdict: Following on from the discovery of a dead Borg last time, we (sort of) meet the Collective here. Chakotay is well used here, and the plot is quite good. If there's a disappointment, it's that the reactivation of the Borg cube would have made a hell of a good cliffhanger, had this aired the week before 'Scorpion'. Instead we get an irritating *deus ex machina*. 7/10.

#161: 'The Darkling'

by Brannon Braga and Alex Singer

Directed by Alex Singer
Music by Paul Baillargeon
US air date 19-02-97

Plot: Stardate 50693.2. The Doctor attempts to enhance his program by recreating the personalities of some of history's most brilliant minds. Unfortunately, he forgets that they all had their dark sides. Meanwhile, Kes has built up a relationship with a local traveller. When he is attacked, everyone blames a rival traveller, but then the Doctor's behaviour continues to grow stranger.

Déjà Vu?: Well, it's Jekyll and Hyde, isn't it?

Tales of a planet-sized organism remind one of Magla in the *Doctor Who* story 'Destiny of the Daleks' or Zil's planet in the *Blake's 7* episode 'Trial'.

And then there's the Doctor-Master joke . . .

***Voyager* Database:** Janeway was the acknowledged master of the all-nighter (partying all night and doing homework at breakfast before it was due) at the Academy. She also took a course in Klingon physiology.

Tarkan sentries take ships as trophies and it will take a few months to go around their space.

(Lack of) Continuity: T'Pau now looks Oriental.

Kes's recent break-up with Neelix ('Warlord') is mentioned.

Ye Canna Change the Laws o' Physics: The Doctor blames B'Elanna's unconsciousness on anaphylactic shock, though in fact he drugged her himself with ketalene.

Residual holographic signatures remain behind at the scene of the Doctor's attack on Zahir. How is this possible? He's just a projection after all.

Puzzles: Where did the Doctor get his native clothes?

Why doesn't Kes take the phaser when the Doctor leaves it beside her to beat up Nakahn?

Bloopers: The ledge on the studio set doesn't match the visual-effect long-shot.

Learn Your Lines: Kes: 'Everyone seems to treat me like I'm still a child – I'm three years old now!'

Darkling (referring to the Doctor): 'What a hollow excuse for a life – pathetic, servile, at the beck and call of anyone who invokes his name.'

Highs: The Doctor's bedside manner with B'Elanna.

There's a completely nonhumanoid alien by the fireplace in the inn at one point – I thought it was a piece of furniture at first, until it moved!

The Doctor jumps off the cliff with Kes, proving his pursuers wrong.

Lows: The Doctor's evil self is portrayed in a clichéd manner.

Verdict: Bob Picardo does his best with this take on Jekyll and Hyde, but can't save it. He's good at doing the hunched-over leering Darkling, but there's no good reason why the Darkling *should* be hunched over and leering, other than that it's the cliché for Mr Hyde.

Kes's new boyfriend is pretty limp too. Still, Lien and Picardo make a good pair. 5/10.

#160: 'Rise'

by Brannon Braga
from a story by Jimmy Diggs

Directed by Robert Scheerer
Music by Jay Chattaway
US air date 26-02-97

Plot: Trying to help the inhabitants of the planet Nezu stave off a meteorite bombardment, a shuttle carrying Tuvok, Neelix and some Nezu crashes near a gallacite mine. With a meteorite due to destroy the area in hours, their only hope of getting a signal to *Voyager* is to ascend a nearby orbital tether. A carriage is repaired and activated, but it soon becomes apparent that a murderer is on board, desperate to protect a secret.

Déjà Vu?: Arthur C Clarke's novel *The Fountains of Paradise* introduced the concept of an orbital elevator.

***Voyager* Database:** Neelix spent two years working on tether maintenance on Rinax, and helped rebuild twelve carriages. These turn out to have been one-tenth scale models for the prototype.

The presence of trianium alloy in the asteroids proves they are artificial.

The Itanian Order fake natural disasters, and take over abandoned planets when their populations have evacuated them.

(Lack of) Continuity: Neelix envisions and talks to his dead family every night, and names the carriage Alixia, after his sister (see 'Jetrel').

Tuvok gives everyone tri-ox shots to oxygenate the blood (TOS – 'Amok Time').

Ye Canna Change the Laws o' Physics: The idea of an orbital elevator is a real one championed by some scientists, though I personally can't see how it wouldn't get mangled by coriolis forces . . . It would operate by magnetic levitation, already used for some trains in Japan. Stopping the carriage would risk losing maglev cohesion, which is true, though the Japanese trains needn't worry, as they don't travel vertically.

Puzzles: How were Tuvok and company beamed back during a battle? The shields would have to be down for transport, and that would leave the ship vulnerable.

When did Tuvok catch the padd? He was rather occupied when it was blown out of the carriage.

Bloopers: In the opening bridge scene, Garrett Wang can be seen relaxing at the back, clearly thinking he's not in shot.

There's no sign of the toroidal antenna that is supposed to be on the shuttle's hull.

The side-on view of the carriage shows it to be a different design from when seen from the top.

When Neelix opens the carriage door, everyone acts as if they're fighting against the depressurisation – but objects on the seats rest quite comfortably with no sign of being ruffled.

Learn Your Lines: Doc: 'Vulcans are notoriously difficult to impress. Mr Tuvok rarely acknowledges my brilliance.'

Highs: Tuvok demonstrates his strength to the miner. Sklar gives Neelix a kicking. The last scene is very Riggs and Murtaugh.

Lows: The shots of the carriage – the sparks are like something out of *Flash Gordon*.

Tuvok once again apologising to the person whose fault the problem is.

Verdict: Neelix's complaint about having no respect from Tuvok totally contradicts the past two years' experience for them – and after Tuvix they must both know that. The main plot is a fairly straightforward mystery with an easily guessable resolution, and the characters are real rejects from *Scooby Doo*. This episode also has possibly the worst visual effects in the show's history, to show the carriage rising up the orbital tether. The use of Tuvok is getting worse by the week, as here he thanks Neelix for letting him into the carriage, after it was Neelix who forced him out to start with. 5/10.

#162: 'Favorite Son'

by Lisa Klink

Directed by Marvin Rush
Music by Dennis McCarthy
US air date 19-03-97

Plot: Stardate 50732.4. Harry fires on a Nisari ship without authority, somehow knowing that it was hostile. Confined to quarters, he begins to develop a rash as the ship approaches

Tauresia. Harry suddenly realises that he isn't really human, but Tauresian, which is why the Nisari were hostile – they fire on any ship carrying a Tauresian. The female population welcome Harry as an honoured guest, and invite him to stay, as men are so rare.

Déjà Vu?: Harry Kim at Castle Anthrax!

Behind the Scenes: The Tauresian ships are a reuse of the Miradorn ship from the *DS9* episode 'Vortex', which was also the mercenary ship in *TNG* two-parter 'Gambit', while the Nisari ships are resprays of the Romulan scout vessel from *TNG* episode 'The Defector', with the cockpit pod moved to the rear of the ship from the front.

***Voyager* Database:** Harry had the Mendakan pox when he was nine.

(Lack of) Continuity: B'Elanna thinks Harry's zits are cute, like a speckled Targ.

Ye Canna Change the Laws o' Physics: Tuvok defines *déjà vu* as a paradoxical, state-dependent, associative phenomenon, which is close enough.

Puzzles: How and when did Harry get this condition? Exactly how do the Tauresians kill their men?

Learn Your Lines: Harry theorising about what might be happening to him: 'Space-time anomalies, alien telepathy, alternate realities . . . The list gets weirder as it goes on.'

Highs: Garrett had, allegedly, been suspended for two weeks, for showing up for work late. With that in mind, Tom's final comments to Harry when he returns to the ship are very funny.

Lows: Everything on the planet. Even the 'beautiful' girls aren't.

Verdict: Truly, truly silly. Garrett struggles, as Harry Kim is taken to a planet of women who want to breed from him. Most reasonable SF fans would say this sort of nonsense died out in the 50s, but here we are. 2/10.

#163: 'Before and After'

by Ken Biller

Directed by Allan Kroeker
Music by Jay Chattaway
US air date 09-04-97

Plot: Stardate 57600 (approximately). Kes is put in a bio-temporal chamber, and wakes up an old woman. Chakotay is captain, and the Doctor has hair. She's going through the morlogium, the Ocampa death. Suddenly she's in her quarters, and has memories only of the people who were with her at the biotemporal chamber, and is taken to sickbay. Then it's her ninth birthday . . . It soon becomes clear that Kes is in fact living her life backwards through time.

Behind the Scenes: Kes gains long hair in this episode, which remains for the rest of her time on the show. The reason for it is that Jennifer Lien was suffering a reaction to the adhesive used to attach her Ocampa ears, and this way they could dispense with the prosthetics by simply hiding the ears.

***Voyager* Database:** Janeway, Carey and B'Elanna died during the Year of Hell, which started around Stardate 50973. Kes is one of the ship's doctors after the Year of Hell. She and Tom were married and have a daughter, Linnis, who is married to Harry, and they in turn have a son, Andrew. Linnis is also a member of the medical staff.

Neelix is now the security chief, while Tuvok is first officer.

The Yqttho in the Beta Quadrant can predict the future.

The Year of Hell saw the ship under attack from the Krenim, who use chroniton-based torpedoes, which are out of temporal phase and can pass through the shields. A fragment of one lodged in a Jeffries tube and irradiated the crew; its precise phase variance is 1.47 microseconds.

The Doctor was off line for months during the Year of Hell. Linnis was born during that year.

Ocampa babies are born from between the shoulder blades.

Kes's normal body temperature is 16.3 degrees C, compared with 37 degrees for a human. She is three years and two months old at this point in Season Three.

Kes makes a report on the Krenim.

(Lack of) Continuity: Stardate 56947 is six years after the current season. Tom says the Year of Hell was three years ago, but it must have been five or so, because, in the present, the Year of Hell is six months in the future.

The Doctor six years on calls himself Van Gogh. Before that it's Dr Mozart.

Ye Canna Change the Laws o' Physics: Kes is time-travelling because, like everyone else, she was irradiated by the chroniton particles (particles of time!) in the torpedo fragment. Unlike everyone else, however, who was decontaminated, she was put into a biotemporal chamber intended to slow down her personal time, which reactivated the dormant chronitons.

Bloopers: Chakotay's log claims Stardate 55836.2 is two days after 56947! Though the Year of Hell begins six months in the future, the torpedo that gets stuck is eleven months away – but is in the first attack . . .

Newborn Kes has human ears.

Learn Your Lines: Kes: 'I do have memories. They just don't coincide with everyone else's.'

Kes: 'If there's one thing this experience has taught me, it's that there's no time like the present.'

Highs: The Year of Hell background. There's also something strangely pleasing and triumphant when Kes reaches a time in which Janeway is still alive.

Lows: Kes as a foetus, then an ovum . . .

Verdict: Stunning. A few holes in the plot, but basically a great episode, with another *tour-de-force* performance from Jennifer Lien, as Kes lives her life backwards. The various stages of old-age make-up for her are excellent, though

Picardo's toupee is less so. There's something discomforting about Harry having married Tom and Kes's daughter, but otherwise this is one of *Voyager*'s most impressive SF episodes. It's also a great teaser for the 'Year of Hell' to come, and makes the wait for that episode almost interminable. 9/10.

#164: 'Real Life'

by Jeri Taylor
from a story by Harry Doc Kloor

Directed by Anson Williams
Music by Dennis McCarthy
US air date 23-04-97

Plot: Stardate 50836.2. The Doctor gives himself a holographic family, including a wife and two children. When B'Elanna sees how unrealistic they are, she reprograms the simulation. The Doctor is particularly concerned about his son consorting with Klingons, and his daughter playing dangerous sports, and takes it out on Tom, who has volunteered for a dangerous shuttle mission. Then the Doctor discovers that his daughter has had an accident.

Déjà Vu?: The Doctor's original family, before B'Elanna's 'improvements', are like a Stepford family.

The Doctor seeks a second opinion on Belle's injuries from Dr Finlay!

Behind the Scenes: Just for this episode, B'Elanna has a new hairstyle, with a tied braid hanging down one side.

Voyager **Database:** According to the Doctor, events in his family unfold as a natural evolution of probabilities within the program. B'Elanna modifies it by adding randomised behaviour algorithms. The program is called Family Program Beta-Rho on Holodeck 2.

Neelix serves Pleeka-rinds and grub-meal casserole four days running.

B'Elanna reads a Klingon equivalent of Mills and Boon romances called *Women Warriors at the River of Blood*. The title sounds more like a bad 50s sword-and-sorcery tale for a school-age audience.

'Vulky' is a disparaging term for anything associated with Vulcans – e.g., 'Diplomacy is a Vulky idea.'

(Lack) of Continuity: The Doctor is known to his family as Kenneth (after Ken Biller). He is surprisingly racist, disapproving of his son's association with Klingons (maybe it's because of who reprogrammed the simulation) and would prefer him to have Vulcan friends.

Belle plays Parrises Squares (first mentioned in *TNG* episode '11001001').

The shuttle is the *Cochrane* from 'Threshold'.

Ye Canna Change the Laws o' Physics: The Vostegii space station is destroyed, leaving debris of boronide, sorium and carbon 60 (buckyballs).

Plasma particles in subspace may be a wake.

Astral eddies are formed at the confluence of space and subspace, and matter is sucked into an interfold layer.

Puzzles: Is the script seriously suggesting (in the scene about the Qu'tlech dagger) that we accept random attacks of violence if it's the way of another culture?

Bloopers: Tom takes the right-hand seat in the shuttle – which is the copilot's seat, not the pilot's.

Learn Your Lines: B'Elanna: 'Klingons do have what you might call a romantic side – it's just a little more vigorous than most.'

Highs: B'Elanna's reaction to the Doctor's family.

Lindsey Haun is surprisingly good for a child actor.

Picardo is excellent, of course.

Lows: The Doctor's uncharacteristic bigotry. The appalling swathe of clichés at the end, right down to the manipulative violin music.

Verdict: Not a great episode, but with some unintentional hilarity – the deathbed scene had me rolling about with laughter as it seemed to be aiming for the highest number of soap-opera clichés used within a single scene. As usual, Picardo is on great form, and the kid playing Belle is pretty good in her otherwise amusing death scene.

However, there are so many clichés, and so much padding, that it's an almost unbearable task to not hit the fast-forward button. The Doctor's racism is also very out of character, even if it is only about fictional aliens – can you imagine the uproar if he'd told his son, 'I don't want you seeing those Jewish boys again – get yourself some nice Japanese friends' (or insert race/nationality of choice for both of these categories)? Put bluntly, this isn't a *Voyager* episode: it's a cheesy daytime soap episode. 0/10.

#165: 'Distant Origin'

by Brannon Braga and Joe Menosky

Directed by David Livingston
Music by David Bell
US air date 30-04-97

Plot: A Voth scientist, Gegen, and his assistant discover Hogan's remains on Hanon IV, and follow the leads from Bahrat's space station until they find *Voyager*, whose crew they believe to have originated on the same planet they did. They board the ship with personal cloaking devices, but are discovered by Harry. One is captured, but the other escapes, abducting Chakotay. They themselves are then caught by the Voth Cityship, as the Voth government intends to charge Gegen with scientific heresy for challenging the belief that the Voth always lived in the Delta Quadrant. Back on *Voyager*, the Doctor discovers that the comatose Voth has genetic markers from Earth, and that he evolved from dinosaurs.

Déjà Vu?: The Voth are evolved from Earth dinosaurs, and they regard humans as inferior, upstart apes – as in the *Doctor Who* story, 'Doctor Who and the Silurions'.

The females' head ridges resemble the 'Warriors of the Deep' Silurians, right down to having a spot for the third eye.

Gegen's assistant is called Vir, which also happens to be the name of Londo's attaché in *Babylon 5*.

Behind the Scenes: The Hanon IV landscape is an unused establishing shot filmed for 'Basics' Part II.

The stock set from 'The Chute', 'Fair Trade' and 'Unity' is used again.

Voyager **Database:** Human cranial capacity is 22 per cent less than that of the Voth. The Voth's delytus lobe gives them a superior sense of smell. The Voth are insectivores and have a matriachal society. They evolved on a remote area of Earth which was destroyed by natural disaster, and left the planet 70 million years ago. They can voluntarily enter protective hibernation.

Gegen is a molecular palaeontologist.

(Lack of) Continuity: Hogan died more than a year ago, according to the state of bone decalcification. The Voth then visit Bahrat's station from 'Fair Trade' and examine a canister of warp plasma.

There are 148 people on *Voyager*, about twenty more than the last time the crew complement was mentioned.

Tom wants B'Elanna to teach him Klingon martial arts involving the Ba'telh, like the Mok'bara which Worf taught on the *Enterprise* in *TNG*.

The mess hall is in Section 12 of Deck 2.

There are other Saurian races, and indeed we saw one in 'Parturition'.

Ye Canna Change the Laws o' Physics: The Voth describe human bones as having a cartilaginous microstructure which is extremely porous. Bones are porous, but cartilage isn't a part of bone.

Endotherm just means warm-blooded.

Voth and humans share 47 genetic markers.

The Voth have interphasing cloaks that allow them to walk around the ship undetected, by being slightly out of phase with the space-time continuum. If they're invisible, how can they still see? Light would have to be shifted around them, and if it was shifted around their retinas they'd be blind. If the light wasn't shifted around the retinas, then the retinas at least would be visible. And if you're out of phase with space-time, then photons will have a hard time reaching your eyes.

Puzzles: The Voth skin tone changes under different lighting – is this a deliberate attempt to show mood changes? Certainly Gegen makes a note about the colour of Vir's scales when his daughter is around.

Bloopers: The scrap of Hogan's uniform found by Gegen has a section of grey rollneck and a piece of yellow tunic in one piece of material, when they should be two separate garments.

The canister of warp plasma so important in 'Fair Trade' wasn't from *Voyager* and was destroyed – so the Voth are looking at something that shouldn't exist.

Learn Your Lines: Chakotay: 'I won't bite.'

Odala: 'It would be in your best interests if I never saw you again.'

Highs: Gegen and Vir touring the ship, observing Tom and B'Elanna.

Henry Woronicz is great.

Chakotay makes a good speech when trying to convince Odala of a more positive way to view Gegen's theory.

Lows: When Picardo is explaining about the dinosaurs, his delivery is very slow, and it sounds as if he's reading the pronunciations from cue cards.

Verdict: Pretty good – a smart plot, a decent appearance from Chakotay . . . But the episode's real grace is the wonderful Henry Woronicz, who is probably the best guest since Joel Grey in 'Resistance'. In a nice variation on the storytelling structure, the Voth lead us to *Voyager*. There are some other neat touches of the Voth's alien nature – such as the lights that have flies buzzing around for them to eat.

Bravely, there's no real happy ending. 8/10.

#166: 'Displaced'

by Lisa Klink

Directed by Allan Kroeker
Music by Jay Chattaway
US air date 07-05-97

Plot: Stardate 50912.4. Surprised Nyrians begin appearing on the ship, accusing the crew of abducting them. At the same time each Nyrian arrives, a *Voyager* crew member vanishes. B'Elanna tries to find the cause, thinking it's natural, but the Nyrian with her stuns her – they are doing it deliberately. Before long, only Chakotay is left, and the Nyrians are swarming over the ship. Then he too finds himself in an artificial habitat with the rest of the crew.

Déjà Vu?: The Vulcan rite of Tal-oth is a test to survive in the wild for four months with only a knife. It's probably derived from the similar test of endurance in TOS episode 'Yesteryear'.

Behind the Scenes: The section of corridor and door outside Cargo Bay 2 is the same one outside the holodecks and shuttle bay.

The Nyrians are armed with the Romulan rifles seen in *TNG* episodes 'Unification' and 'Starship Mine' – here they have an extension added to the barrel. The stripped-down Romulan pistol also reappears.

The Ocampa ruins from 'Caretaker' and the Bajoran camp from *TNG* episode 'Ensign Ro' are briefly seen as other environments aboard the station. The station corridors are a revamp of the Borg-cube sets from 'Unity'.

***Voyager* Database:** Displacements occur every 9 minutes and 20 seconds. It takes 18 hours for the whole crew to go. With only 140 crew it should take 15 hours and 3 minutes, give or take a few seconds.

Larson, Crewman Gennaro and Ensign Molina (all male) are named.

The *Voyager* crew environment contains ten compounds

spread over four square kilometres. There are 94 separate environments of the Nyrian station. The Argala habitat is at minus 20 degrees Celsius, which the Nyrians can't handle.

(Lack of) Continuity: Tom and B'Elanna have had a Klingon martial-arts session following a bet in the previous episode.

Sickbay is on Deck 5.

Making weapons out of available parts reminds Chakotay of Academy training – shouldn't it remind him of being in the Maquis with guerrilla necessities?

Ye Canna Change the Laws o' Physics: There's a surge of polaron particles every time a displacement switch is made. These create a spatial distortion around the victim. The translocator that causes it is described as being like an artificial wormhole.

Puzzles: Since there are no combadges and therefore no Universal Translator, how come Jolath, the Saurian from a neighbouring environment, speaks English?

Learn Your Lines: B'Elanna: 'You may find all this Klingon stuff fascinating, but I don't.'

Highs: The nice shot from B'Elanna's point of view as she is translocated.

Chakotay's attempt at *Die Hard* on the ship.

Janeway's revenge on the Nyrians.

The Doctor interrupting Tom and B'Elanna's conversation.

Lows: The Tom and B'Elanna subplot.

Verdict: Nothing particularly special, but a harmlessly entertaining runaround that's neither a classic nor a disaster. Pretty much everybody gets some nice scenes, though it wouldn't have done any harm to lose the Tom/B'Elanna romance bits, which are pure padding. And I'd be very worried about two people who sunbathe fully clothed in uniform . . .

On the good side, it's a nice touch that they thought to mention the Nyrians deciding to download the ship's computer and a translation algorithm, so that for once there's a reason why our heroes can understand an alien system. 7/10.

#167: 'Worst Case Scenario'

by Ken Biller

Directed by Alex Singer
Music by Dennis McCarthy
US air date 14-05-97

Plot: Stardate 50953.4. B'Elanna finds a new holonovel about a Maquis mutiny on the ship, in which the person running the program plays a security officer whom Chakotay approaches to take part in the mutiny. Seska is also one of the mutineers. This program is soon the talk of the ship, and it transpires that Tuvok wrote it as a training simulation for his team soon after the two crews merged. However, he gave up when he saw there would be no mutiny, and never finished the story. Janeway all but orders him to finish it, as everyone wants to know how it would turn out. He and Tom collaborate, and go to the holodeck to access the program. However, the program malfunctions, trapping them inside with the safeties off.

Déjà Vu?: Holodeck-gone-wrong story.

Behind the Scenes: Jonas's voice over the intercom is not Raphael Sbarge.

Voyager **Database:** The mutiny program is titled 'Insurrection Alpha'.

The crew pester Tuvok for a sequel – Janeway wants a Western, B'Elanna wants a detective story, and Neelix wants a biography of himself. So far there's been no follow up – though it'd be interesting to speculate that the 'Killing Game' World War Two scenario is one he wrote.

(Lack of) Continuity: Tom expected to find B'Elanna playing pool at Sandrine's.

The holographic Janeway has a *First Contact*-style compression rifle in what is supposed to be Season One.

Seska has been dead for over a year, and Stardate 48167.2 was a month before she left – in fact that date equates to two months before 'Caretaker'.

Ye Canna Change the Laws o' Physics: The brig's doorway is an electrostatic force field.

The fake Doctor injects Tom's neck with 20 c.c.s of nitric acid – that would be fatal.

Bloopers: Ayalla has had a sex change, and is now male (maybe a transporter malfunction . . .).

The holographic Chakotay doesn't have his Season One grey hairs.

Learn Your Lines: Janeway: 'With all due respect, Mr Tuvok, loosen up.'

Highs: Tuvok arguing with people over how the plot should continue – he wants logical characterisation, but B'Elanna wants romance, while Tom wants plot twists.

Tuvok's clever resolution to the problem.

Lows: A lot of plot holes and bloopers.

Verdict: Another good piece of entertainment. Chakotay is at his best since Season One, even being so animated as to grin like a loon throughout the briefing-room scene, while Tom and Tuvok make a great team as they try to defeat Seska's trap. Intriguingly, her motives are pro-Maquis rather than anti-*Voyager*. The episode is really made up of two stories, one segueing into the other halfway through, and it's a shame the second half is another holodeck-goes-wrong-trapping-our-heroes-inside episode. But that doesn't hurt too much in this case, and it certainly looks as if the season is going out on a run of good shows. Oh, and Tom suits the gold uniform better than the red one. 8/10.

#168: 'Scorpion'

by Brannon Braga and Joe Menosky

Directed by David Livingston
Music by Jay Chattaway
US airdate 21-05-97

Plot: Stardate 50984.3. A probe lets *Voyager* know in advance that they've reached Borg space. The only safe way through looks like being a narrow corridor full of gravimetric distortions, which they nickname the Northwest Passage. Heading for it, Janeway has the Doctor begin replicating nanoprobe antibodies from the dead Borg from 'Unity'. Soon the ship is passed by fifteen Borg cubes, who ignore the ship. Shortly afterwards, *Voyager* finds their wreckage. An alien ship is attached, and its occupant attacks Harry when an away team beam aboard. *Voyager* narrowly escapes, but the crew now know that these aliens, Species 8472, are as dangerous as the Borg.

Against Chakotay's advice, Janeway seeks an alliance with the Borg, offering them the means to defeat 8472 in return for safe passage. While she is aboard a cube, 8472 attack in force, destroying a planet. Janeway is knocked cold, and the cube flies off, dragging *Voyager* in its tractor beam.

Déjà Vu?: *Babylon 5* Shadows flying Vorlon ships . . .

Behind the Scenes: Many people had noted the similarities between Species 8472 and the Shadows from *Babylon 5*, as well as the similarities between the 8472 bioships and Vorlon ships from *B5*. This comparison is actually true. Foundation Imaging, which did the CGI for *Babylon 5*'s first three seasons, came over to *Voyager* this season, and were faced with a hurried deadline to supply 8472 and their ships. Mojo (Adam Leitowitz, effects supervisor from Foundation Imaging) has admitted that, to get the job done, Foundation modified the Vorlon ships and Shadows at the wire-frame stage, and gave them new skin textures.

The cubes are the ones from *Star Trek: First Contact*, as are the costumes and much of the Borg's furnishings.

In the script, 8472 are described as humanoids of inhuman proportions, and are simply referred to as bio-aliens.

John Rhys-Davies (Leonardo) was a regular on *Sliders*, and is best remembered as Sallah in the Indiana Jones movies.

***Voyager* Database:** 8472 fly bioships. Their cells are the most densely coded the Doctor has ever seen, with 100 times the amount of DNA found in other species. Their cells are aggressive, as is their immune system, which destroys Borg nanoprobes, so the Borg can't assimilate them.

Janeway has a new holoprogram, where she is an apprentice to Leonardo da Vinci.

(Lack of) Continuity: Though fan lore and noncanonical novels had long since pegged the Borg's home space as being in the Delta Quadrant, this wasn't actually confirmed until Beverly Crusher said so in *Star Trek: First Contact*.

The Borg's transwarp capabilities first appeared in *TNG* episode 'Descent'.

The Borg can understand only what they assimilate, which contradicts their early episodes. Borg drones have assimilation tubules in their knuckles, as seen in *First Contact*.

Ye Canna Change the Laws o' Physics: Vaccines are created for cultures of the cells, toxin or venom to be protected against, so it's a logical step to have nanoprobe antibodies made from reprogrammed nanoprobes. The Doctor reprograms nanoprobes to emit 8472 cells' biochemical signature, so as not to trigger an immune response – again a realistic concept.

Bloopers: The bioships are reported to have weapons too strong for *Voyager* to withstand, and are seen to blow Borg cubes into a million pieces with one shot. Despite that, a direct hit to *Voyager* merely knocks it aside, undamaged.

Learn Your Lines: The Borg: 'We are the Borg. Existence as you know it is over. We will add your biological and technological distinctiveness to our own. Resistance is futile.'

Puzzles: Why doesn't Janeway just offer to trade the modified nanoprobes for a transwarp drive?

Highs: The music, the effects, the whole tone of the piece.

Lows: Chakotay's parable from which the episode title derives.

Verdict: Bringing back old enemies always carries the danger of pandering to fans at the expense of casual viewers, but there's no such problem here. The Borg are back, and they are very well used. There's plenty of spectacle, and the whole crew get their share of the action.

The Borg's enemy, Species 8472, are an impressively menacing creation, with whom there is no negotiating: it's kill or be killed. Add to this a great sense of impending doom, the best musical score since 'Heroes and Demons' and a good cliffhanger, and you have a recipe for rounding out the season on a very high note. 10/10.

Interlude

Between Seasons Three and Four all the producers agreed that a new cast member was needed, and that, in Braga's words, 'it would be cool' to have a Borg crew member. Originally this might have been a man, but they soon decided on a woman instead, and, after auditions, they settled on Jeri Lynn Ryan, who had previously been a late addition to *Dark Skies*.

The official line is that Jennifer Lien left by mutual consent, and that the writers couldn't find a way to use her properly because of Kes's nine-year life span.

Fourth Season

Regular cast:
As Season Three, but with Jeri Ryan as Seven of Nine
instead of Jennifer Lien as Kes.

#169: 'Scorpion' Part II

by Brannon Braga and Joe Menosky

Directed by Winrich Kolbe
Music by Jay Chattaway
US air date 03-09-97

Plot: Stardate 51003.7. Janeway contacts Chakotay to say their deal has been accepted, and that Tuvok should join her. On the Borg cube, Janeway is introduced to her liaison with the Collective – Seven of Nine, Tertiary Adjunct to Unimatrix Zero-One. They decide to modify torpedoes to carry Borg nanoprobes, as 8472's ships are made of the same type of cells as the creatures themselves. Unfortunately, Kes is still in telepathic contact with 8472, which means they can read her mind, and know what is planned.

Déjà Vu?: Species 8472 are still Shadows flying Vorlon ships.

Behind the Scenes: The CG schematic of the multikinetic neutronic mine that Seven shows to Janeway on a monitor, is the 'unbalanced' Borg ship from *TNG* episode 'Descent'.

***Voyager* Database:** Species 8472 come from fluidic space. The Borg started the war by invading fluidic space and attempting to assimilate 8472 (though this contradicts the teaser to Part I).

A multikinetic neutronic mine with a yield of 5 million isotons will disperse nanoprobes over five light years. A torpedo would have a yield of 200 isotons. Seven was once human, and was assimilated eighteen years ago.

(Lack of) Continuity: One of the biggest blunders of the series has Chakotay use the Borg neural link from 'Unity' to sever Seven's link to the Collective. So we're supposed to believe that this one man, who is totally overpowered by half a dozen ex-Borg in 'Unity', has a stronger will than the *entire* Borg Collective of *billions*.

Seven doesn't have an electronically modulated voice the way all other drones (and even Locutus) did. She also has obvious breasts, which none of the other female Borg do. The only other Borg ever to have either breasts or an unmodulated voice is the Queen, which – along with the label 'Tertiary Adjunct to Unimatrix Zero-One' – suggests that Seven is being groomed to be a Queen. The name Seven of Nine slightly deviates from Borg designation conventions mentioned in *TNG* episode 'I Borg'. There, Hugh is designated Third of Five, and so presumably Seven *should* actually be called Seventh of Nine.

Ye Canna Change the Laws o' Physics: Seven says the multikinetic neutronic mine's shockwave will disperse nanoprobes over five light years from the point of explosion. Er, and what exactly are these nanoprobes being propelled by, or propagating through? Even if they were going out as radiation, they'd still be limited to the speed of light, and take five years to spread out.

A coherent graviton beam opens singularities into fluidic space.

Puzzles: The producers seem to have forgotten that the airponics garden was in Cargo Bay 2 in the earlier seasons. I wonder what happened to it.

Learn Your Lines: Doc: 'Don't worry, I'll delete myself at the first sign of trouble.Well, perhaps not the first sign . . .'

Seven on humanity: 'You are erratic, conflicted, disorganised. Every decision is debated, every action questioned, every individual entitled to their own opinion. You lack harmony, cohesion, greatness. It will be your undoing.'

Highs: Seven makes an immediate impression.

Great effects, music score . . .

The whole thing is thrilling and exciting.

Verdict: For possibly the first time, the second half of a *Trek* two-parter exceeds the quality of the first half by some way – and that's especially impressive considering how good the first half of this story was. All the comments made in the entry for Part I still apply – this is a wonderfully exciting good-guys-versus-bad-guys spectacle. It is, of course, also the introduction of Seven of Nine, Kes's replacement in the regular cast. Oddly, Jeri Ryan's very good acting is actually the one thing that doesn't sit well in the episode. Believe it or not, she's too good. Seriously. She's supposed to be a Borg drone – cold and unemotional – but actually gives a great semi-villainous ice-queen performance, which is too individual for the Borg. But, if my speculation about her being a Queen in training is correct, then that does fit. In any case, this episode is still a great start to the season. 10/10.

#170: 'The Gift'

by Joe Menosky

Directed by Anson Williams
Music by Dennis McCarthy
US air date 10-09-97

Plot: Stardate not given. Having separated Seven of Nine from the Collective, the Doctor is forced to operate on her, as her human tissue begins rejecting the Borg implants. Essentially she's a Borg being assimilated by humanity. Meanwhile, Kes is developing strange powers, and evolving due to the new neural pathways forced open by her contact with 8472.

Déjà Vu?: Kes's evolution is very reminiscent of Wesley's in *TNG* episode 'Journey's End'.

Behind the Scenes: Stock footage of burning atoms from 'Meld' reappears.

The last shuttle goes, so this is an opportune moment to look at what the makers have to say. Brannon Braga and Bryan Fuller say they just replicate new ones. Jeri Taylor says the Maquis crew are kept below decks building them. Lolita Fatjo (script co-ordinator) says the shuttle numbers are a mistake and that they simply lost track.

Voyager **Database:** The Doctor says he can't treat a patient against his or her wishes.

Seven's real name is Annika. Her parents were explorers who wanted nothing to do with Starfleet or the Federation, and were last heard of in the Omega Sector.

Galactic Cluster Three is a transmaterial energy plane intersecting 22 billion omnicordial life forms. Species 259 live there.

The Doctor designs Seven's catsuit, claiming it's medically beneficial.

(Lack of) Continuity: Kes is given a shuttle to take with her when she leaves the ship. There are now none left.

Janeway has met several Borg who were separated from the Collective.

Kes throws *Voyager* 10,000 light years past Borg space, shaving ten years off the trip home.

Puzzles: Why remove all the improved Borg shields and weapons? Wouldn't it be better to keep them?

Learn Your Lines: Janeway: 'I can't give you back to the Borg. But you're not alone: you're part of a human community now, a human Collective! We may be individuals but we live and work together. You can get some of the unity you require right here on *Voyager*.'

Seven: 'Your attempts to assimilate this drone will fail. You can alter our physiology but you cannot change our nature. We will betray you; we are Borg.'

Highs: Tuvok sparring with the Doctor.

Seven going gaga.

The final shot.

Lows: A lack of cohesive story.

Verdict: A rather odd episode, this, because it's basically a collection of leftover plot threads from previous episodes being tied up, rather than having a cohesive plot of its own. And yet, it works beautifully. Kes's departure is rather rushed, and Jeri Ryan continues to impress (especially in her rubber-and-duct-tape half-Borg costume). Tuvok and Neelix also get good scenes, and overall it has an air of change. After this, the show will never be quite the same again . . . 7/10.

#172: 'Day of Honor'

by Jeri Taylor

Directed by Jesus Trevino
Music by Dennis McCarthy
US air date 17-09-97

Plot: *Voyager* encounters the Cataati, most of whose race were assimilated by the Borg. They are seeking thorium isotopes. Meanwhile, B'Elanna is trying to avoid taking part in the Day of Honor, a Klingon holiday. When an accident forces the ejection of the warp core, Tom and B'Elanna take a shuttle to retrieve it. Their shuttle is destroyed by the Cataati, who steal the warp core and leave the pair in spacesuits with the air running out.

Behind the Scenes: Michael Jan Friedman wrote the novelisation, to tie in with the Pocket Books miniseries *Day of Honor* – for which this episode is pretty much a commercial.

The spacesuits are the ones from *Star trek: First Contact*.

***Voyager* Database:** Cataati technology is based on the use of thorium isotopes. They were assimilated a year ago, but thirty ships escaped.

It should be possible to open a transwarp conduit using a tachyon burst from a modified main deflector while the ship is at warp 2.

The Day of Honor is for reviewing the year to see if one has lived up to the behavioural standards expected of a Klingon.

Eating the heart of a sanctified targ gives a warrior courage.

Tom and B'Elanna co-wrote the 'Day of Honor' holo-program.

B'Elanna found her mother's Klingon rituals hateful as a child.

Deception is impossible among the Borg.

There is a six-week spacewalking course in the third year of Starfleet Academy.

Tom thinks that constantly pushing people away is a sure way not to get hurt.

(Lack of) Continuity: The shuttlecraft that's destroyed is the *Cochrane*, from 'Threshold'.

B'Elanna says she's defeated no enemies in battle, over-looking the Vidiians in 'Faces', and Vorik.

Tom seems to be trying to chat up Seven even though he's already seeing B'Elanna.

B'Elanna is nauseated by zero-g, like Worf in *First Contact* (but contradicting 'Macrocosm').

Ye Canna Change the Laws o' Physics: An acoustic inverter is part of a sonic shower.

Eating the heart of an enemy for courage is a ritual among many of Earth's primitive cultures.

The two spacesuits' communications systems can be inter-plexed to form a phase carrier wave.

Puzzles: Why keep all the Borg regeneration alcoves in Cargo Bay 2, and not just Seven's?

How can B'Elanna work with Vorik as if 'Blood Fever' never happened? Maybe we're lucky and they're trying to erase it from canon.

What does B'Elanna try to disable the tractor beam with?

Bloopers: When Vorik calls Janeway from Engineering, you can see that he's standing on the bridge set, despite the tight angle.

Learn Your Lines: Seven: 'This crew is inefficient and con-tentious, but it is capable of surprising acts of compassion.'

Highs: Neelix's offer to let B'Elanna take out her frustrations on him is as sweet as he is stupid.

Lows: The lead Cataati has awfully slow delivery.

There's not much tension over whether Tom and B'Elanna will survive.

Being able to recover the warp core is such a cop-out.

Verdict: Oh dear. We're plunged right back into lame soap-opera territory, as Tom and B'Elanna are put in a contrived situation where they'll be forced to admit their love for each other. The subplot about the Cataati is a laboured refugees-versus-the-West story that eventually says yes, they are thieves and spongers. Dawson's always worth watching, but this episode is just too contrived and unconvincing to entertain or to advance the characters. The novelisation's got amazingly clumsy prose too. Pathetic. 3/10.

#171: 'Nemesis

by Ken Biller

Directed by Alex Singer
Music by David Bell
US air date 24-09-97

Plot: Stardate 51082.4. Chakotay's shuttle is shot down on a war-torn planet. He is rescued by the Vorri, humanoid soldiers engaged in a war with the Krayden, whom they call the Nemesis. The Nemesis defile the dead and are thoroughly evil. Chakotay makes friends with the soldiers, some of whom get killed, then finds himself in a Vorri village which is occupied and ethnically cleansed by the Krayden.

Meanwhile, Janeway is playing host to the Krayden Ambassador.

Déjà Vu?: The Treen were the Venusian race ruled by the Mekon in the old *Dan Dare* comic strips.

The episode is also very much in the mould of the ground-based episodes of *Space Above and Beyond*.

Ugly enemies being the good guys is a cliché most amusingly used in Harry Harrison's book *Star Smashers of the Galaxy Rangers*.

Tuvok as a Krayden has a Dalek voice, though the real Krayden don't.

Behind the Scenes: All the weapons are contemporary.

Neither Seven nor B'Elanna appears in this episode.

The Krayden attack plane is a Harrier, modified by CGI.

The Krayden soldiers' uniforms are Mokra uniforms from 'Resistance.'

***Voyager* Database:** Chakotay was on a survey mission.

The Vorri use biochemical weapons, according to the Krayden.

The Krayden defile the dead and murder women and children, according to the Vorri.

(Lack of) Continuity: Neelix knows this war, and that it has been going on for a decade, which is odd, since his experience ended 10,000 light years back.

Ye Canna Change the Laws o' Physics: The Vorri use a combination of photometric projections, emotional stimuli and psychotropic drugs to brainwash Chakotay. I assume photometric projections are some kind of holodeck, but the other two elements are used in real-life brainwashing, such as the CIA's notorious MK-Ultra experiments of the 70s.

Puzzles: How much of what the Vorri said about the Krayden was true, and vice versa?

Learn Your Lines: Doc: 'They had you so mixed up they could have convinced you your own mother was a turnip.' Proof of Chakotay's vegetable DNA?

Highs: Chakotay is quite good here, and the action scenes are well handled.

Lows: The Patrol are a right bunch of war-movie clichés.

Verdict: Basically a Vietnam movie with Chakotay in it. It's actually quite good, with the brainwashing twist being very well done (though the twist of the ugly aliens not being the evil ones is exceedingly hoary). Biller's use of language is also very clever where the Vorri are concerned – their slang is just different enough to be alien, but not too different to be incomprehensible. It even has its own understandable colloquialisms. For example, 'glimpse' means see, appearance or eye, depending on context. Very well done. 7/10.

#173: 'Revulsion'

by Lisa Klink

Directed by Ken Biller
Music by David Bell
US air date 01-10-97

Plot: Stardate 51186.2. After Tuvok attends a ceremony to promote him to lieutenant commander, the ship answers a distress call from an alien vessel containing a hologram who claims that an accident killed the crew. The Doctor and B'Elanna go to help, and find a far better candidate for the title of 'android version of Norman Bates' than Kryten ever was.

Déjà Vu?: HD25's gold skin is reminiscent of Data's in *TNG*. His obsession with cleanliness seems to be inherited from Kryten (*Red Dwarf*), and his lethal disgust for human infestation suggests that the *Doctor Who* story 'Paradise Towers' was also an influence.

The design of the room where B'Elanna finds the bodies is vaguely like the computer room in *Alien*.

HD25 sticking his hand in to crush B'Elanna's heart is like Mola Ram's attempt to do the same to Indy in *Indiana Jones and the Temple of Doom*. It's also Judge Death's favourite method of dispensing justice in the *Judge Dredd* comic strips.

Behind the Scenes: In real life Tim Russ is the biggest joker on set, and is more likely to play jokes on McNeill and Wang than the other way around.

***Voyager* Database:** Tom and Harry play jokes on Tuvok.

Tuvok once dressed down Janeway in front of three admirals for not following proper tactical protocols on her first command.

HD25 is an isomorphic projection designed for tasks too menial or dangerous for a human, such as cleaning out the reactor core.

The tool for pulling out Borg nodes used to be part of Seven's thoraccic assembly. A cut hand would have regenerated in seconds when she was a Drone. Her hand exoskeleton can take touching 5,000 volts.

Tuvok is promoted to Lt. Commander.

(Lack of) Continuity: Neelix is being given his first official mission as ambassador ('Macrocosm').

Tom is critical of Seven as a former Borg, which contradicts his attitude in the previous episode. Maybe he's just annoyed that she doesn't fancy him.

Borg have no time for single-cell fertilisation – though they do have babies in *TNG* episode 'Q Who'.

Ye Canna Change the Laws o' Physics: Tom says it has been three days since the Day of Honor.

Culhane (male) is named as a crew member.

Antimatter radiation dissolves human flesh in seconds – yeah, right . . .

Puzzles: How could B'Elanna and the Doctor possibly not notice right from the start that HD25 is totally barking?

Bloopers: In the last shot of the scene where B'Elanna discovers the bodies, you can see a reflection of a boom mike on the shiny console surface behind her.

Learn Your Lines: Tuvok: 'In my three years on *Voyager* I have grown to respect many of you. Others I have learned to tolerate!'

Seven: 'It may not be apparent, but I'm often amused by human behaviour.'

Highs: Leland Orser.

Seven winding up Harry by calling his bluff over sex.

Lows: The Doctor is out of character when being nosy about Tom and B'Elanna.

Verdict: Hmm. An excellent performance from Leland Orser, and of course from Dawson and Picardo. Unfortunately the unoriginal plot is hamstrung by Dawson and Picardo having to be mind-bogglingly stupid not to notice that HD is completely out of his tree. The resolution is blatantly telegraphed very early on. ('An isomagnetic conduit that will destabilise your matrix? That'll be handy if you turn out to be a psycho and I have to fight you off.') 5/10.

#174: 'The Raven'

by Bryan Fuller
from a story by him and Harry Doc Kloor

Directed by LeVar Burton
Music by Dennis McCarthy
US air date 08-10-97

Plot: While Janeway is negotiating for passage through B'omar space, Seven begins to have hallucinations of being attacked by a raven. Borg implants regrow, and she steals a ship to follow the Borg signal she is receiving. Tuvok follows, and together they make an intriguing discovery about the source of her visions.

Déjà Vu?: 'The Raven' was an Edgar Allan Poe poem.

Behind the Scenes: Seven gets a new brown catsuit.

The Borg sets in Seven's flashback are from 'Scorpion'.

The cargo-bay set has expanded, gaining the upstairs gantry and office previously seen only in 'Learning Curve'.

The mirrored shot of a model shuttle from 'Initiations' is used again.

The original title was 'Resurrection.'

***Voyager* Database:** The B'omar maintain links with the Nazardene, and want visitors to their space to pass through a strictly controlled course under strict conditions. They are afraid of the Borg.

All Borg have an implant that allows them to pick up resonance homing beacons.

(Lack of) Continuity: The Borg voice Seven hears refers to her as 'Seven of Nine, grid nine-two of subjunction twelve'. Unfortunately, grid nine-two of subjunction twelve was the room in the Borg cube where Seven was supposed to work with Janeway and Tuvok, not her full Borg designation.

Seven was assimilated aged six, which makes her 24 now.

Seven's parents were known in the Federation for unorthodox scientific ideas.

Sickbay is on Deck 8 in this episode, instead of Deck 5 as usual.

Ye Canna Change the Laws o' Physics: The Doctor prepares a genetic resequencer that would neutralise Borg nanoprobes. But nanoprobes are mechanical – they don't have genes to resequence.

Bloopers: Jeri Ryan has trouble keeping a straight face while Neelix teaches her how to eat. Neelix says her food will be steamed – then stir-fries it.

The bridge rail wobbles when Chakotay swings himself around it.

Highs: Tuvok and Seven have a great chemistry.

Jeri Ryan is especially impressive while reliving her childhood assimilation.

Lows: The B'omar are dull.

Verdict: Quite a good episode, looking at Seven's repressed memories coming back as she regains her humanity. The teasing hints about life aboard the SS *Raven* are also interesting. Ryan and Russ display a wonderful chemistry once Tuvok beams to her shuttle, too. If only they were paired more often. As is common with Season Four, the rest of the episode is rather dull, with the aliens (who all look even more alike than usual this year) being the most boring lot so far. 6/10.

#175: 'Scientific Method

by Lisa Klink
from a story by Sherry Klein and Harry Doc Kloor

Directed by David Livingston
Music by Jay Chattaway
US air date 29-10-97

Plot: Stardate 51244.3. Strange things are afoot on the ship – Janeway has a migraine, Tom and B'Elanna are caught canoodling in Engineering, and Chakotay has been aged about fifty years overnight. The Doctor modifies Seven's optical implant to search for a cause, and she discovers that the ship is overrun by cloaked aliens who are experimenting on the crew. But how can the crew be warned without alerting the aliens who are monitoring them?

Déjà Vu?: Aliens experimenting on the crew in this fashion was the plot of *TNG* episode 'Schisms'.

Out-of-phase observers infiltrating the ship were previously used in 'Distant Origin'.

***Voyager* Database:** There are 257 rooms aboard *Voyager*.
Seven is now assigned to the astrometrics lab.
Progeria was wiped out in the twenty-second century.
Neelix's great-grandfather was Myliian, from a neighbouring planet. That makes an eighth of his DNA Myliian, and this is hyperstimulated by the aliens.
There are at least 56 aliens on board.
Experiments on animals have long since been declared unacceptable even for survival.

(Lack of) Continuity: Tuvok and Janeway make a date to split a bottle of wine.

Ye Canna Change the Laws o' Physics: Chakotay is affected by progeria – early ageing, a condition that really exists in children. He suffers bone decalcification and tissue necrosis, also signs of ageing. The metabolism regulator in his DNA has been hyperstimulated.

The aliens' phase variance is 0.15 – 0.15 what?

The alveoli in B'Elanna's lungs stop processing oxygen.

Neuroleptic shock will disable the aliens' tags in the crew's DNA, if delivered to the whole crew simultaneously by modifying the EPS conduits (these run throughout the ship).

Puzzles: Why doesn't Seven tell Tuvok what's happening? She can see in the ready room that he isn't yet being shadowed by any aliens.

Learn Your Lines: Tuvok: 'Shall I have them whipped, as well?'

Highs: The see-through kiss is disgusting but very well done!

Chakotay's hair falling out is nicely done too, though it doesn't follow either of the standard male patterns of baldness.

The make-up is also good.

Janeway's rant to Tuvok, and his reply.

Lows: B'Elanna and Tom acting like a couple of kids – though to be fair this is the fault of the aliens messing with their hormones. Beltran doesn't even try to act older, or change his voice.

Chakotay and Neelix swapping ailments.

Verdict: A relatively entertaining episode, but with plot holes that a Borg cube could be driven through. The basic plot, with only Seven against the aliens, is harmless fun, but before long it all starts to fall apart: out-of-phase aliens are becoming commonplace, and there's no reason why Seven shouldn't tell Tuvok what's happening (he's not an alien target yet).

The attempt to justify the episode with some heavy-handed lecturing about vivisection actually works against it, because of clichéd dialogue, and the fact that it's tagged on in the way little moral messages used to be tagged on to the end of the *He-Man* cartoons in the 80s. The Doctor in tights is amusing, though. 5/10.

#176: 'Year of Hell'

by Brannon Braga and Joe Menosky

Directed by Allan Kroeker
Music by Dennis McCarthy
US air date 05-11-97

Plot: Stardate 51252.3. *Voyager* is transporting a Zahl ambassador, when the ship encounters a small Krenim vessel. Abruptly, a temporal shockwave hits them, the Zahl disappears, and the Krenim ship is much larger and more powerful. Janeway fights them off, but over the next few months the ship is battered by Krenim attacks. In fact the temporal wave was caused by Annorax, using a temporal incursion weapon to try changing history. When he encounters *Voyager*, Annorax abducts Tom and Chakotay. As Krenim attacks continue, *Voyager* has to be abandoned.

Déjà Vu?: The story is about the remnants of an empire from a couple of centuries ago, who use a large time weapon which also keeps them immortal and protected from time, to erase their enemies from history. A bit like the *Doctor Who* novel *The Dark Path*.

Annorax, apart from 'anorak' derivation, is play on the name 'Arronax', from *20,000 Leagues Under The Sea*.

Behind the Scenes: Originally, this script was written to be the Season Three cliffhanger. However, with the changes in cast structure, a new story had to be written to execute that, and 'Year of Hell' was pushed back to the Sweeps. When the episode finally aired on the BBC, it was shown as a feature-length movie, though the only episode intended to be viewed that way is 'Dark Frontier'.

Kurtwood Smith (Annorax) was the villain in *Robocop*, and also appeared in *DS9* and *Star Trek VI*.

***Voyager* Database:** The crew of the weapon ship have been on this mission for 200 years.

The astrometrics lab is officially opened. It measures the radiometric output of three million stars and computes the position of the ship relative to the centre of the galaxy.

Harry is a sports aficionado.

Ensign Strickland and Crewman Emanuel are killed when the Doctor shuts the hatch on them.

Janeway's birthday is on 20 May, which is somewhere between Day 47 and Day 70.

(Lack of) Continuity: The Doctor claims to have been activated on Stardate 48315, which is correct, for a change.

Seven knows the Borg were involved in the first warp flight (*Star Trek: First Contact*).

Tom now has a general fixation with history rather than just automobiles ('The 37s') or twentieth-century USA ('Future's End').

Presumably Kes's information changed things, as not only does neither Janeway nor B'Elanna die, but the year didn't start at Stardate 50973 as she predicted.

In the alternate timeline, Tuvok wears full commander's pips, and therefore outranks Chakotay.

Neelix finally gets his wish to be a security officer.

Janeway has made it her goal in life to avoid time travel ('Future's End').

Ye Canna Change the Laws o' Physics: Tom bases his safety idea on the design of the *Titanic* – specifically, transverse bulkheads, which in the *Titanic* were meant to stop water flooding the ship if any one section was holed.

Tuvok has a tactile interface on his console while he's blind.

Ships are identified by hull markings and biospectral frequency.

Ironically, the temporal shields prevent *Voyager* from being restored when Annorax gets an incursion wrong (I like that irony).

The weapon ship exists in a state of temporal flux, outside space-time.

Bloopers: Tuvok bleeds red instead of green when he cuts himself shaving.

Learn Your Lines: Annorax: 'Target *Voyager*. Put Janeway out of her misery.'

Janeway: 'We're going through this space, whether they like it or not.' And what about Starfleet principles?

Highs: Kurtwood Smith as Annorax.
The effects.
The clever plot.
Harry and B'Elanna's chemistry in the lift.
Great cliffhanger.

Lows: The pure padding about Janeway's birthday.

Verdict: A distinct threat to the ship and crew this time. It suffers from some padding – notably the whole thing about Chakotay replicating a watch as a birthday present for Janeway – but for the most part this shapes up to be another good annual Braga-and-Menosky epic. Seven coming to help Tuvok with his 'personal grooming' clearly means something too.

Great effects, good acting from all concerned, and a clever plot make for the best episode since 'Scorpion'. *Voyager* may come in for a lot of stick when compared with the other *Treks*, but it undeniably has the two-part epic down pat, unlike the other branches of the franchise. 9/10.

#177: 'Year of Hell', Part II

by Brannon Braga and Joe Menosky

Directed by Mike Vejar
Music by Dennis McCarthy
US air date 12-11-97

Plot: Stardate 51425.4 (Day 133). While Chakotay fraternises with Annorax, Tom discovers that some of the Krenim are tired of their mission, and may be willing to rebel. Meanwhile, Janeway decides it's time to stop running, get reinforcements from the Nalhydrin and Mawasi, and go after the weapon ship.

Déjà Vu?: As before. Tom also refers to Annorax as both Captain Bligh and Captain Nemo.

Voyager **Database:** After evacuation, only nine people remain on *Voyager*: Janeway, B'Elanna, Seven, Harry, the Doctor, Neelix, Tuvok and two unnamed others.

Annorax keeps trophies of the erased worlds, but for his conscience rather than triumph.

Chakotay failed Professor Fassbinder's course in temporal mechanics at the Academy, and proceeds to prove it by getting temporal calculations wrong.

Neelix serves puréed ration cubes as a drink (with Talaxian spices).

Starfleet Medical regulation 121-A lets the Doctor relieve a captain of command.

(Lack of) Continuity: Trioxin rather than tri-ox compound helps people breathe more easily.

The Doctor was off line for some time but is repaired.

Voyager entered Krenim space to avoid a rogue comet.

Janeway suffers third-degree burns to 60 per cent of her body – that would be fatal. She also has post-traumatic-stress syndrome.

Ye Canna Change the Laws o' Physics: OK. The temporal mechanics of the end do work: the temporal incursion weapon erases itself from history.

Puzzles: There must be something between Janeway and Tuvok, going by the way she touches his face.

Opinion varies on whether the last scene, set 200 years ago, means that Annorax didn't create the weapon. No it doesn't – the padd clearly shows its schematics under development. Basically, he's caught in a time loop, which *Voyager* went round once and then came out the other side.

Learn Your Lines: Annorax: 'Past, present and future – they exist as one. They breathe together.'

Chakotay: 'You're trying to rationalise genocide. One species is significant – one life is significant.'

Highs: Kurtwood Smith as Annorax.

Janeway's speech about the ship.

The music when she remains alone on *Voyager* for her kamikaze run.

The shots of the damaged *Voyager*.

Lows: More dodgy radio-style writing when Annorax tells Obris that Obris is turning off the temporal core.

Verdict: Once again it lives up to the promise of the first half, something *TNG* and *DS9* two-parters never did. The plot remains fiendishly clever, but the real clincher is Annorax himself: despite Tom's speeches to Chakotay, it's pretty clear that Annorax isn't actually evil; and Kurtwood Smith plays him beautifully. Though Joel Grey in 'Resistance' remains the best guest star to date, Smith as Annorax is a close runner-up, and is certainly the best villain *Voyager* has had so far. Throw in good work from the rest of the cast, and stunning visuals, and you have a real treat in store. 9.5/10.

#178: 'Random Thoughts'

by Ken Biller

Directed by Alex Singer
Music by Jay Chattaway
US air date 19-11-97

Plot: Stardate 51367.2. On the planet Mhari, an away team are trading supplies. When a man commits a brutal assault shortly after bumping into B'Elanna, she is arrested. His violent thoughts sparked the crime (the Mhari are telepaths). Nevertheless, she is responsible. Unwilling to let her be punished for this, Janeway has Tuvok investigate.

Déjà Vu?: Thought police. Psi Cops. You get the picture. The trade in violent thoughts and memories is similar to *Strange Days*.

A murder investigation leading to an exploration of Tuvok's dark side – can we say 'Meld' here?

Behind the Scenes: The first mind-meld includes a number of interesting shots: a knife, a green monster biting an arm, the explosion of the warp-plasma sample ('Fair Trade'), a Rottweiler, a screaming mouth, a SWAT team firing tear gas (news footage from the Rodney King riots), and a Borg cube exploding ('Scorpion').

The second mind-meld entails even more interesting clips: Enterprise-E crewmen from Borg viewpoint (*Star Trek: First Contact*); a crewman covered in cuts with his eyes gouged out (*Event Horizon*); Sam Neill's character on hire (*Event Horizon*); the Nexus ribbon (*Star Trek: Generations*); a creature appearing to be a Vidiian or Tom Paris from 'Threshold'; Veridian III, exploding (*Star Trek: Generations*); Tuvok as Krayden ('Nemesis'); and the Lakul, exploding (*Star Trek: Generations*).

The neurogenic restructuring machine used to be in *TNG* sickbay.

***Voyager* Database:** There are very few telepaths in Starfleet.

The brig has been occupied for less than 1 per cent of the trip so far.

Tuvok is impressed by the lack of crime on Mhari. Crime on Vulcan before Surak also used to be the result of other people's violent thoughts.

(Lack of) Continuity: This episode has Tuvok's annual mind-meld.

Ye Canna Change the Laws o' Physics: Neurogenic restructuring is the punishment for thought crimes on Mhari, to remove violent thoughts.

Puzzles: If B'Elanna's thought of punching Frayn was more than the Mhari could handle, then surely Tuvok's dark side would have driven Guill completely bananas.

Learn Your Lines: Janeway: 'You know the rules, Tom – we can't just pick and choose which laws we'll respect and which we won't.'

Highs: Tuvok shows off his dark side again.

Lows: Silly premise.

Neelix and the girl, and Neelix's seeking romantic advice from Tom.

The Mhari city is the usual boring plaster and pastels. Are all Delta Quadrant settlements built by the same architect?

Verdict: In spite of the incredibly silly version of a thought crime that B'Elanna is accused of – and a considerable lack of originality – this is a reasonable episode. Tim Russ gets to show Tuvok's dark side again, and the trade in mental images is good, but in the end it's all been done better in previous episodes, most notably 'Ex Post Facto' and 'Meld'. This retread is really just a timewaster, especially since the best bits – Tuvok looking pissed off excepted – come from spotting the clips in the flashbacks. 7/10.

#179: 'Concerning Flight'

by Joe Menosky
from a story by him and Jimmy Diggs

Directed by Jesus Trevino
Music by Dennis McCarthy
US air date 26-11-97

Plot: Stardate 51386.4. *Voyager* is attacked by alien ships which steal the computer core among other things, and take them to a nearby planet to fence. When Janeway and Tuvok beam down to investigate, they discover that, because the da Vinci program was running at the time, he was stolen too – and the Doctor's mobile emitter lets him stay active. Janeway must team up with Leonardo to recover the computer core.

Behind the Scenes: The city is optically dumped atop the Santa Monica hills. Leonardo wears the mobile emitter upside down on his chest, rather than on his arm. The guards have the Romulan/'Starship Mine' rifles.

***Voyager* Database:** Leonardo thinks he's been abducted to America by Spanish sailors and that Janeway followed him in a Portuguese ship. He describes his new patron as being as ruthless as a Borgia.

The main computer has simultaneous access to 47 million data channels and transluminal (faster-than-light) processing at 575 trillion operations per nanosecond. Its operational temperature margins are from 10 to 1,790 degrees Kelvin.

There is a pause button on the mobile emitter.

Seven has to report to the Doctor for maintenance once a week. He wants to hear gossip while he's confined to sickbay by the loss of the mobile emitter.

(Lack of) Continuity: Leonardo refers to Vulcan as an island off Sicily. He should mean Sicily itself – Mount Etna was traditionally Vulcan's Forge.

Tuvok tells Leonardo that he's from Scandinavia!

Janeway mentions that Kirk claimed to have met Leonardo (TOS – 'Requiem for Methuselah').

Ye Canna Change the Laws o' Physics: Command override Janeway pi 110 makes the computer core's abduction protocol overload it. Would it be destroyed or damaged if it overloaded?

The fortress has a door facing the sunset so that attackers will have the light in their eyes. Surely this depends on when they attack.

Puzzles: How long is there between *Voyager*'s 'mugging' and reaching the planet, for Leonardo to find employment?

Bloopers: That's a very gentle slope that Janeway and Leonardo pedal off, not a cliff.

Learn Your Lines: Leonardo: 'When are we not in prison? When are our lives free from the influence of those who have more power than us?'

Highs: Tuvok, when ordered to make small talk.

John Rhys-Davies is excellent as Leonardo.

Lows: Harry's interest in Seven is still cringeworthy.

Verdict: This one's a frequently forgotten episode, but is noteworthy for the greater than usual amount of location filming. It's also pleasantly amusing: Rhys-Davies is always fun to watch, and all concerned seem to be having a good time. Da Vinci seems to accept the twenty-fourth-century marvels too readily even by his standards, but otherwise there's much to enjoy here, in the sparkling dialogue, if not in the plot or characterisation. 8/10.

#180: 'Mortal Coil'

by Bryan Fuller

Directed by Allan Kroeker
Music by Paul Baillargeon
US air date 03-12-97

Plot: Stardate 51449.2. While collecting samples of protomatter in a shuttle, Neelix is killed in a freak accident. Seven uses her nanoprobes to bring him back, but the lack of an afterlife during his experience disturbs him.

Déjà Vu?: Life after death . . . Spock, Sheridan . . . There's a long list of people who had that in SF. The dream sequences are handled exactly like the Orb/Prophet experiences in *DS9*. Conversely, Picard had an afterlife experience in *TNG* episode 'Tapestry', as did Janeway in 'Coda'.

Voyager **Database:** A Class-1 nebula contains protomatter. Neelix dealt with this substance while a trader. It's the most powerful energy source in the quadrant.

The Kazon are Species 329 and were deemed unworthy of assimilation by the Borg – why assimilate a species that would actually detract from perfection? This is the first mention that the Borg seek perfection.

Prixan is the Talaxian Observance of Family Alliance.

Wildman's daughter is named Naomi. Neelix is her godfather, and the only person who can get her to sleep at night, after checking under the bed for monsters.

Because the memories and experiences of all drones

remain in the Collective, the Borg are essentially immortal. Children assimilated by the Borg are placed in maturation chambers for seventeen cycles (however long that is).

(Lack of) Continuity: Protomatter was used in the creation of the Genesis torpedo, according to *Star Trek III: The Search for Spock*.

'Phage' is mentioned again.

Neelix's canister is the one from 'Fair Trade' – which was destroyed – but he says he nearly lost it to the Kazon the last time he used it.

The Borg can revive dead drones up to 73 hours after death, though the one in 'Unity' was briefly activated after five years (albeit protected from decay by vacuum). This is silly – she could, and says she would, revive any and all casualties from now on (but doesn't, of course).

Neelix is dead for 18 hours, 49 minutes and 13 seconds – a new world record. (In real life it's more like eight minutes before irreversible brain death.)

We see Neelix's sister, Alixia, in the Vision Quest ('Jetrel').

Ye Canna Change the Laws o' Physics: Nanoprobes reverse cellular necrosis (the breakdown of dead cells) while the cerebral cortex is stimulated by neuroelectric isopulse. The nanoprobes compensate for any cellular degeneration. This resuscitation technique was assimilated from Species 149.

Puzzles: When Tom says Chakotay's suggestions to revive Neelix won't work, is it true, or is he just considering the morale value of getting rid of him?

Bloopers: Before approaching Neelix in the teaser, Chakotay is posed as if chatting with someone just off screen. Unfortunately the angle is a little too wide, and you can see there's no one there.

Naomi sounds choked full of a cold.

Learn Your Lines: Seven: 'You are a peculiar creature, Neelix.'

Highs: Neelix dies. Don't all cheer at once – it doesn't last long.

The Doctor's reaction to working under Seven's instructions.
Chakotay's teachings about the Vision Quest, surprisingly.
Neelix and Samantha Wildman would make a good pair.
Seven and Tuvok's discussion of death.

Lows: Neelix comes back to life. You may groan now.
Neelix talking to himself.
Naomi.

Verdict: Watching this is like having teeth pulled, except it lasts about twenty times longer. Though Ethan Phillips is usually better at dramatic episodes than comedy, this is an exception. Neelix absolutely sucks in this episode. Though the idea of having a character face a loss of faith is a good one, it doesn't work when the person in question is Neelix. The episode also makes a mistake in having Seven restore him with nanoprobes – either this means any deaths on board can be reversed, or else it's a vital major development which will be forgotten immediately. It's not too hard to guess which will be the case.

The story might have worked if it had set up an arc dealing with how one comes to terms with the destruction of a dearly held belief, but instead it uses Naomi as a reset button to make Neelix feel back to normal. Basically, this is an excruciatingly dire episode in which the best thing is Chakotay. 3/10.

#181: 'Waking Moments'

by André Bormanis

Directed by Alex Singer
Music by David Bell
US air date 10-12-97

Plot: Stardate 51471.3. Tuvok shows up for work naked, Seven flings herself at Harry, Tom dies in a shuttle crash, and Janeway meets the dead crewmen she's got killed. All nightmares shared by the crew, which also include a fairly typical *Voyager* alien. When Chakotay goes on a Vision Quest, he wakes up to find that the ship has been taken over by aliens to whom dreams are more real than the waking world.

Déjà Vu?: In *Babylon 5*, Ivanova also once dreamed of turning up for work naked. Reality within unreality has also been the theme of previous *Treks*, such as *TNG* episode 'Frame of Mind' and 'Projections'.

Behind the Scenes: For Tuvok's 'nude' scene in the teaser, Tim Russ had the make-up department mould a ridiculously large . . . er, attribute for him. When he came on to the set and removed his dressing gown to reveal that instead of underwear, the whole cast and crew just collapsed with the giggles.

Roxann Dawson is given a new Engineering smock to try to hide her pregnancy.

***Voyager* Database:** Tuvok doesn't sleep nude, though he dreams that he does. Nobody does in *Trek*, actually.

Chakotay always refused to hunt deer as a boy.

Harry's quarters are on Deck 6, Room 105-2.

Tuvok's security code is Security clearance Tuvok zeta-9.

Inimocene prevents sleep.

Chakotay refers to Australian aboriginal mythology of the Dream Time.

The aliens live in unfurnished caves.

(Lack of) Continuity: A neurogenic field is imposing the same dream on everyone.

Ye Canna Change the Laws o' Physics: Sleep deprivation doesn't actually prevent dreams – after three or four days, they would start manifesting as hallucinations while one is awake, because they are that important to the functioning of the brain.

Learn Your Lines: Janeway: 'Either I've become impervious to antimatter explosions, or we're still dreaming.'

Highs: Seven's 'diversion'.

Nice segue between Janeway touching the back of her hand, and Chakotay dreaming she's awake.

Lows: Very bland aliens.

Verdict: Quite a nice episode, though no classic. The dream-within-a-dream card has been played too often in *Trek* in recent years to be really effective, but everybody's on good form, and there's a nice mixture of humour, action and tension. If you can tell the difference between these aliens and almost any others except the Krayden that we've seen since 'Fair Trade', though, then you're a better man than I am, Gunga Din. Also, that's as close as Harry will ever get to wooing Seven. 7/10.

#182: 'Message in a Bottle'

by Lisa Klink from a story by Rick Williams

Directed by Nancy Malone
Music by Paul Baillargeon
US air date 21-01-98

Plot: Seven has discovered a network of subspace relay stations, which carry signals all the way to the Alpha Quadrant, where a Federation ship can be seen. Janeway decides to transmit the Doctor's program through. When he arrives, he finds the crew dead and the experimental ship under Romulan control. The ship does have new mark-two EMH, however, and the two Doctors must work together to save the ship from the Romulans.

Déjà Vu?: Two eccentric nameless Doctors don't get on, but work together . . . They could just have called it 'The Two Doctors'.

Behind the Scenes: The Defiant-Class ships are simply *DS9*'s Defiant with new markings, and are CGI. The other ship is a CGI Akira-Class vessel from *Star Trek: First Contact*. A Nebula-Class ship also appears, as do Romulan warbirds.

The *Prometheus* bridge is a redress of the *Enterprise-E* bridge.

Voyager Database: There are 27 Romulans aboard the USS *Prometheus*. The *Prometheus* has multivector attack mode, which means it splits into three sections to outnumber an enemy ship on its own. It also has regenerative shields, ablative hull armour, and holoemitters throughout.

Starfleet Security Protocol 28, Subsection 2, says that in the event of a hostile takeover the EMH should deactivate himself and await rescue.

Neither EMH was designed with sex organs, but the Doctor has modified his program . . .

Chakotay has a cousin in Ohio.

Neelix researches US cuisine to have marketable job skills when he reaches Earth. He starts by cooking Rodeo Red's Red-Hot Rootin' Tootin' Chili. That sounds good, actually.

The relay network belongs to the Hirogen.

Voyager was declared officially lost fourteen months ago.

(Lack of) Continuity: The USS *Prometheus*'s registry is NX-59660. The NX prefix means it's an experimental prototype, as established by the *Excelsior* (NX-2000) in *Star Trek III: The Search for Spock*. The Tal Shiar are Romulan Intelligence (*TNG* – 'Face of the Enemy').

Voyager is 60,000 light years from home.

The Federation is at war with the Dominion, but the Romulans aren't involved (until the *DS9* episode 'In the Pale Moonlight').

The Doctor refers to having combated alien macroviruses ('macrocosm') and alien invaders ('Basics'), having crossed Borg space ('Scorpion') and having travelled through time ('Future's End').

There's a reference to the Terellian plague (*TNG* – 'Haven').

Harry is an expert in holotechnology.

Leonard McCoy's *Comparative Alien Physiology* is as important a medical text as *Gray's Anatomy*. The Doctor passes on news of *Voyager*'s situation to Starfleet.

Ye Canna Change the Laws o' Physics: The Doctor is transmitted by optronic data-transmission stream.

Algorithm extraction and decompiling are tortures for holograms.

Microbiotic contamination makes the air vents open. Should it make them close? Otherwise they'd just make it easier for the contamination to spread.

Puzzles: The 'thrombic modulator' sounds more as if it belonged in *Rocky Horror* . . .

Learn Your Lines: Doc: 'I was saving *Voyager* when you were only a gleam in your programmer's eye!'

Highs: Anything with the two Docs.

Seven dealing with the Hirogen.

Harry and Tom trying to create a new EMH just in case the Doctor doesn't make it back.

Verdict: The funniest episode since 'False Profits'. The script itself isn't that witty, and the jokes are somewhat obvious, but the performances of Picardo and Andy Dick as EMH2 are just so manic that they make the whole thing into a comic masterpiece. Throw in a great space battle, some impressive new ships and sets, and you have a really good stand-alone episode. A word of advice, though – try to see it with others. It's a worthwhile experience. 10/10.

#183: 'Hunters'

by Jeri Taylor

Directed by David Livingston
Music by Jay Chattaway
US air date 11-02-98

Plot: Stardate 51501.4. Starfleet send an encoded message back through the relay network from the previous episode. However, the Hirogen are not pleased by this trespassing, and decide to hunt *Voyager* down. Meanwhile, almost everyone gets some mail from home.

Déjà Vu?: Let's see: a race of reptilian humanoids in powered armour, who hunt other intelligent species for sport, and keep their skulls as trophies? In other words, predators, as in the movie of the same name.

Behind the Scenes: The relay station is a redress of the Caretaker's array.

The recaps of the previous episode were put in so that reruns could air between that one and this.

***Voyager* Database:** Seven is supposed to regenerate in her alcove for three hours per day. Starfleet have sent an encoded message and star charts encoded in a latent data stream under the letters from the crew's relatives.

B'Elanna and Chakotay learn of the Maquis's destruction.

Neelix reads the mail he delivers.

Tuvok's eldest son, Sek, has had pon farr and had a daughter called T'Meni, which is Tuvok's mother's name.

Hirogen measure distance in 'Ketriks'.

The Alpha Hirogen survives having his throat slit by Tuvok.

(Lack of) Continuity: The station uses a quantum singularity for power. Chakotay is amazed at this, though Romulan Warbirds use them as well (*TNG* – 'Timescape').

Mark Johnson gave Janeway up for dead and married someone else. Is this a reason for Janeway's inconsistent behaviour in future episodes? Has she a death wish?

Since T'Pel didn't know Tuvok was alive, their telepathic marriage bond must be severed.

Tom's father is Admiral Owen Paris.

Janeway is suddenly fascinated by archaeological puzzles, as Picard was, or Chakotay in 'Future's End'.

Ye Canna Change the Laws o' Physics: We're told that an osteotomy means being gutted, but actually it would mean having your bones removed.

Radiometric decay ratios – i.e. half-life – indicate that the station is 100,000 years old.

Tom and Harry confirm that a quantum singularity is a black hole (see the entry on 'Parallax').

A polaron pulse should stabilise the station's containment field, but an antithoron burst destabilise it.

Hirogen ships use a subnucleonic scanning beam.

The station puts out as much energy in a day as a star does in a year.

A warp field while at sublight speed protects the ship from the black hole's gravity well. Nonsense. And the black hole puts out a lovely – and equally nonsensical – swirly glow.

Puzzles: Did the Hirogen build the relay stations? Highly unlikely.

Bloopers: Tom's letter from his dad doesn't make it in time – but it was already being decoded in the previous act.

Learn Your Lines: Seven asks the Alpha Hirogen: 'What possible use could you make of my intestine?' and gets the answer: 'Unusual relics are prized. Yours will make me envied by men, and pursued by women.'

Highs: Seven and Tuvok on the Hirogen ship.

Lows: Neelix to Tuvok, calling him 'Gramps'.

Despite both actresses' talents, the Seven–Janeway conversations are becoming tiresome by now, but not nearly as much as Harry's schoolboy crush on Seven.

A very clunky final Janeway–Chakotay scene.

Verdict: Very disappointing, in the way that 'The Swarm' was, and for the same reason: the titular aliens, though a fascinating prospect, hardly appear. Instead, most of the episode is devoted to more soap about the crew's families, when they get mail from home. Now, looking into the characterisation ought to be a good thing, but not when it's so laboured, and you've actually stopped the plot for it. There are no surprises in the messages either, and the whole thing is obviously (and ham-fistedly) contrived to leave Janeway free for Chakotay. Boring. 4/10.

#184: 'Prey'

by Brannon Braga

Directed by Allan Eastman
Music by Dennis McCarthy
US air date 18-02-98

Plot: Stardate 51652.3. *Voyager* picks up an injured Hirogen, who had been tracking a prey who was too much for him to handle. When the prey also slips aboard *Voyager*, it is revealed to be an 8472. The Hirogen wants to kill it, and Seven supports him, but Janeway isn't so sure.

Déjà Vu?: 8472's *Alien*-type theme is heard when Tuvok and Harry find the blood.

Behind the Scenes: For some reason, a few notes of the *DS9* theme are heard when the episode title appears.

***Voyager* Database:** The Doctor is teaching Seven the social graces. Exercise 17 is 'Bridge Banter for Beginners'.

The Hirogen are nomadic, with no homeworld. They follow their prey wherever it goes, and may eat parts of suitable quarry. All of their culture is based on the hunt.

The Hirogen body resists all sedatives.

(Lack of) Continuity: Tuvok can communicate with 8472 just as Kes did in 'Scorpion'.

Janeway says 8472 was immune to sensors last time – which it wasn't.

Phaser rifles are modified to fire nanoprobe bursts.

This 8472 was left behind when the war ended, then hunted by the Hirogen for six months.

Janeway revokes Seven's access to primary systems even though she clearly did the right thing.

Ye Canna Change the Laws o' Physics: 8472's blood is a mixture of DNA and polyfluidic compounds. Since polyfluidic just means different types of liquids, then you could describe human blood the same way.

Learn Your Lines: Alpha Hirogen: 'The way a creature behaves when wounded is the key to its destruction.'

Highs: The Doctor/Seven social-graces exercise.

A lovely shot of 8472 crawling across *Voyager*'s hull.

Tony Todd is great as Alpha Hirogen, doing the gravelly voice without the modulation that Tiny Ron needed in the previous episodes.

Lows: 8472 being wimpified. Once again they take a great scary villain, and try to make it a sympathetic character.

Verdict: Hmm. A bit of a mixed bag. On the one hand, it's very well done, with lots of good, character-based conflict, and a definite threat to the ship. However, it also wimpifies Species 8472 rather earlier than might be expected. Tony Todd is an excellent guest as usual, though his character is not that interesting beyond being a threat. Seven is quite right that Janeway seems to be punishing her simply for not thinking like Janeway.

Ryan, Russ, Beltran and Picardo all get good scenes, and all work fairly well together again – if only they did these ensemble pieces more often . . . 7/10.

#185: 'Retrospect'

by Lisa Klink and Bryan Fuller
from a story by Mark Gaberman and
Andrew Shepard Price

Directed by Jesus Trevino
Music by Jay Chattaway
US air date 25-02-98

Plot: Stardate 51679.4. Janeway is looking to upgrade *Voyager*'s weapons systems from an arms dealer, Kovin. When Seven attacks him, the Doctor finds evidence of suppressed memories. Soon, Seven recalls that Kovin extracted some of her nanoprobes when they were in his lab.

Behind the Scenes: A rifle from 'Waking Moments' is held by Kovin's assistant. The stripped-down Romulan pistol appears again.

Voyager **Database:** The target buoy is made of monotanium.

Medical tricorders are 7.6 cm by 9.8 cm by 3.2 cm and have a duritanium alloy casing.

Janeway is willing to trade astrometric charts and isolinear chips for weapons.

A metagenic pulse promotes nanoprobe growth.

Under Entharan law, being accused is itself a serious crime, which damages the accused.

(Lack of) Continuity: Seven is given access to primary systems again, for good behaviour.

Reference is made to Seven's hallucinations in 'The Raven'.

Ye Canna Change the Laws o' Physics: Biogenic amnions in Seven's hippocampus block her memories. Tuvok points out that recovered memories are unreliable. He is correct, as witnessed by several child-abuse witch hunts in the 80s and early 90s.

Puzzles: What actually caused these memories, if Seven hadn't in fact been 'violated'? Telling a tale about false memories is one thing, but they could at least have told us whether she hallucinated, was getting confused with other memories, was being led by the Doctor, or whatever.

Learn Your Lines: Seven's 'I believe I'm beginning to feel anger' is followed by the Doctor's, 'Good: that's a perfectly healthy response; and when Kovin gets what he deserves you're going to feel much better.'

Highs: The Doctor and Seven, of course.

The basic idea of looking at recovered memories and the burden of proof in sex-offence cases.

Lows: The handling of the plot makes no sense, and there's no ending.

Verdict: I'd fast-forward past 'Retrospect', actually. The idea of doing a story based on the issue of recovered memories probably seemed like a good idea. Tuvok oddly doesn't even suggest a mind meld to find out the truth. Much of the first half of the episode is quite good, and the mystery is very intriguing. Unfortunately, the episode falls apart in the second half, as story and logic are sacrificed in the name of laborious social comment. Everybody seems to blame Seven. Ordinarily I'd never reveal the end of a story in a review anyway, but here there *isn't* an end to reveal! It's like an Agatha Christie book with the last ten pages ripped out. Still, Ryan and Picardo are excellent, even if it's obvious that none of the crew are concerned about what really happened to Seven. 5/10.

#186: 'The Killing Game'

by Brannon Braga and Joe Menosky

Directed by Victor Lobl
Music by David Bell
US air date 04-03-98

Plot: Stardate not given. The crew are members of the French Resistance in the city of Saint-Claire in 1944. The new German commandant, however, is a Hirogen. In fact, the Hirogen have taken over the ship, and are forcing the crew to undergo experimental hunts in expanded holodecks.

Déjà Vu?: *Trek* previously had a Nazi setting in TOS episode 'Patterns of Force', in which a somewhat foolish Federation historian had tried to assist a planet by showing them Nazi efficiency. The Resistance map is on the back of a nude painting – surely not ze fallen Madonna with ze big boobies?

Behind the Scenes: Though originally made as a two-parter, both episodes aired on the same night in the US. It had been hoped that it would be shown as one double-length movie, in the end the two episodes were merely aired together.

Familiar backlot is seen in lots of old shows/movies.

Roxann Dawson was pregnant during filming. For most of the season the bulge is (badly) disguised by her new Engineering jacket. Almost the whole stock of prop weapons turns up in the ready room.

***Voyager* Database:** Janeway is Katrine, B'Elanna is Brigitte, Neelix is the Baker, Tuvok is the bartender, Tom is Bobby and Chakotay is Captain Hiller. Harry is kept in the ship, to maintain the holodecks.

(Lack of) Continuity: It's confirmed that there are only two holodecks. After WW2, the Alpha Hirogen intends to refight Wolf 359, the battle with the Borg from *TNG* episode 'Best of Both Worlds'.

Ye Canna Change the Laws o' Physics: The neural interfaces implanted by the Hirogen link the brain's neocortex directly to the holodeck, making the wearer believe he or she is the character being played. (Despite this, they seem to retain their own personae.) St Claire is in a vital strategic position – any ground assault into Germany must go through it.

It's Sunday, 2 October 1944. Bakers and shops at work in France on a Sunday in the 40s? Not a hope in hell!

There's no such place in England as Sonnenshire.

The SS guards standing outside the town's HQ wear British-style khaki puttees. This isn't entirely unknown for German troops in WW2, but it's rare, and certainly would never be the case for guard duty at HQ's front door!

Puzzles: Where did the Resistance get a crate of US hand grenades?

There isn't actually much similarity between Hirogen and Nazis, despite the holographic Nazi's attempts to talk about hunting.

The Borg would have been a better comparison (and Tom makes that comparison in Part II).

Bloopers: Mulgrew (as a Klingon) mispronounces petaQ as 'poo-targh'. The holographic Nazi who is the father of B'Elanna's faux baby should, by the pips on his collar, outrank the Beta Hirogen (Teranj). Perhaps the Hirogen programmed the simulation to have all holocharacters defer to them regardless of apparent rank.

It's odd that all the German troops in the episode are SS troops – no Wehrmacht at all.

J Paul Boehmer can't pronounce Praxiteles.

These Hirogen are shorter and don't have electronically modulated voices.

Learn Your Lines: Karr: 'Never underestimate your prey or disrespect its abilities. If you do, you will become the hunted.'

Highs: Seven in that dress, and singing.

Tuvok with a trench coat and Tommy gun (the flat cap is iffy, though).

The ingenious intellectual conflict between Nazi and Hirogen beliefs, exemplified by the scenes between the Alpha Hirogen Karr and the holographic Nazi. J Paul Boehmer is very good at being a Nazi, despite a wandering accent. When with B'Elanna he seems almost likable, but just wait till Part II . . .

The forward-thinking Karr.

Lovely explosion blowing Janeway and Seven off their feet when the Nazi HQ goes up.

Lows: Tom reminiscing about 'Brigitte'.

'Hiller' thinks a futuristic room in midair (Decks 4–6 exposed by the blast) are an *underground* bunker. How dumb is that?

Verdict: Think *Predator* versus *Allo Allo* and you're not far off. Braga and Menosky have turned in the most watchable episode since 'Year of Hell'. True, it isn't very intelligent, even by *Voyager* standards. The Hirogen are a lot smaller, and the view of the Nazis is amazingly simplistic, but it's great fun! This is simply good entertainment, without taxing the brain cells.

The Resistance cell are the most interesting characters – notably Seven (a very good singer), Janeway and Tuvok – who looks very cool running around with an overcoat and Tommy gun.

Jeri Ryan proves to be a fine singer, especially when singing 'That Old Black Magic'. The cliffhanger is silly but good. 9/10.

#187: 'The Killing Game', Part II
by Brannon Braga and Joe Menosky

Directed by David Livingston
Music by David Bell
US air date 04-03-98

Plot: Stardate 51715.2. The Doctor has enabled Seven to throw off the effect of the neural interface, and do the same for Janeway. Now, with American troops invading the city, the pair must get the Resistance and Americans to help them retake the ship.

Behind the Scenes: So many Klingon uniforms were required that there's quite a mixture on show – as well as the usual *TNG* uniforms, a number of *Star Trek VI* ones show up too.

***Voyager* Database:** Karr is running these simulations for the sake of his people. Their nomadic hunting is driving them to extinction, but holodeck technology would enable them to settle down and still have the hunt.

(Lack of) Continuity: Chakotay is now called Captain Miller.

Ye Canna Change the Laws o' Physics: A photonic burst will be harmless to organic tissue but disrupt all holographic activity within twenty metres.

Puzzles: How many crew actually die?

After what the Hirogen did, Janeway just ups and gives them the holodeck technology? Isn't this both rewarding their attacks, and breaking all sorts of rules?

Bloopers: There's a very anachronistic building in the background when Chakotay calls the ceasefire.

The Klingons (and Neelix) keep their daggers in their pistol-holsters.

Boehmer pronounces Reich as 'Reisch'.

Learn Your Lines: Tom (describing the Nazis to Seven): 'Totalitarian fanatics bent on world conquest – the Borg of their day. No offence.' A gross oversimplification, but . . .

Highs: Janeway looks good in black.

Wounded Janeway being hunted by Teranj, and her cunning victory.

The Nazi showing his evil side, especially when he corrupts the Teranj into mutiny by his fanaticism.

Nice night shooting on the backlot.

The Klingon invasion, and Teranj's dive.

Lows: Still 'Bobby' and 'Brigitte' reminiscing.

'Miller' is incredibly dumb to shoot past his prisoner at two other Hirogen instead of dropping that one first.

Janeway handing over the holodeck technology. (Remember when she wouldn't even let the Kazon have a food replicator? And the Kazon are a lot less dangerous than the Hirogen.)

Verdict: As before, it's entertaining froth. Nothing serious, but just good old-fashioned escapism. For one thing, Harry's survival when Tom finds him is totally unbelievable. Neelix as a Klingon is somehow unpalatable too. Despite this, the episode is an improvement on Part I, not least because of the improved direction. A captive Tuvok and Seven have a nice scene with regard to a threat to her life, while there's plenty of tension from Janeway being stalked by one of the Hirogen.

As is so often the case with *Voyager*, the ending is very rushed, not to mention rather stupid, but that's forgivable in light of the episode's entertainment value. It's a moment when Karr realises he's underestimated Janeway, as mentioned in Part I. 10/10.

#188: 'Vis à Vis'
by Robert J Doherty

Directed by Jesus Trevino
Music by Dennis McCarthy
US air date 08-04-98

Plot: Stardate 51762.4. Tom befriends a test pilot (Steth) and helps him repair his experimental ship. However, the pilot is an impostor, and swaps identities with Tom.

Déjà Vu?: Swapped identities, farcical scenes of Steth wandering into successors of Tom's conversations . . . The *X Files* episode 'Dreamland' is especially similar, though that came after this.

Behind the Scenes: The scriptwriter, Robert J Doherty, has taken over a staff position for Season Six, in the wake of Ron Moore's departure.

***Voyager* Database:** Advanced subspace geometry was the only Academy class in which Tom paid attention. Tom and Harry play golf with Ensign Kaplan (a neat trick, considering that she got killed in 'Unity'). Seven has an eidetic memory.

(Lack of) Continuity: Tom's hobby of antique cars was introduced in 'The 37s'.

He's been press-ganged by sickbay several times, most recently in 'Revulsion' and 'Message in a Bottle'.

Steth claims to be from the fourth planet in the Bentham system – but it's called Benthos in Act One and Bentha in Act Five.

Ye Canna Change the Laws o' Physics: Steth's ship is powered by coaxial warp drive – space folding. It works by having a coaxial induction drive take in subatomic particles and reconfigure their internal geometry. A symmetric warp field should contain anomalies in a space-folding core. A carburettor mixes air with fuel – something is needed to dilute the stream of subatomic particles into the coaxial induction drive, such as a polaric modulator from the impulse engines.

Once installed, this makes the engine a differential induction drive. Chromoelectric bursts to the modulator will disrupt the engines.

Genome reversion after so long, and replacement by copying others? He samples DNA and deposits his DNA into his victims – but, since he also retains his own DNA, there's no reason why they would swap appearances (DNA is a set of instructions, and this sort of swapping would affect only the offspring of a victim – if it worked at all).

Puzzles: Doesn't Steth have the sense to realise that it's dumb to take a new form in a heavily populated ship, where he doesn't know anything about how Tom fits in? He'll obviously be detected quickly.

Learn Your Lines: Doc: 'I had no idea my superior abilities were affecting your psyche so strongly.'

Highs: The guest star Dan Butler (Steth) is incredible, playing five different roles – all unique. The main one is intensely slimy and obviously a villain, but still . . .

Nice-coloured glow around the alien ship. Nice morphs, too.

The Bentham ships are stunning – it would have been nice to see them again.

Lows: Tom and B'Elanna bitching even before he gets replaced by Steth.

Verdict: Here, an alien takes on the appearance of first Tom, then Janeway, leaving Tom looking alien and Janeway looking like Tom. The biggest liability is Robert Duncan McNeill. He's OK as Tom, but when he's the alien he's just the same writ a little larger, especially since Tom is already acting oddly before being replaced by Steth. And the less said about his attempt at Janeway, the better. Mulgrew is more skilful, making subtle changes to her performance that show the truth without giving the game away too much. Overall this proves once again that most actors forget how to act when called upon to play evil versions of their usual characters. 6/10.

#189: 'The Omega Directive'

by Lisa Klink
from a story by Jimmy Diggs and Steve J Kay

Directed by Victor Lobl
Music by Paul Baillargeon
US air date 15-04-98

Plot: Stardate 51781.2. The sensors detect Omega particles, which only captains know about. Because of a disaster with them a hundred years earlier, the particles are to be destroyed, and even the Prime Directive is rescinded to allow this. Seven, meanwhile, also knows of the particle, but wants to stabilise it and study it, as it is the Borg's equivalent of the Holy Grail – a symbol of perfection. Of course, the particles' rightful owners would also rather keep the stuff to themselves.

Behind the Scenes: The research centre in the Lentaru sector is the spaceborne office built for *Star Trek: The Motion Picture*, used in numerous *TNG* and *DS9* episodes, and best known as the Regula 1 science lab in *Star Trek II: The Wrath of Khan*.

The alien lab is again made of stock sets, and their ships look like a revamp of the Saurian ship from 'Parturition'.

The original title was 'The Omega Effect'.

***Voyager* Database:** The Doctor has recommended that Seven read *A Christmas Carol*. Each Borg drone's experiences are processed by the Collective, and only useful information is kept.

Seven knows about the Omega Directive through assimilated Starfleet captains.

The Borg consider Omega to be perfection and stabilised a single molecule for a trillionth of a second, blowing 29 cubes and 600,000 drones in the process.

Only Starfleet captains and flag officers have been briefed on Omega.

The Omega molecule was first synthesised a century ago in

the Lentaru sector. It's impossible to go to warp there, but a cover-up said it was a natural phenomenon.

The Borg got their information on Omega from thirteen different species, and call it Particle Zero-One-Zero. All drones are programmed to assimilate it if possible.

(Lack of) Continuity: Tuvok and Harry started playing Kal-to in 'Alter Ego'. Seven describes it as elementary spatial harmonics.

Janeway's clearance code is Janeway one one five three red, clearance level ten.

Harry says it's theoretically possible to blow up a type-six protostar and turn it into a wormhole home.

Ye Canna Change the Laws o' Physics: Omega destroys subspace when unstable. In theory, if it were stabilised, it would be a limitless energy source. A single molecule contains as much energy as a warp core. The aliens have synthesised 200 million. The Omega particle is also referred to as a molecule.

Puzzles: Weren't the alien race a bit miffed at *Voyager* for stealing their technology? How did they get Allos home, or is he still on board?

Bloopers: One of the FAP spotlights to illuminate the container of omega molecules in the lab comes on too early, casting a little disc of blue light on the outside of the doors before Janeway and Tuvok have got it fully open.

Learn Your Lines: Janeway: 'The final frontier still has some boundaries that shouldn't be crossed.'

Highs: Seven is actually useful.

Harry and Tuvok working on the torpedo.

Seven's little Collective, having adapted Starfleet rank protocols.

Lows: These interminable Janeway/Seven playlets are getting so boring.

Verdict: It starts with a vaguely misleading suggestion of being a covert-ops story. The plot and science don't bear scrutiny, but this succeeds as a superior *Voyager* episode by having decent dialogue, reasonable characterisation, and – most importantly – a solid role for everyone in the cast. Harry gets an amusing scene that doesn't rely on making a fool of Tuvok; Seven gives us a surprising insight into the Borg; and Tuvok gets to display that superior Vulcan strength on an away team.

On the downside, there have been way too many Janeway/ Seven mother/daughter scenes this season already. The acting is mostly above average, however – especially Tim Russ, as usual, and Jeri Ryan, who is here really being an important and relevant character, not just window dressing with an attitude. Finally, the idea of a Borg having a religious experience is just irresistible. Definitely one of the better episodes of the season. 8/10.

#190: 'Unforgettable'
by Greg Elliot and Michael Perricone

Directed by Andrew J Robinson
Music by Jay Chattaway
US air date 22-04-98

Plot: Stardate 51813.4. *Voyager* receives a call for help from Kellin, who claims to know Chakotay. Brought on board, she explains she tracks runaways from her planet, but that when she visited *Voyager* in pursuit of one she fell in love with Chakotay. Now she herself is on the run, to be with him. He is doubtful at first, having no memory of her. Her race generate pheromones that block the long-term memories of other species. Chakotay soon begins to fall for her. However, another of her people will be coming for her.

Behind the Scenes: Robert Beltran was very happy to work with Virginia Madsen (Kellin), and says he loved every minute of it.

Robinson was very glad to be able to get Madsen for this episode, and makes more use of hand-held-camera-work (as in 'Blood Fever') to try to draw the audience in and give a more intimate and personal view.

***Voyager* Database:** *Voyager* is now searching for deuterium for refuelling, which more or less fits in with the timescale mentioned in 'Innocence'. The search for deuterium leads into 'Demon'.

Chakotay describes Kellin as a bounty hunter (who hunts people trying to remove their world). More bounty hunters will turn up next season, in 'Think Tank'.

Beta Squad has the shipboard reputation of being the best security team.

(Lack of) Continuity: Kellin says she spent several weeks on *Voyager* up to a month ago, which would have been between 'Killing Game' and 'Vis a Vis'.

Ye Canna Change the Laws o' Physics: Kellin's species' pheromones block long-term memory engrams (and as luck would have it are inexplicably immune to tricorders and transporter locks).

In real life, a remora is a type of fish that accompanies sharks, and feeds off their table scraps.

A neurolytic emitter wipes Remoran memories of the outside world and makes them content with their planet.

The Remorans use proton-based particle weapons capable of penetrating any shields, even if the modulations are changed (as is often done to protect against Borg adaptations).

Tying baryon sensors into deflector control should scatter the beams.

Puzzles: Kellin was aboard undetected for two days. How did she eat or go to the bathroom without being noticed?

Though he has a phaser in hand, Chakotay is still shouting 'drop it' twice while the Tracer is zapping Kellin – does he care so little that he won't fire even as his girl is getting shot?

Learn Your Lines: Tuvok: 'I'd rather not engage in speculation; it is a dangerous pastime.'

Highs: Excellent direction.
Madsen is OK.

Tuvok cracks a joke!

Seven and Harry about courtship rituals.

Lows: The whole Chakotay–Kellin romance, which is utterly unconvincing.

Silly plot contrivances to explain lack of knowledge about Kellin (phereomones, computer viruses, and eventually not even bothering to try explaining why tricorders and medical scanners don't work).

You can see the 'twist' outcome (that before long he'll fall for her and she'll have her mind wiped) coming a mile off.

Verdict: The plot – designed to clear up any threads about Janeway/Chakotay – doesn't make any sense whatsoever, and, given the whole memory-wiping thing, is totally inconsequential anyway. That said, the idea of a society whose two main laws are 'nobody leaves' and 'nobody reveals anything about it' is somewhat creepy – especially when the Tracer says that the reason they don't let the few dissidents go is because that would suggest the government doesn't care about them. It's the sort of character-based episode that *DS9* does well, and could have worked there. There's no chemistry or spark between Kellin and Chakotay. Ignore 'Unforgettable', unless you need a cure for insomnia. 1/10.

#191: 'Living Witness'

by Brannon Braga, Bryan Fuller and Joe Menosky from a story by Braga

Directed by Tim Russ
Music by Dennis McCarthy
US air date 29-04-98

Plot: Seven hundred years in the future, the evil crew of the warship *Voyager* are the centrepiece of a museum on the Kyrian homeworld. One of the exhibits is a data module containing a backup of the Doctor's program. Hardly has the Doctor got used to the idea that it's 700 years on, than he finds himself having to defend the crew's reputation against charges of war crimes.

Déjà Vu?: Hydrospanners were Han Solo's favourite tool in *The Empire Strikes Back*.

A peaceful race *now* that started war *then*, before coming full circle – just as in *Doctor Who*'s first Dalek story (whatever it's officially called this week).

And, of course, the holographic representation of the show's heroes for propaganda purposes was also looked at in the *Babylon 5* episode 'Deconstruction of Falling Stars'.

Behind the Scenes: Tim Russ and Roxann Dawson both did the director's course together, but due to Roxann's pregnancy she doesn't have a directing assignment until Season Six, and the episode 'Riddles'. Her pregnancy also meant she was working less towards the end of this season, and in fact she's absent from this episode altogether because her baby was delivered in the week in which it was filmed.

The main museum set is reused in *Star Trek: Insurrection*. Other *Voyager* sets reused there include Main Engineering, which is redressed as the *Enterprise-E*'s library (though most of the library scene is cut from the finished film).

***Voyager* Database:** The evil Doc has yellow eyes like Data, as the Kyrians believed he was an android. Evil Chakotay's look makes him resemble a TOS Klingon, while evil Janeway wears one glove, à la Michael Jackson. The evil Seven is a full Borg, and has a little Collective in the cargo bay.

The Kyrians believe that *Voyager* sided with the Vaskins in a war, using biogenic weapons on Kyrian cities after murdering the leader. In fact *Voyager* was trading with the Vaskins, when Kyrian terrorists attacked.

(Lack of) Continuity: In several previous episodes – notably 'The Swarm', 'Future's End' and 'Message in a Bottle' – it's made clear that the Doctor can't be backed up. But here we see a backup module. Though this story is set 700 years in the future, so they may yet find a way to back him up.

As in 'Message in a Bottle' the Doctor's program is in the form of an optronic data stream.

The rioters use photon grenades.

The Doctor points out that *Voyager* wasn't a warship, but in 'The Thaw' Harry says it was mainly designed for combat performance.

Ye Canna Change the Laws o' Physics: Punishment for a hologram is having his program decompiled.

Puzzles: How much stuff did the Kyrian raiders take? There must have been quite a lot.

Learn Your Lines: Janeway: 'Defeat, genocide . . . Why quibble with semantics?'

Quarren's 'Please, this isn't about race' only gets the Kyrian Commissioner to say: 'It's always about race.'

Doc: 'Facts be damned! Names, dates, places . . . It's all open to interpretation. Who's to say what really happened?'

Highs: Janeway has a cooler hairstyle.

Seven as a full Borg, and her little Collective in Cargo Bay 2.

Everybody being evil – this crew is so much better, and better acted, than the normal one.

Subtle differences in the 'evil' *Voyager* – no combadges, black gloves and rollnecks, Tuvok's larger ears.

Picardo and Henry Woronicz (Quarren) are great together.

Lows: Only the fact that the evil crew aren't the real ones!

Verdict: Seems at first glance to be a *Voyager* version of *B5*'s 'Deconstruction of Falling Stars'. It's a surprisingly dark episode. Tim Russ's direction is exceptional, and the evil crew don't fall into the cliché trap. Chakotay and Harry are especially improved by being made thugs, Janeway has a single personality, and Tuvok is downright chilling. It's a shame that B'Elanna is absent from the episode, so we don't see what her evil double is like. Where the *B5* episode was a self-indulgent one that merely reiterated how heroic the heroes were, this episode takes far more risks by perverting the show and the audience's expectations in a most wonderful way. Everyone knows that history is written by the victors, and that what we 'know' as history isn't always true. In real life, for example, Rasputin was more Oliver Reed than the evil master manipulator. And that's even before it gets on to the racial themes, with two ethnic groups blaming each other for past violence (and race riots) or the war-crime trial element. And of course, Quarren as a kid had a fascination for *Voyager* even though they were the bad guys – just like a lot of people.

This is a truly multilayered and intelligent story as well as being hugely entertaining and well done. It also has a much more powerful impact on the alien culture of the week than is usually the case. If the episode has any cons, they're only nits – the Doctor can suddenly be backed up when he couldn't in 'Message in a Bottle', and the riot sequence is let down by the budget. But that doesn't really matter. By far the best episode of the season. 10/10.

#192: 'Demon'

by Ken Biller
from a story by André Bormanis

Directed by Anson Williams
Music by David Bell
US air date 05-05-98

Plot: Stardate not given. Running out of deuterium, the ship visits a Class-Y planet, known as a Demon planet, which shows signs of having deuterium deposits. Tom and Harry take a shuttle down, but both their spacesuits are punctured, and they collapse. *Voyager* is then forced to land, and Chakotay and Seven find Tom and Harry apparently healthy – without spacesuits. When the pair return to the ship, they can no long breathe normal air.

Behind the Scenes: The deuterium pools are commercial silver model paint, if I recall correctly.

***Voyager* Database:** G'rex is the greatest writer in Talaxian history – Neelix can't sleep without reading a few pages.

Class-Y planets are Demon-class, filled with thermionic radiation and 500K temperatures.

Nazawa is a male transporter ensign.

Janeway lets the crew be copied to form a newly sentient populace. There goes the Prime Directive in a big way . . . Creating a new evolutionary stage of this species has got to be a major violation.

(Lack of) Continuity: It was established in *TNG* episode 'Relics' that the matter and antimatter in Starfleet warp engines are deuterium and antihydrogen respectively.

Neelix threatens to sing a Talaxian Rodno, a Klingon opera and a Vulcan funeral dirge ('Tuvix').

We were told in 'Innocence' that the warp core would need to be refuelled after three years, which just about equates to here.

Ye Canna Change the Laws o' Physics: The geophysics department is trying to synthesise deuterium (this isn't what geophysics means – it means studying the physical body of the planet). Deuterium is a hydrogen isotope, composed of a single electron orbiting a nucleus made up of only a single proton and single neutron. So, let's get this straight: the ship has run out of the most abundant element in the universe, and they're failing to create it! Can't the replicators or transporters modify hydrogen atoms from the water supply?

When Harry's and Tom's suits are punctured, oxygen starts leaking out. OK, but shouldn't the planet's poisonous atmosphere and heat also be leaking *in*?

Twenty kilos of deuterium is enough to get main systems on line.

Bioforming: opposite of terraforming – adapting physiology at cellular level to suit an environment. The artificial version is called pantropy.

The Silver Blood contains deuterium, hydrogen sulphates, dichromates and organic proteins.

A Nadion burst from phaser emitters may weaken the EM properties of the Silver Blood.

The Silver Blood has mimetic properties – chemical memory – and reads DNA and copies it.

Puzzles: Why are they looking for new beds anyway? There's only the same number of rooms.

How did the real Tom and Harry survive, trapped unconscious in punctured suits? Even with backup life support, the poison atmosphere and temperature would still get in and kill them.

How did the Silver Blood copy their memories and personalities as well as their shapes?

B'Elanna's experience in sickbay suggests it's only form that is copied, as does the Doctor's theory about bioforming.

Copying human DNA gave it awareness and sentience?

Since the ship is back to normal for takeoff, presumably they got enough deuterium – but isn't the deuterium part of the life form? Isn't this vampirism of the new life?

Bloopers: When the Doc orders the lights to maximum illumination, the lighting isn't as bright as it has been in some previous episodes (but then, systems are low-powered . . .).

Tuvok seems to be still wearing the larger ears from the evil *Voyager* in 'Living Witness' while on the bridge.

Learn Your Lines: Tuvok: 'I could give you a litany of damaged systems, Captain. But suffice it to say: now that we're down, we won't be going up again soon.'

Highs: The visual effects of the landing.

Wang is quite good in the last act.

Neelix trying to set up a temporary dorm in sickbay.

It's a nice touch that the fake Tom and Harry aren't evil doubles – and in fact don't know they're doubles.

Lows: Harry and Tom about Tuvok.

A very unrealistic planet surface – almost reminiscent of TOS.

Seven being too dumb to look for footprints.

Verdict: Diabolical, appropriately. Some of the worst science ever scripted ('500 degrees Kelvin' etc.) combines with a limp plot (*Voyager* has run out of gas, as Paris puts it, and must find more fuel), inconsistent characterisation, and glossing over of consequences to produce the last dire episode of the season. To be fair, Anson Williams's direction is pretty good, the effects of the ship's landing are excellent, and Garrett Wang is great in the last act.

However, it's all dragged down by monumental stupidity: Harry dresses down a superior officer, Tuvok, in front of the command staff with impunity (and Paris not only thinks he deserves it, but also implies that this is a good way to attract promotion!), though the Vulcan has more lines than usual for this season. There's no mention of the ethical questions, which were given precedence in *TNG* episode 'Up the Long Ladder'. And Janeway's unilateral hostility at the end is outrageously out of line, especially compared with the points made in 'Living Witness'. What else can you say about an episode where the best thing is Neelix trying to find a new bed for the night? 4/10.

#193: 'One'

by Jeri Taylor and Jim Swallow (uncredited) from a story by John Devins (uncredited)

Directed by Ken Biller
Music by Jay Chattaway
US air date 13-05-98

Plot: Stardate 51929.3. Radiation from a Mutara-Class nebula would kill the crew when they went through it, unless they make the month-long trip in stasis. This means leaving Seven and the Doctor in sole charge of the ship. However, as the journey continues, the radiation damages the Doctor's mobile emitter, leaving Seven truly alone.

Déjà Vu?: The idea of a social being having become isolated is a very old one: in TV SF it dates back to the *Twilight Zone* pilot, 'Where Is Everybody?' or TOS episode 'The Mark of Gideon'. In *Star Trek* terms, the story is most reminiscent of the fourth-season *TNG* episode 'Remember Me', with a touch of the earlier *Voyager* episode 'Projections'. Of course I suspect most of the (predominantly male) viewers will find shots of Seven in her catsuit slinking down the corridors a lot more memorable than Dr Crusher looking baffled in 'Remember Me'.

Behind the Scenes: The stasis tubes were first seen in 'Resolutions', and the stasis room on Deck 14 is a revamp of the cargo-bay set.

The Borg cube interior is a single frame of an optical from *Star Trek: First Contact* (it's from quite late in the long pullback in the opening scene).

The Borg drone costume doesn't have the exoskeletal armour, and is not as impressive to look at.

***Voyager* Database:** The nebula extends 110 light years and would take a month to cross. Doing a quick calculation, at that rate *Voyager* should have been only 53.3 years from home when it arrived in the Delta Quadrant. This conflicts with both the premise's seventy-year figure, and the results of calculating from the maximum speed mentioned in 'Scorpion'.

This time there are 151 crew members in total, including the guy who popped his clogs at the beginning of the episode.

(Lack of) Continuity: In 'The 37s' it was explicitly stated that the ship couldn't be operated by fewer than a hundred people.

The nebula is called 'a Mutara Nebula', in a reference to the nebula in *Star Trek II: The Wrath of Khan*, but it clearly has totally different properties from those of the original Mutara Nebula (which didn't have the deadly radiation).

In spite of having had the questionable taste to resurrect Neelix a few episodes previously, Seven keeps her nanoprobes to herself when the nameless crew member bites the dust at the beginning of this episode. Since it doesn't even occur to anyone else to suggest she bring him back too, we can only assume that he was the ship's YTS trainee, and they were all glad to see the back of him.

Ye Canna Change the Laws o' Physics: The nebula puts out vast quantities of subnucleonic radiation. Which sounds good, but doesn't really mean much. Apparently it damages human flesh almost instantly.

Puzzles: How come the radiation doesn't affect Seven's organic parts? She doesn't have that much Borg technology left in her, and it should affect her flesh just as quickly as everybody else's – unless her nanoprobes were constantly regenerating her from minute to minute.

Tim Russ's sidelining continues: the ship is about to be handed into the sole control of a hologram and a former Borg, yet the security/tactical officer isn't even present at the briefing? Isn't this just a little dumb?

Who is Trajis anyway? All of Seven's other hallucinations relate to her internal doubts about being able to complete the mission, but Trajis's presence makes no sense in this context.

It's odd that Seven first reroutes stasis power to the engines, then life support to the stasis tubes. Surely that Borg efficiency of hers would be more likely to cut life support to all decks except the Bridge and reroute that to the engines. There's no need to mess with the power to the stasis tubes, and the end result would be identical. In fact it'd be better, as she wouldn't lose consciousness.

Bloopers: The Borg drone doesn't have a modulated voice, and has a most un-Borg-like line in insults. This may be a deliberate hint at its nature as a hallucination, but there's no indication of that in the script.

The timescale in the last act doesn't even remotely hold water. In the astrometrics lab at the beginning of Act Five, there are seventeen hours and eleven minutes to go before the ship is out of the nebula. Seven walks to the turbolift (talking to hallucinations), is taken to a view of a Borg cube, then to the bridge – at which point there are only 41 minutes to go, and that's with the engines going off line!

Learn Your Lines: The Doctor comments on Tom's sleep-walking: 'Leave it to Mr Paris to be just as much trouble now as when he's awake.'

Highs: The whole scene in which Seven perverts the Doctor's holodeck program to help her conduct maintenance.

Also Seven's brief and eerie dream.

Lows: Yet another variant on the very small joke line in 'The Trouble with Tribbles'.

Trajis says things like 'I have an ample supply.' (No real person talks like that. Then again, he isn't real, so maybe that's a good point!)

Trajis's cheap sexist banter about getting to know each other.

Verdict: The subject of Seven's handling of solitude – surely a fate worse than death for a Borg – is quite well handled, and of course Jeri Ryan is excellent as usual. The direction makes her solitude reasonably eerie, and is in fact quite reminiscent of some parts of the astronauts' shots in 2001. Unfortunately there are rather too many shots of Seven walking along the empty corridors, doing nothing. Though the script is good for Seven's character, there are plenty of problems with the plot. Still, it's fairly solid, and Ryan carries it along nicely. 7/10.

#194: 'Hope and Fear'

by Brannon Braga and Joe Menosky
from a story by them and Rick Berman

Directed by Winrich Kolbe
Music by Dennis McCarthy
US air date 20-05-98

Plot: Stardate 51978.2. The ship takes aboard Arturis, a linguist who claims to be able to decode the Starfleet message. It gives directions to a location where the crew find the USS *Dauntless*, a new ship with Quantum Slipstream technology, which could get them home in three months. But all is not well, and Harry and Tuvok find alien technology behind the Starfleet disguise.

Déjà Vu?: The *Dauntless* isn't Starfleet grey, but has a hint of salmon pink, and resembles the Mon Calamari cruisers seen in *Return of the Jedi*. Arturis's double pistol strongly resembles the handguns from the Disney film *The Black Hole*.

Behind the Scenes: The engine core is one of those novelty plasma globes – in fact the same one already seen in 'Rise' – surrounded by a set of those water-bubble tubes you get in gadget shops.

The console outside the brig is from the Doctor's office in sickbay.

***Voyager* Database:** Arturis's race are Species 116. The Borg weren't able to assimilate them until the past year. Fewer than 20,000 survived, and Arturis wants revenge, by programming the *Dauntless* to take *Voyager*'s crew into Borg Space.

Arturis knows 4,000 languages. Janeway still struggles with basic Klingon.

The *Dauntless*'s registry is NX-01A. It was supposedly launched on Stardate 51472 after 47 trials, but that's a lie on Arturis's part.

(Lack of) Continuity: The Borg were able to assimilate Species 116 because *Voyager* had helped them defeat 8472. Arturis blames Janeway for the destruction of his people.

It has been five months since the coded Starfleet message was received ('Hunters').

Ye Canna Change the Laws o' Physics: Arturis says decoding the message was a simple matter of extracting the iconometric elements and triaxilating a recursion matrix.

They don't even try to explain how the Quantum Slipstream drive works.

Puzzles: How did B'Elanna get a brief Slipstream out of *Voyager* when the *Dauntless* is actually an alien ship and not of Starfleet?

Bloopers: Although the *Dauntless*'s interior has reverted to its true appearance, when Seven accesses the brig console, there's still a little Starfleet signage sticker on top of it, even though all the Okudagrams have changed. Some fans on the

Internet suggested that the Starfleet consoles remaining in the *Dauntless*'s engine room were a blooper, but the script specifies that only the bridge should change.

Learn Your Lines: Arturis: 'The Borg Collective is like a force of nature. You don't feel anger towards a storm; you just avoid it.'

Highs: Tuvok and Janeway have a chat reminiscent of those in earlier seasons.
  Seven's Kryten impression.
  The *Dauntless* looks . . . interesting.

Lows: Janeway has a very silly minidress in the teaser.
  Arturis's head looks silly.
  The engine core.

Verdict: This episode marks the resolution of the Janeway/Seven mother/daughter arc, but is also a pretty good (and rare!) ensemble piece for the whole cast. Everybody gets some good lines, though the highlight is Seven's Kryten impression – her joke is very reminiscent of the 'deadpan-mode' scene from 'The Last Day' (last episode of *Red Dwarf*). Though not a cliffhanger, this is a quite decent season finale, and gives a decent sense of closure to Season Four. 7/10.

Interlude

At the end of Season Four, Jeri Taylor retired from the day-to-day grind of overseeing the show, to spend more time with her family. This left Brannon Braga in more or less sole charge of the show, while Rick Berman still oversaw the *Trek* franchise as a whole.

Lisa Klink departs, and later claims to have left because she didn't like the way the female characters were written – a strange complaint from the woman who, as story editor, was in charge of that . . . Bryan Fuller replaced her as story editor. Also, Michael Taylor came over from *DS9* to join the writing staff.

During the hiatus, several of *Voyager*'s sets were used for filming *Star Trek: Insurrection*. This most notably included the Main Engineering set, which was redressed as the *Enterprise-E*'s library; the Jeffries tubes; and the standard Officers' Cabin set, which became Riker's quarters.

Fifth Season

Regular cast:
as season Four

Recurring cast:
Scarlett Pomers as Naomi Wildman

#195: 'Night'

by Brannon Braga and Joe Menosky

Directed by David Livingston
Music by Jay Chattaway
US air date 14-10-98

Plot: Stardate 52081.2. Janeway is sulking while everybody is bored stiff as the ship passes through an area with no stars or planets. Tom, meanwhile, has begun a new holonovel, *The Adventures of Captain Proton*. When the ship is attacked by aliens who live in the void, it turns out that a race called the Malon are dumping their toxic waste in this region, regardless of the dangers to the native aliens.

Déjà Vu?: Very obviously the *Captain Proton* holonovel is a pastiche of the 1930s *Flash Gordon* and *Buck Rogers* serials with Buster Crabbe. Proton's (Tom's) rocket pack and controls are clearly derived from *King of the Rocket Men*, and its successors (*Commando Cody* and later *The Rocketeer*).

Behind the Scenes: Every element of the Malon design is set to look like industrial decay – their ships and costumes are rusted and patched and have verdigris, and leak green steam. The Malon themselves have sallow skin and zits.

***Voyager* Database:** The new holodeck program, *The Adventures of Captain Proton*, debuts. The final chapter of *Captain Proton* is 'Satan's Robot', named after the hench-thing of the same name.

There are no stars for at least another 500 light years. They've been in the starless expanse for 53 days, and have two years to go.

Tuvok meditates by the stars, visualising each star as a thought.

Janeway was once a commander on the USS *Billings*.

Janeway implies that hanging is still a punishment for mutiny on the Federation statute books.

(Lack of) Continuity: Neelix is still looking to take up tactical training ('Fair Trade' etc.).

Harry is assigned to turn Cargo Bay 2 into a third holodeck. Where would Seven live?

Tom seems to think B'Elanna likes only games involving Klingon pain sticks etc., contradicting all the previous times we're told she hates all that Klingon stuff.

Harry plays his clarinet again.

Janeway says there's no one she trusts more than Chakotay – formally ending the original status of Tuvok as her most trusted friend.

Ye Canna Change the Laws o' Physics: Heavy concentrations of theta radiation are occluding the sensors.

Nylophobia is the fear of nothingness.

A warp flare is a sustained polyluminous burst.

The Malon dump contaminated antimatter. Six billion isotons are produced every day by their civilisation. What exactly is an isoton, and what can antimatter be contaminated with? How come it doesn't explode?

Voyager's residual antimatter (waste) is broken down by a transkinetic chamber into subatomic particles (er, they'd still be antiparticles, just smaller ones!).

The theta radiation produced is absorbed by radiometric converters to use for recycled energy.

The spatial vortex must be destroyed from the end with the weaker dimensional radius.

Puzzles: The lights in the holodeck go off, but the setting remains, because the holodeck is on a different power grid. So why did the holographic lights go off?

Learn Your Lines: Doc: 'Does the phrase "To be continued" mean anything to you?'
  Chakotay: 'I want good news; that's an order.'
  Janeway: 'Time to take out the garbage . . .' I love it when she gets tough.

Highs: The *Captain Proton* teaser, and Seven's later part in the program.
  Nice steadicam work, and segues between scenes.
  Finally the crew mutinies – but only a little.
  Lovely nebula when they get out of the void.

Lows: Neelix has hideously tasteless pyjamas.
  Dodgy effect of *Voyager* flying through spatial charges.

Verdict: *Star Trek* returns to its allegorical roots, with the first of this year's green fables. 'Night' is, like the previous season's finale, a fine ensemble piece. Though it seems as if ideas for two or three episodes are being bandied about here, none of them outstay their welcome. The plotlines are simple but effective, but the character vignettes are the best – notably Harry playing the clarinet for Tuvok.
  It's also nice to finally see the crew note that Janeway isn't the most psychologically stable person in Starfleet. Frankly she's halfway to becoming Colonel Kurtz from *Apocalypse Now*. Quite cleverly, there's a recap of how and why the ship got stranded, to help ease new viewers into it. 8/10.

#196: 'Drone'

by Bryan Fuller, Brannon Braga and Joe Menosky
from a story by Fuller and Harry Doc Kloor

Directed by Les Landau
Music by Dennis McCarthy
US air date 21-10-98

Plot: An accident fuses some of Seven's nanoprobes with the Doctor's mobile emitter. This fusion then assimilates DNA from a crewman to gestate a new twenty-ninth-century Borg. Although this Borg is not a member of the Collective, and so is not hostile, the Collective are soon on their way to assimilate both him and his 500 years in advance technology.

Déjà Vu?: Basically a combination of *TNG* episodes 'The Child' and 'I Borg'. The back of One's head makes him resemble a helmetless Robocop, and he has a mound on his chest just like that of the creature in the *B5* episode 'Infection', where the ancient technology grabbed its victim there and assimilated him.

Behind the Scenes: The entrance to Cargo Bay 2 has been slightly modified, with a different door and some barrels before the Borg alcoves.

As a future Borg, One is far more streamlined than usual, though this makes him less visually interesting.

Clips from 'Scorpion' Part II are seen when Janeway and Seven show One the Borg on the big screen in Astrometrics.

The Borg Sphere from *Star Trek: First Contact* reappears. The documentation for that film's production describes the sphere as a scout ship, though it is described otherwise in this episode.

The UK video sleeve says 'Bryan Full' instead of 'Bryan Fuller'.

***Voyager* Database:** The Doctor has taken up holo-imaging (twenty-fourth-century photography) as a hobby.

One has reactive body armour, multidimensional adaptability and internal transporter nodes – all far in advance of current Borg technology.

When the emitter begins to assimilate the science-lab console, the Okudagrams on it become Borg control panels.

One identifies *Voyager* as having a duranium hull and tri-cyclic life-support system.

He matures 25 times faster than a regular drone, and assimilates 47 billion teraquads of information.

Cargo Bay 2 is on Deck 8, Section 2.

Neelix suggests that Tom should try building a new shuttle – which he does, in time for the next episode.

(Lack of) Continuity: The little bullet-shaped shuttle is the Class 2 (though the same interior is used for various types).

One is created from the Doc's mobile emitter, some of Seven's nanoprobes, and a sample of Ensign Mulcahy's (male) DNA. That makes him a cybernetically enhanced clone, and Seven states that the Borg never reproduce in this way (compare the babies in 'Q Who').

We're reminded that the mobile emitter is from the twenty-ninth century (in 'Future's End').

Main Engineering is on Deck 11, Section 32.

B'Elanna says there is still an airponics bay.

The Borg Sphere is described as a long-range tactical vessel.

The scale of the Borg Sphere model makes it the same size in relation to *Voyager* as the cubes in 'Scorpion' were.

The Doc tries to treat One despite his refusal – a direct contradiction of the ethics he refers to in 'The Gift', where he isn't allowed to treat someone who refuses treatment.

Ye Canna Change the Laws o' Physics: The shuttle is caught in the shear-line of the nebula.

When One needs to regenerate, his neural patterns show signs of degradation – does this happen to all Borg? The mobile emitter regulates One's central nervous system from the neocortex.

The warp core produces 4,000 teradynes of energy per second.

A multispatial algorithm will predict the nebula's rate of expansion. A multispatial force field protects One from the destruction of the Sphere, but not by much.

Puzzles: Seven points out that Borg must face outwards while regenerating – a nice touch of humour but I can see no reason why it should be true.

How come all the Borg alcoves in Cargo Bay 2 are active when only Seven and One need them? Weirder still that, when One is gone, she shuts off his alcove but leaves all the others on.

I also wonder how the Doctor will explain why he looted One's body for the mobile emitter, which he has regained in future episodes.

Bloopers: One says tricylic instead of tricyclic when identifying *Voyager*'s life-support system.

Learn Your Lines: Doc: 'The Borg – party-poopers of the galaxy.'

Seven: 'The lure of perfection is powerful, Captain.'

Seven: '*Voyager* is my Collective.'

Highs: One is simply wonderful – just look at his face when he assimilates the Borg data node. If only they could have kept him for a little while longer (say until 'Dark Frontier'). And he pronounces 'futile' with a long 'i' which Seven never does.

Verdict: Jeri Ryan truly excels here, especially at the end, but the real revelation is J Paul Boehmer as the drone – he's stunning, and completely different from his role as a Nazi in 'Killing Game'. The expressions that cross his face when he first assimilates a data node are almost worth the admission price alone. Though another 'innocent' regular would be a bad move, it's a shame they couldn't hang on to him for an arc of three or four episodes.

One's stance is funny – very reminiscent of Kryten in *Red Dwarf*, though it may simply be a result of how the costume feels.

On the downside, it *is* really just a cross between *TNG* episodes 'The Child' and 'I Borg'. However, it's better than either of those. 10/10.

#197: 'Extreme Risk'

by Ken Biller

Directed by Cliff Bole
Music by David Bell
US air date 28-10-98

Plot: When a probe is lost in the atmosphere of a gas giant, *Voyager*'s crew get into a race with the crew of a Malon freighter, to see who can be the first to build a shuttle capable of entering the atmosphere and retrieving the probe intact. Unfortunately, Chief Engineer B'Elanna is acting oddly, taking part in extremely dangerous sports with the holodeck safeties off.

Déjà Vu?: The probe actually resembles the Sith Intruder flown by Darth Maul in *The Phantom Menace*, though in this case the *Voyager* version came first. A new smaller ship to set stories on – sounds a bit like the shift to *Starbug* in *Red Dwarf III*.

Behind the Scenes: The sky-diving costume was designed for *Star Trek: Generations*, though Dawson is better in it than Shatner . . . The actual figure of B'Elanna sky diving is CGI.

***Voyager* Database:** The Cardassian-bashing program is called 'Torres 216'. The Maquis-slaughter one is 'Torres Zeta 1'.

B'Elanna's grandmother used to make her banana pancakes. Her father left when she was six, she was kicked out of Starfleet Academy at 19, and was only 'a few years' older in 'Caretaker'.

The *Delta Flyer* has ultra-aerodynamic contours, retractable warp nacelles, parametallic hull plating, unimatrix shielding designed by Tuvok, and Borg photonic missiles. Tom has old-style controls put in, rather than touch-sensitive panels.

(Lack of) Continuity: The planet is referred to as a Class-6 gas giant, though before now Starfleet protocol classified planets by letter, not number.

The Maquis were finally finished off by the Jem'Hadar in the *DS9* episode 'Blaze of Glory'.

Neelix is continuing with security training.

B'Elanna has been engaging in these holodeck risks since the day after she heard about the end of the Maquis. That was in 'Hunters', though there was no sign of her condition in any episode between then and now.

Ye Canna Change the Laws o' Physics: The nameless holographic pilot warns that B'Elanna could 'thermalise' jumping from 200 kilometres.

A Polaron burst could disrupt the tractor beam.

The planet has a layer of liquid hydrogen and methane 10,000 kilometres below the upper atmosphere.

The probe had unimatrix shields, as does the *Delta Flyer*, which also has a hull made of tetrabirniam alloys with polymetallic plating.

B'Elanna originally intended building the *Delta Flyer*'s hull out of titanium.

Seven uses a coherent neutrino beam to spy inside the Malon ship. Some real science at last – neutrinos will indeed penetrate any matter, though how she gets the reflections back to tell what they've passed through is another question entirely . . .

The display is a polythermal image – just like a thermal camera today.

Doc diagnoses B'Elanna as clinically depressed.

Puzzles: Chakotay lets B'Elanna go in the *Delta Flyer* in his place, though he was ordered to go. Shouldn't he have gone *as well*, or was he just using it as an excuse to chicken out?

What's this force-field thing made with a phaser, EPS relay and another bit of metal?

Bloopers: In the close-up of B'Elanna's face when she's called to Engineering, you can see the line where her prosthetic make-up joins her real face.

Learn Your Lines: Tuvok (in response to Tom's plan to fly into the atmosphere): 'Perhaps you weren't paying attention when the Malon freighter imploded.'

Tuvok: 'Proposing the same flawed strategy over and over will not make it more effective.'

Highs: Dawson is very good.

The *Delta Flyer* is way cool, and does look better without the ridiculous tailfins.

Lows: Well, Vorik is in it for a start.

Verdict: *Déjà vu* is the main feeling inspired as B'Elanna starts acting oddly around Day of Honor time. Dawson gets a chance to get her teeth into a better role than usual, and everyone else gets a scene too, but the episode is really nothing remarkable. It follows on nicely from B'Elanna's persona in the second half of last season, but doesn't make any changes or introduce anything new other than the *Delta Flyer* itself. Chakotay is reasonably effective when brutally forcing B'Elanna to confront the truth.

Essentially harmless but forgettable. 5/10.

#198: 'In the Flesh'

by Nick Sagan

Directed by David Livingston
Music by Jay Chattaway
US air date 04-11-98

Plot: Stardate 52136.4. Tuvok and Chakotay have infiltrated a fake Starfleet Academy/Starfleet HQ in a space station. There, they find that the personnel are aliens, genetically modified to pass as human, ready to infiltrate the real Starfleet. Investigating a dead lieutenant, the Doctor discovers that these aliens are actually Species 8472, who have judged humans to be hostile because of their alliance with the Borg in 'Scorpion'. Meanwhile, Chakotay has a date with one of the 8472s.

Déjà Vu?: Sagan's acknowledged intent was to do a variation on the Cold War KGB training camps of myth – as seen in the *Mission Impossible* episode 'The Carriers'. The *Doctor Who* story 'The Android Invasion' has a similar basis.

The outcome, inspecting each other's technology, is very much like the US–USSR agreements that ended the Cold War.

Behind the Scenes: Nick Sagan is the son of the famed cosmologist Carl Sagan, who wrote the novel and movie

Contact, and presented the 70s astronomical series *Cosmos*. He's is also the story editor for this season.

Chakotay's alias of Jason Hayek is probably named after Salma Hayek.

The brief shot of the night-time Golden Gate from *Star Trek II*, seen in 'Non Sequitur', is used again when Archer and Chakotay return to her quarters.

Species 8472's musical theme from 'Scorpion' is reused in this score when Chakotay is captured.

Voyager Database: The Academy Officers' Club is the Quantum Café.

A Klingon Martini is made of vermouth, gin and bloodwine.

8472 don't sleep or breathe oxygen.

Seven gets a new blue catsuit.

Chakotay resigned his commission in Starfleet on 3 March 2368.

The Doctor confirms Chakotay is 100 per cent human.

Starfleet Directive zero one zero states: 'Before engaging alien species in battle, any and all attempts to make first contact and achieve non-military resolution must be made.'

Chakotay's service number is 47-alpha-612.

Voyager's weapon range is 3,800 kilometres.

There are a dozen more recreations throughout the quadrant; this one is terasphere 8.

Boothby promises to get in touch when the 8472 leaders decide on peace or war. So far there has been no follow-up.

(Lack of) Continuity: Ray Walston previously played Boothby in *TNG* episode 'The First Duty'.

There's at least one Ferengi at this ersatz Academy – presumably 8472 spied on it while Nog was there, as he is the only Ferengi in Starfleet. There are also Bolians and Vulcans there, both of whom seem to be quite common in Starfleet (not least because they have cheaper make-up).

There are 128 crew on *Voyager*, counting the Doctor.

Harry wonders what it would be like to date an alien, obviously forgetting (wisely, I wish I could as well) his adventures in 'Favorite Son'.

Nuclear bombs killed 600 million people in World War Three.

Janeway says 8472 killed 4 million Borg.

Ye Canna Change the Laws o' Physics: The fake Starfleet HQ is on a space station, and created from a mixture of holograms and particle synthesis. It's powered by thirteen thermionic generators.

Cytokinetic injection triggers a DNA reversion from human to alien. Isomorphic injections help 8472 maintain their genetically altered human form.

Genetic change is detectable only at microcellular level.

Puzzles: Is Janeway lying or amnesiac when she says they've had no contact with Earth for four years (forgetting 'Message in a Bottle', 'Hunters' and 'Hope and Fear')? How did 8472 get their information about Starfleet HQ and Academy? By being there, from the Borg, from infiltrating *Voyager* (probably not, as they don't know *Voyager* is the only Federation vessel in the delta quadrant), or by some other means?

Bloopers: At the end, when Tuvok and Neelix visit the habitat, Tuvok is wearing the one gold and one black pip of a lieutenant j.g., rather than a lieutenant commander's two gold and one black.

Learn Your Lines: Archer: 'The concept of being unconscious for eight hours a night – it's so alien.'

Chakotay (quoting Shaw): 'The only secrets are the secrets that keep themselves.'

Highs: Chakotay trying to avoid being kissed by 8472.

Lows: Chakotay changing his mind and kissing 8472 back.

The retcon that 8472 were only defending themselves and didn't really mean it when they said the galaxy would be purged!

Verdict: In many ways it's a TOS story, being based on the Cold War. Species 8472 responding to diplomacy does detract from them as villains to be feared, but, with decent writing, I'm not going to complain too much. The mystery is

very well handled, and the effects excellent. Very funny
Chakotay-as-tourist scene too. In all, a clever and involving
episode. 7.5/10.

#199: 'Once Upon a Time'

by Michael Taylor

Directed by John Kretchmer
Music by David Bell
US air date 11-11-98

Plot: The *Delta Flyer* crashes, carrying Tom, Tuvok and a
badly injured Samantha Wildman. While rescue teams
search, Neelix tries to hide the truth from Wildman's daughter, Naomi, by taking her into a series of children's holodeck
adventures about Flotter and Trevis.

Déjà Vu?: The music is reminiscent of Danny Elfman's score
for *Batman*.

Behind the Scenes: Michael Taylor is no relation to Jeri
Taylor. He co-wrote the Hong Kong action movie *Guns of the
Dragon*.

The UK video sleeve describes Ensign Wildman as an
engineering officer, when she's a science officer.

Harry makes a Flotter doll – anybody think they were
hoping people would ask for them to be made as merchandise?

Scarlett Pomers is a different Naomi from the one in
'Mortal Coil' and her quarters are a larger set than in that
episode.

***Voyager* Database:** Educational programs like the Flotter
one list the 'Elements of Earth', 'Water' and 'Plasma'.

Naomi is scared of Seven – unfortunately this won't last
long.

The Doctor is teaching her, as the ship has no schoolroom.

Harry loved the Flotter programs when he was a kid –
especially the one where Flotter thinks Trevis is a rubber tree.

Starfleet Regulation 476-9 states that all away teams must

report to the Bridge at least once every 24 hours.

For the first time that I can think of in *Trek*, a whole ship is transported – the *Delta Flyer* being beamed to the shuttlebay.

(Lack of) Continuity: Ah, an ion storm hit the *Delta Flyer* – that familiar threat to space travellers from TOS.

We're told that Neelix had sisters (plural), though in 'Jetrel' we were told of only one, Alixia.

Neelix has a nightmare about the Metreon Cascade, which we're told in 'Jetrel' destroyed his home colony. It doesn't look as impressive as might be imagined, and would have been been better left unseen.

Tuvok's youngest child is a daughter.

Ye Canna Change the Laws o' Physics: The moon has a fluorine atmosphere.

Naomi describes the mitochondria as the warp core of the cell.

Polarising the hull will make it more visible to sensors.

The *Flyer* is buried under kilotons of Benamite.

Puzzles: Naomi is scared of aliens, but not of Flotter and Trevis, even though they're made up as completely as any regular aliens in the series. Is Janeway OK? She actually says she's 'had enough' coffee!

Bloopers: When looking for Neelix, who is on the bridge, Naomi leaves her quarters carrying the Flotter doll, but when she emerges from the turbolift it's gone. Neelix later finds it still in her quarters.

The amount of rock covering the shuttle varies between 30 and 50 kilotons, depending on who's speaking.

Learn Your Lines: Tuvok: 'Did you envision a more heroic death?' Tom: 'I didn't envision dying at all!' Tuvok: 'In accepting the inevitable, one finds peace.' Tom: 'If that's another Vulcan saying, Tuvok, I'll stick with "Live long and prosper".'

Highs: Lovely crash site.

The Doc teaching Naomi about mitochondria and cells.

Again Neelix is best when dramatic and enraged, this time

in his argument with Janeway over whether to tell Naomi about the situation.

Tuvok talking to Samantha about their kids.

Lows: Naomi is excruciating, and already fancies being captain's assistant on the bridge à la Wesley Crusher.

The computer voice narrating the story is pretty awful, too.

Verdict: Anything that's promised as a Neelix episode is usually something to be wary of, and 'Once Upon a Time' is no exception. Though it debuted only two episodes previously, the *Delta Flyer* already gets its first crash. Much of the episode follows up on material from 'Mortal Coil' about Flotter and the Great Forest, as Neelix takes Naomi to a holodeck recreation of it to ease her mind. Ethan Phillips is a good actor, but this material is simply uninteresting.

There are a few good moments, though, especially the scene in which Tuvok and Samantha talk about their respective children, which is quite moving. Longtime viewers will find the Ogre of Fire's destruction of the forest rather interesting – given what happened to Neelix's home and family. In the end, though, this is rather dull. 1/10.

#200: 'Timeless'

by Brannon Braga and Joe Menosky
from a story by them and Rick Berman

Directed by LeVar Burton
Music by Dennis McCarthy
US air date 18-11-98

Plot: Fifteen years in the future, Chakotay and Harry Kim are the only survivors of *Voyager*, which crashed while attempting an experimental quantum slipstream journey on Stardate 52143.6. Harry, flying ahead in the *Delta Flyer*, had miscalculated and sent the wrong phase corrections to *Voyager*. With a stolen ship, the pair intend to get a message back to their earlier selves and prevent the disaster – if they can evade Starfleet Captain Geordi LaForge of the USS *Challenger*.

Déjà Vu?: Chakotay's 'Now would be a good time' is delivered very much like Chekov's use of the line in *Star Trek IV*.

Behind the Scenes: The USS *Challenger* is named for the space shuttle *Challenger*, which exploded in 1986.

This is an anniversary episode, being the 100th episode of *Voyager*.

The future *Delta Flyer* is slightly modified – notably the rear door.

The *Enterprise-D* model used is the new one from *Star Trek: Generations*.

Voyager Database: At the time of its doomed flight, on Stardate 52143.6, *Voyager* has been in the Delta Quadrant for four years, two months and twelve days. The Quantum Slipstream drive comprises a quantum matrix, bendamite crystals (synthesised, though the substance was on the planet in the previous episode) and Borg technology.

Seven died on Stardate 52164.3, which is supposed to be the same day, but is actually two weeks later.

Janeway orders Chakotay to have a date with her. She can cook (vegetable biryani), based on her grandmother's recipes.

Voyager crashed on a planet in the T'kara Sector, just outside the Alpha Quadrant border.

The *Delta Flyer* made it to Earth.

Seven has an interplexing beacon, which allows Borg drones to communicate with each other. They can contact the earlier Seven by using a Borg temporal transmitter, which was found in the wreckage of a cube in the Beta Quadrant.

(Lack of) Continuity: The future communicators are the ones from *TNG* episode 'All Good Things'. The Quantum Slipstream drive was first mentioned in 'Hope and Fear'.

The USS *Challenger* is a Galaxy-Class ship – the *Enterprise-D* model.

There are 153 people on *Voyager*, counting the Doctor. Where did they pick up the extra 25 people since 'In the Flesh'?

Ye Canna Change the Laws o' Physics: The ship hit the ice at full impulse, which is about half the speed of light. There shouldn't be anything left of the planetoid, let alone the ship.

The bodies are preserved well enough to be recognisable, but don't resemble real-life ones that have been preserved in glaciers and are now seen in museums.

Inaprovaline combats drunkenness.

Tom refers to the new drive as an Edsel – a US car that was withdrawn amid scandal after proving to be a notorious deathtrap in the 1950s.

The slipstream becomes unstable because of a shift in phase variance, which throws the ship out of slipstream and splats it.

Puzzles: Again, why should it take years to synthesise crystals when you can simply use the replicator to . . . well, replicate them.

How did the *Flyer* get to slipstream – when only *Voyager* has the new engine core.

Bloopers: When introducing the Quantum Slipstream drive, Janeway says 'instellar' propulsion instead of 'interstellar'.

Learn Your Lines: Janeway: 'My advice on making sense of time paradoxes is very simple: don't even try.'

Highs: Garrett Wang is very good. So is the frozen version of the set.

Seven getting pissed – the Borg can't hold their liquor.

The crash is pretty amazing.

Lows: The grey-hair make-up.

Verdict: An anniversary episode is also something to be wary of: usually they're either truly dire or truly brilliant. Thankfully, 'Timeless', the 100th *Voyager* episode, is closer to the latter. It looks unpromising at first, being largely a Chakotay-and-Harry episode, but recovers quickly. Garrett Wang proves to any doubters that he can deliver the goods when called upon with a good story; there's very little sign of the immature ensign here. The other regulars still get some brief moments in flashback scenes, the best of which is Seven getting drunk – almost worth the admission price alone.

Between good direction, a clever script and an improved performance from Wang, this makes the tape worth getting. 8/10.

#201: 'Infinite Regress'

by Robert J Doherty
from a story by him and Jimmy Diggs

Directed by David Livingston
Music by Dennis McCarthy
US air date 25-11-98

Plot: Stardate 52356.9 is a week after the events of the episode (the only stardate we're given in it). Seven begins manifesting multiple personalities and acting oddly. It soon becomes apparent that a Borg vinculum in a nearby debris field is causing her cranial implants to generate the personae of others assimilated by the Borg. *Voyager* must shut down the vinculum, but the alien Species 6339 have other ideas.

Déjà Vu?: *Quantum Leap*'s mirror trick is used a couple of times, to show the people whose personalities Seven is manifesting.

The midnight snacker that Neelix has been complaining about seems to be a takeoff of the Lunch Bandit arc in *Homicide Life on the Streets*. It would have worked better if this midnight snacker had been mentioned in a previous episode.

The *Voyager* novel 'Seven of Nine' covers similar ground.

Behind the Scenes: They've stuck a floor light under Seven's alcove, which flashes to highlight her breasts in yet another new way. Nice to see the producers are keeping their priorities in order.

***Voyager* Database:** A Borg cube's atmosphere contains tetryon particles. Seven describes Naomi as 'subunit of Ensign Wildman'.

Naomi is now studying Seven to find out how to be perfect.

She intends to be captain by the time *Voyager* gets home.

There are 47 suborders to the Prime Directive.

Cottiscott is a children's game with green and red pieces.

Seven's new personalities include an unknown little girl, a Klingon warrior, a Vulcan subaltern, a Starfleet science officer, an alien woman, a Ferengi, the mother of an officer of the USS *Melbourne*, a Bolian manicurist, a Krenim scientist, a Cardassian, a Hirogen, a Bajoran . . .

Drones with personality damage are immediately destroyed.

The starship *Tombaugh* (named for Clyde Tombaugh, discoverer of Pluto) was assimilated thirteen years ago.

For once, Janeway is actually concerned about beaming a potentially dangerous object aboard. But then she does it anyway.

A Borg vinculum regulates the Collective by seeking out and purging any stray individual thoughts, and making sure every drone stays focused.

(Lack of) Continuity: The USS *Melbourne* was destroyed at Wolf 359, and the wreckage was seen in *TNG* episode 'Best of Both Worlds' Part II.

Ferengi are Species 180. Since Species 6339 were discovered only four years ago, how long ago were the Ferengi discovered? Are there more Ferengi in the Delta Quadrant?

Tuvok gets his annual mind meld.

Ye Canna Change the Laws o' Physics: Spikes in the frontal synapses indicate sleepwalking.

The Doc refers to Species 6339 as Typhoid Mary.

Puzzles: Seven makes Naomi a bridge assistant but doesn't thank Tuvok for risking his life?

Learn Your Lines: Doc to Tuvok: 'With all of these new personalities floating around it's a shame we can't find one for you.'

Highs: Wow, what a *tour de force* from Jeri Ryan, as she switches between personalities, especially the little-girl one – her trying to start mating with B'Elanna is fun too.

And as for the Ferengi . . .

The nightmarish mind meld (with unusually memorable thudding music score).

Lows: The Doctor's dismissal of a mind meld as Vulcan mumbo-jumbo is utterly out of character.

Verdict: Another fairly harmless episode, which gives us yet more unnecessary layers to Borg technology, and a lovely opportunity for Jeri Ryan to strut her stuff. Ryan's performance is the main element of the show, of course, and she handles it well, but every new addition to Borg lore just makes it more top-heavy and unbelievable. Tuvok's annual mind meld isn't very imaginative use of him either, though at least the nightmare visions within the meld are a good touch. 8/10.

#202: 'Nothing Human'

by Jeri Taylor

Directed by David Livingston
Music by Dennis McCarthy
US air date 02-12-98

Plot: An alien parasite merges with B'Elanna, and the Doctor's database isn't large enough to hold enough exobiology knowledge to cover the problem. He gets help from a holographic re-creation of the noted Cardassian exobiologist Krell Moset – but a Bajoran crewman recognises Moset as a war criminal who murdered hundreds of people in medical experiments.

Déjà Vu?: Like that other hologram, Arnold J Rimmer, the Doc enjoys torturing his crewmates with excruciating slideshows of his exploits. At least there are no telegraph poles among them.

The Krell were the aliens who built the underground complex on Altair IV in *Forbidden Planet*, and were destroyed by the monsters from their subconscious.

'The Taybor' was an episode of *Space: 1999*.

Behind the Scenes: Bob Picardo had put forward the idea of
the holodoc needing another hologram for a complex operation way back in Season Two. The original idea, however,
was that he would require a backup version of himself, which
would have none of the personality traits he had evolved
since 'Caretaker', and that naturally the two Docs wouldn't
be able to stand each other. The idea has since been split into
several elements: Dr Zimmerman in 'The Swarm', a rival
holodoc in 'Message in a Bottle', the need for an assistant
hologram in this episode, and reversion to the original
memory settings in both 'The Swarm' and 'Latent Image'.

The original title was 'Not Human'.

***Voyager* Database:** The Doc's matrix isn't big enough to
contain *everything* in his database, and exobiology isn't in
there as standard. Putting the exobiology database into a new
hologram will help.

Krell Moset cured the Phostosa virus, but experimented on
prisoners to do so.

(Lack of) Continuity: In 'The Gift' we're told the Doc can't
treat a patient against their wishes. Here, however, B'Elanna
refuses treatment, and he treats her anyway.

The Doc criticises B'Elanna for making generalisations
based on race – forgetting his own anti-Klingon stance in
'Real Life', also written by Taylor.

Ye Canna Change the Laws o' Physics: Palomar is not a
'fetid mud pit', but the southern California mountain topped
by the famous observatory.

The energy wave left a residual ion trail which can be
tracked.

The alien uses biochemical secretions to interface with its
ship's controls.

The parasite is a cytoplasmic life form – this merely means
it has living cells. It has multiple neocortices along its
primary nerve. Neurostatic shock to one will cause chain
reaction making the creature lose motor function.

Inaprovaline here is used to deal with cytotoxic shock.

The alien comm signal has triaxillating wavelengths.

Puzzles: Why use a Cardassian appearance? Why not just use a second Doc (as originally planned)? This makes no sense. Even though he's an expert in nonhumanoid exobiology, they could pick and choose any appearance they liked. Moset's knowledge could go into any form.

Why delete the Moset hologram? It's only a programmed reconstruction of him, not the actual person, however bad that person was. They could keep his knowledge in a different hologram But, then, the Doc has always had a tendency to veer from one extreme to the other – and deleting Moset will put further crewmen at risk in future. Taybor suggests deleting all of Moset's research from the database – what, even the cures for various diseases? This is dumb.

Didn't the Moset hologram have ethical subroutines – and, if not, why not?

Learn Your Lines: Tom: 'Fine, let's just deactivate the evil hologram and let B'Elanna die. At least we'd have our morals intact.'

Krell: 'Ethics, morality, conscience . . . Funny how they all go out the airlock when we need something.'

Highs: The Doc's slideshow.

Chakotay actually gets a laugh (when refusing to rescue the captain from the Doc's slideshow).

The briefing-room exchange, even though Tuvok is hardly putting forth a logical argument.

Lows: The Vulcan reproductive organ as art . . .

The rubber alien.

By an amazing stroke of luck our one-time Bajoran crewman had his family murdered by Krell Moset.

Verdict: A study on ethics in medicine – experiments on animals or people. Moset's experiments – operating on conscious patients, blinding people, exposing them to polytrinic acid or nadion radiation – are obviously based on Dr Mengele and his ilk, or possibly the Japanese scientist of Unit 731.

David Clennon is excellent as the Cardassian doctor and it really is a shame they couldn't have kept him handy for future episodes. Jad Mager is less impressive as Taybor, and of course Picardo is his usual watchable self.

What's really disturbing is that, although this episode is clearly designed to be thought-provoking, too little thought seems to have gone into the moral dilemma: the idea that one should abandon any treatment found to have been developed by unethical research is incredibly stupid. Apart from the fact that you simply can't put the genie back in the bottle, how would this affect modern medicine if, for example, aspirin was found to have been developed this way? Would we all immediately stop using painkillers? I think not.

Some nice moments in this episode, but ultimately it fails due to lack of proper thought – not to mention the luck that this week's guest crewman knew Moset. 7/10.

#203: 'Thirty Days'

by Robert J Doherty
from a story by Scott Miller and Ken Biller

Directed by Winrich Kolbe
Music by Paul Baillargeon
US air date 09-12-98

Plot: Stardate: 52179.4. Reduced to the ranks and sentenced to 30 days in the brig, Tom narrates the tale of how he ended up there – how the ship explored a water world being mined by aliens. The aliens were concerned about loss of containment of the field that holds their planet together, but when Tom and one of their scientists, Riga, discovered that the mining was responsible, the alien government refused to change its ways. Tom and the scientist took matters into their own hands . . .

Déjà Vu?: The underwater world has numerous progenitors – from *20,000 Leagues Under the Sea* to the *Red Dwarf* episode 'Back to Reality'.

Captain Proton is finally seen using his rocket pack à la

King of The Rocket Men or *Commando Cody*, and we see a 30s *Flash Gordon*-style rocket ship there too. No, not the brain probe!

Behind the Scenes: The story's premise, of starting with Tom in jail, telling how he screwed up, was from Robbie McNeill, who felt his character needed some of his earlier edge back. In the scene where Tom, as Captain Proton, is seen flying with the aid of a rocket pack, the rocket-pack prop caught fire, nearly roasting Robbie McNeill, and giving his arse (so beloved by many female fans) minor burns. Apparently he vowed never to wear a jetpack again, and who can blame him?

Buster Kincaid is named after Buster Crabbe of course.

The shot of the *Delta Flyer* leaving the ship is the same one used in 'Extreme Risk', but with a different planet composited in.

The original title was 'Down Deep'.

***Voyager* Database:** Tom is reduced in rank to ensign. He reveals he has always been fascinated by the sea, and that ancient sailing ships were always his first love. Even though we've never heard of this before . . .

The Federation Naval Patrol runs seagoing surface ships on Federation planets.

A deflector beam (reverse of a tractor beam) is used to try stabilising the breach in the planet's containment field.

The Meneans believe the planet formed naturally. In fact, aliens used a kinetic transfer system to draw their planet's ocean away and around the field reactor over a period of 200 years.

(Lack of) Continuity: The Delaney sisters have been mentioned many times since 'Parallax', but this is their only appearance to date, playing Malicia and Demonica in the Proton program.

Harry's character is Buster Kincaid.

There's a reference to Harry's crushes on Marayna ('Alter Ego') and Seven (various episodes last season) – the latter infatuation apparently being over.

The water-bubble tubes from the *Dauntless*'s engine room ('Hope and Fear') are now part of Captain Proton's rocket set.

Ye Canna Change the Laws o' Physics: The underwater city is an oxygen refinery and desalination planet. It's built of corrosion-resistant alloys and variable-density ballast.

Multiphasic energy discharges give away the location of a 100,000-year-old field reactor which is generating an anti-gravity field to hold the planet together.

The giant electric eel attacks with a biothermic discharge of over half a million volts.

Six hundred kilometres underwater and Tom tries to stop a leak with his hands – at that depth a stream from a leak would slice through him like the proverbial hot knife through butter. It would not be the neat little shower that we see!

Seven thinks venting plasma along with transporting out nonessential items will help them float.

Water density has been increasing in recent years, due to the removal of oxygen from it.

Phaser fire from *Voyager* will cause a hydrodynamic shockwave.

Puzzles: The brig is one small room with an open wall – where's the toilet, then? Is this the Dark Ages? Take away privileges, yes, but surely he should be allowed a loo. Nor does his bed have any sheets, and 30 days' growth of beard barely gives his face a shadow of stubble (in fact it's not even noticeable until Tuvok mentions it).

Who built the ocean, and why?

Refineries that are shut down would have to be rebuilt? Couldn't they just be switched back on? Or is this merely tacit agreement that by 'shut down' they mean destroyed or severely damaged?

Learn Your Lines: Janeway: 'We can't expect an entire society to change because we think they should.'

Highs: McNeill is better than usual. A dodgy rocket in the *Captain Proton* program!

The underwater city is impressive.

Lows: The distant shots of the planet are a bit iffy, as waves are visible, making it look very underscale.

The Meneans aren't very impressive.

This environmental crusading just doesn't seem like Tom.

Verdict: Robbie McNeill is quite watchable as Paris displays a few signs of growing maturity. However, the problem with the Tom Paris character is that his whole arc, from mercenary to redemption, was done in 'Caretaker', so this episode feels like a throwback. It's not bad, but it would just have fitted better at the beginning of the series – certainly before 'Maneuvers'.

Janeway's devotion to the Prime Directive again is also a bit sudden. Tom's treatment in the brig is harsh for such a supposedly enlightened regime – for 'brig' read 'oubliette'. In the end, though, it's watchable enough, with decent performances from all concerned. 7/10.

#204: 'Counterpoint'

by Michael Taylor

Directed by Les Landau
Music by Gustav Mahler, Peter Tchaikovsky, oh, and Jay Chattaway
US air date 16-12-98

Plot: The ship is passing through Devore space, an area populated by a regime who hate telepaths. This means they have to hide the telepathic crew members, and also some refugee telepaths they've picked up, during frequent Devore inspections. Soon, the lead inspector returns, claiming to want to defect, and strikes up a relationship with Janeway.

Déjà Vu?: People in black uniforms and gloves who hunt fleeing telepaths? Even the costume looks like *B5*'s Psi Corps Bloodhound squad – the uniforms, belts, gloves etc. are all uncannily similar.

The Devore warships look amazingly like overscale Minbari Flyers too.

Kashyyyk, in the *Star Wars* universe, is the homeworld of Wookiees.

The detection grid before the T'hara system, and the means of drifting by to evade detection by warp field of impulse signature, is exactly like that of the B'omar in 'The Raven'.

Behind the Scenes: The UK video sleeve credits the script to 'Michael Tatlor'.

The Devore carry the rifles from 'Waking Moments'.

The original title was 'Refugee'.

***Voyager* Database:** The Devore refer to Seven's interlink node as a bionetic implant.

Although the official line is that the Devore Imperium 'relocates' telepaths, there's more than a little suggestion that they're being relocated to six feet under.

(Lack of) Continuity: Scotty kept himself in a transporter buffer for 75 years in *TNG* episode 'Relics'.

There appear to be only two Vulcans on board – Tuvok and Vorik – though in the past Tuvok has referred to 'other Vulcans' aboard. We're told there's also a Betazoid called Gerat on board, but he isn't among the people rematerialised in the cargo bay.

The nebula is another Mutara-Class (*Star Trek II*, 'One').

Neelix tells some of the telepathic children the story of Flotter, Trevis and the Ogre of Fire, which we saw a part of in 'Once Upon a Time'.

Kashyk and Janeway agree that rescuing the telepaths was a violation of the Prime Directive. Isn't she going to confine herself to the brig now?

Ye Canna Change the Laws o' Physics: Staying in the buffer too long causes pattern decay and thus acute cellular degradation.

Torat's ship is powered by mercurium isochromate; 20 cl is enough to power it for a year.

Dark-matter inversion?

Torat says a wormhole is a layman's term that could be applied to many phenomena. This one is apparently an interspatial flexor, and Torat describes it as an intermittent cyclical vortex. Its aperture is unfixed and manifests infrequently in varying locations. To analyse the wormhole, Janeway and Kashyk apply fractal coefficient, neutrino flux parameters and statistical algorithms to try to work out a pattern that will predict its next appearance (it has appeared four times within twenty light years).

An analysis of subspace harmonics might reveal a subspace counterpoint to the wormhole's normal space appearances.

One photon torpedo will open the wormhole. A second will destabilise its subspace matrix and destroy it.

Puzzles: Why did Janeway let the Devore keep inspecting the ship, when she would rather go around B'omar space in 'The Raven' than let them impose such restrictions on the ship's journey?

Why does Alex Enberg (Vorick) again get a guest-star credit in the opening, when he has only a couple of shots, and no lines?

Janeway has Kashyk's replicator taken off line to prevent him replicating a weapon. Couldn't it simply be programmed with a restriction to produce food only?

Bloopers: We hear a supplemental-log entry at the beginning of Act Two, but no main entry (it was cut for time).

Robert Beltran pronounces 'Torat' differently from everyone else.

Learn Your Lines: When Kashyk asks, 'I suppose you liked me better in uniform,' Janeway tells him, 'I haven't decided whether I like you at all.'

Janeway (on breaking the Prime Directive): 'Let's just say I usually go with my instincts and sort it out later at the board of inquiry. Those admirals and I are on a first-name basis, you know . . .'

Highs: Nice use of music.

The triple cross at the end.

Lows: Look, the Devore are Psi Corps Bloodhound squads, and that's that!

Yet another bland alien appearance.

Janeway resorts to kidnapping someone from whom she wants information, even though he's not even part of an enemy faction.

Verdict: Janeway is uncharacteristic as she has a little romance with a Fascist bully-boy. This tale of an authority hunting telepaths has ended up not being the Tuvok story it was conceived to be, but it does largely succeed, in spite of leaving questions as to why Janeway permits the inspections. Most of the success is down to the acting, though there isn't that much chemistry between Janeway and Kashyk, and the latter is a good study in how to do an 'is he sincere or not?' character.

Mahler and Tchaikovsky taking the place of the usual in-house music style is a nice change. For the second episode in a row, Seven has only a couple of lines, and after a season and a half of nothing but her, it's almost a relief! 7/10.

#205: 'Latent Image'

by Joe Menosky from a story by Eileen Connors, Brannon Braga and Menosky

Directed by Mike Vejar
Music by Paul Baillargeon
US air date 20-01-99

Plot: Stardate 52479. While using his new hobby of holo-imaging as a new medical tool in the crew's annual check-ups, the Doctor discovers that Harry has had an injury and operation that he doesn't remember performing. He soon realises that areas of his memory are missing, and that his program has been tampered with. Investigating further, the Doctor discovers a disturbing secret about his own past.

Déjà Vu?: Sort of a reversal of *TNG* episode 'Clues', this time with the artificial life form being the one whose memory is erased and who tries to find out why.

Behind the Scenes: Picardo compares the episode to *Sophie's Choice*, and describes it as the 'birth of the Doctor's human soul'.

For once in a Mary Sue story, the point of it is that the Mary Sue is dead!

Janeway reads *La Vita Nuova*.

***Voyager* Database:** The female ensign being pictured is Renlay Sharr.

Tuvok has followed sumo wrestling since his youth. Janeway, B'Elanna and Chakotay all seem to be fans too.

(Lack of) Continuity: According to the notations on the Doctor's holoimages, Neelix is ranked as a crewman, rather than a passenger or (unofficial) ambassador, as he was referred to before.

Naomi Wildman has no designation.

Seven's maintenance schedule is doubled (i.e. to twice a week, as she was due weekly maintenance in Season Four).

The operation on Harry was performed eighteen months ago – and the Doctor specifically tells Seven that it was 'before you came aboard'. It was around Stardate 50979 – between 'Worst Case Scenario' and 'Scorpion' – and the Doctor claims he was already taking pictures then. But his hobby didn't become apparent until 'Drone'.

Tom fills in while the Doctor is off line, as in 'Message in a Bottle' etc.

Ye Canna Change the Laws o' Physics: Tuning the holo-imager's resonance spectrum along the subspace band gives a holoimage of a patient down to the subatomic level. The Doc detects operation scarring along the dura mater on Harry's occipital plexus, and in the cranial meninges.

A nascent alien retrovirus has been spreading in Decks 10 and 11, but is harmless.

Janeway's cytometabolism is normal, and her endocrine function is working normally.

Acetylcholine is a choline compound with a pure base.

The alien weapon leaves a residual charge in the neural membranes, working its way up the nervous system to the brain – this should be instantaneous, not take minutes.

The Doctor developed a feedback loop between his ethical and cognitive subroutines because, of the two equal patients, he chose his friend.

Puzzles: There's a major one here. The original incident that led to the Doctor's breakdown, which we see in flashback, happened before Seven came aboard. So where the hell is Kes? She was the Doctor's assistant at that time, and didn't leave till after Seven came aboard.

Where did the Doc beam the alien attacker? Back to its ship or out into space?

Why should making the choice between Jetal and Harry damage the Doctor so much? It's simple triage, and something he's done many times before (though there is a suggestion that he was damaged by the alien weapon first). So both patients have an equal chance. Are we expected to believe that his programmers didn't think of that one?

Neelix replicates the synthetic antigens for the Doctor?

Bloopers: Tom, of course, has his Season Five short hair in the flashbacks.

Learn Your Lines: Doc: 'Et tu, Tuvok?'

Janeway: 'We gave him a soul, B'Elanna. Do we have the right to take that away from him now?'

Highs: Picardo and Mulgrew.

Lows: Naomi is more annoying than Neelix ever was.

Verdict: It's handy that the holoimage forms people's uniforms at the same time as their skin – this is a family show, after all . . . The discussion of whether the Doc is an individual or software is a throwback to Season One – this is something solved long ago, so why go through it again? It's handled well, though, especially when couched in terms of Janeway's bias. The Doc spends two weeks in an armchair, thinking about what happened – but he's still back to his normal self by the next episode. 7/10.

#206: 'Bride of Chaotica'

by Bryan Fuller and Michael Taylor
from a story by Fuller

Directed by Allan Kroeker
Music by David Bell
US air date 27-01-99

Plot: Stardate not given. Photonic aliens make contact with the holodeck while the *Captain Proton* program is running, and get into a war with Dr Chaotica, who believes them to be rivals from the fifth dimension. They believe that only photonic life is real, and can't even detect *Voyager*, but their weapons are harming the ship. Captain Proton (Tom), Buster Kincaid (Harry) and the President of Earth (the Doctor) must team up, but they have an ace up their sleeve – Chaotica's new ally, Queen Arachnea (Janeway!).

Déjà Vu?: Wandering into 30s serials was a feature of Craig Shaw Gardner's Cineverse cycle. Arachnea has a fleet of . . . spider-ships? Are they . . . Shadowy? And of course, more 30s serials than I could probably name . . .

Behind the Scenes: This episode came about to cover the time needed to repair the bridge set after a fire there during a publicity photo shoot with Rick Berman (prompting some wags to claim that 'the lightning missed'). One of the studio arc lamps' bulbs had exploded, and the sparks set fire to the starfield backdrop curtains. Though there was no real fire damage to the bridge set, the sprinklers that doused the fire *did* thoroughly screw the place up! The construction crew and art department used the repairs as an excuse to make a few slight modifications, reupholster the chairs and so on.

***Voyager* Database:** 'Bride of Chaotica' is Chapter 18 of *The Adventures of Captain Proton*. The only alien invaders in the Proton program are supposed to be in 'Captain Proton and the Cosmic Creature'.

Janeway claims to be a dress size 4.

In his role as the President of Earth, the Doctor wears a

United Federation of Planets patch on his pinstripe suit.

Harry now seems to think Tom ran the program for historical study as well.

(Lack of) Continuity: Photonic life forms previously caused problems on the holodeck in 'Heroes and Demons', though nobody in this episode refers to that one. Since these aliens take humanoid shape, it's unlikely they are the same ones from the previous episode.

Janeway was a science officer during her time on the *Al-Batani* ('Caretaker'). This week there are 150 people on *Voyager*, and only four working lavatories – surely the first ever canonical mention of the smallest room in *Star Trek*. (Though the *Enterprise-E* ready-room set in *First Contact* and *Insurrection* has a hexagonal lavatory in an anteroom, which has yet to be seen.

Ye Canna Change the Laws o' Physics: The ship has entered a layer of subspace, and this is disrupting the warp field. The ship has run aground on a subspace sandbar, an area where, according to a trans-spectral analysis, the distinction between space and subspace is unstable. And gravimetric forces are disrupting the ship's control systems. While stuck, they have no access to communications, deflector, weapons, computer core, tactical, holodecks, or all but six replicators.

The photonic aliens from subspace are using photon charges to attack the Fortress of Doom. And Dr Chaotica has a Death Ray and Lightning Shield.

Proton gets messages from Earth by teletype.

Puzzles: The crew seem strangely unconcerned by the mass deaths of the photonic beings. So much for the caring, sharing Starfleet.

It's sometimes implied that 'period' music in the *Proton* holonovel is actually played for the characters, and sometimes just dubbed on as part of the episode's score – I wonder which is supposed to be the case.

B'Elanna says they'll have no holodeck access – but obviously they do!

The aliens say they'll stop shooting and let Proton do his

job, but then their weapons fire is said to have increased. Did they lie, or was it just convenient to forget for a better end-of-act cliffhanger?

Bloopers: The photonic life form who gets zapped has a very hard time keeping his face straight in Chaotica's throne room.

There are a couple of moments in the briefing-room scene where you just make out Beltran having little fits of the giggles.

In the close-up of Proton's microphone, you can see through the grille that it's empty and has no mechanism inside.

Learn Your Lines: Janeway: 'As a fellow ruler of the cosmos, I often have to do things myself,' is immediately understood by Chaotica: 'Ah, because of the incompetence of your inferiors!'

Chaotica: 'Oh, don't worry – I wouldn't kill my bride. Not until *after* our wedding night!'

Highs: Janeway as Arachnea – once she starts getting into the hand gestures of bad acting, she's doing a brilliant Shatner take-off.

Satan's Robot is hilarious, especially when it mutters 'invaders' again after Tom hits it to shut it up.

Verdict: The best episode of the season by a long long way. The plot is suitably silly and yet still makes a kind of sense. Tom and Harry are their usual selves, but this time everyone else gets into the light mood too – even Seven and Tuvok. Chaotica himself is a wonderful spoof British villain, and the costumes of him and his lackeys are hilarious. There's also relatively little technobabble, which is a plus.

It's intriguing that the photonic aliens can't recognise bio-chemical organisms as life forms.

The fun goes right down to the smallest details – the music is reminiscent of the old Saturday-morning serials, the terminology fits, and there are even some editorial tricks in the segues between scenes that perfectly match the inspiration for the show. True, it doesn't fulfil *Trek*'s usual brief to say anything about the human condition, but it's gloriously entertaining, not least because of the self-referential gags, such as the one about planet sets being identical because they're expensive! 10/10.

#207: 'Gravity'

by Nick Sagan and Bryan Fuller
from a story by Sagan, Fuller and Jimmy Diggs

Directed by Terry Windell
Music by Dennis McCarthy
US air date 03-02-99

Plot: Stardate 52438.9. A shuttle carrying Tuvok, Tom and the Doctor crash-lands on a planet inside a subspace sink-hole. There, they meet Noss, an alien woman who is also trapped. As they work together to survive, Noss's closeness to Tuvok forces him to re-evaluate some lessons he learned from a Vulcan Master as a child – the last time he fell in love.

Behind the Scenes: The gold filtering over the camera doesn't hide the fact that it's the usual Vasquez location.

Noss's ship is built of pieces of stock sets. Noss is played by Zori Petty (Tank Girl).

***Voyager* Database:** *Voyager* is now 50,000 light years from Vulcan.

The desert planet is Class D.

The hostile aliens use photon grenades.

(Lack of) Continuity: Tuvok specifically states that he only ever loved one woman – not his wife. (It was an unrequited love for the daughter of a Terellian diplomat.) This contradicts 'Tuvix' and the following episode, 'Bliss' – in both of which he is stated to love his wife – and also 'Caretaker' and 'Persistence of Vision'. It was this love that led him from the path of Vulcan logic, and resulted in his being sent to study under the Vulcan Master.

Tuvok refers to pon farr (which we saw in 'Blood Fever') for which he is overdue.

Tuvok, Tom and one other were previously crashed in 'Once Upon a Time'.

Voyager's crew is 152 this week.

Ye Canna Change the Laws o' Physics: The planet is part of a solar system that is stuck in a pocket of subspace. The system is trapped in a gravity well, and a distortion field damages ships that fall into it. It's a subspace sinkhole that grabs ships in a gravimetric shear, and is out of phase with normal space. Its aperture is 600 metres across. The subspace layer inside contains a G-type star and three planets. Time also runs faster inside the sinkhole than it does outside.

Puzzles: Vulcans are vegetarians, as far as we know – what did Tuvok eat when Noss and Tom were tucking into their baked spiders?

Tom and Tuvok's Universal Translator is broken, but the Doctor has one written into his program. Hang on, though – in 'The 37s' we're told that Universal Translators are built into the combadges.

Wouldn't the temporal differential interfere with the transport process?

Learn Your Lines: Tuvok: 'Is there a point to your pessimism?'

Vulcan Master: 'Son hal lok, love, is the most dangerous emotion of all; it produces many other emotions – jealousy, shame, rage, grief. You must learn to suppress them all, otherwise they will consume you.'

Highs: The young Tuvok looks quite like a young Tim Russ.

Joseph Ruskin is great as the Vulcan Master, and there's lots of wisdom in what his character says.

Tuvok showing off some Vulcan martial arts.

It's a lovely shot of Tuvok meditating against the sunrise.

Lows: Tom and Noss spider-hunting is pure padding. It would have been better to show the attack that wounded Tuvok.

Verdict: Lori Petty's performance as Noss is . . . interesting. She's good with the alien language, but, as her English skills develop, she also drops into a bog-standard Hollywood accent, and becomes blander. One of the most moving things is that Tuvok was a victim of unrequited love in his youth, and now pretends to Noss that her love is unrequited. . . . The Tuvok–Tom scene in the corridor before dropping Noss off at home is pleasantly reminiscent of the old Spock/McCoy scenes. 6/10.

#208: 'Bliss'

by Robert J Doherty
from a story by Bill Prady

Directed by Cliff Bole
Music by Dennis McCarthy
US air date 10-02-99

Plot: Stardate 52542.3. The ship comes across what appears to be a wormhole leading straight to Earth's solar system. However, in reality, it is a bioplasmic entity which uses a telepathic lure, and eats ships and their crews. Only Seven, the Doctor and Naomi are not affected, and must try to get the ship out of danger. Luckily they have help from an alien called Qatai, who has been hunting the creature for most of his life.

Déjà Vu?: Well, it's *Moby Dick* for a start, with Qatai as Ahab. Then there's the whole thing of spaceship-eating creature . . . The Doctor even specifically describes himself as an Ishmael to Qatai's Ahab. 'Where Silence has Lease' also features a huge creature fooling people's perceptions.

Blake's 7 – 'Terminal' – where an organic spaceborne life form dissolves the *Liberator*'s hull.

Behind the Scenes: The fake view of the wormhole interior appears to be stock footage from the *DS9* episode 'The Emissary'. It's a different actress playing T'Pel from the one in 'Persistence of Vision'.

The mess-hall set is used as a windowed corridor.

There are lots of stock bits and pieces in Qatai's ship – you can spot the distress beacon from the previous episode next to his chair.

***Voyager* Database:** Chakotay's ambition is to be reinstated to Starfleet with a full pardon, and given a professorship in anthropology. Neelix's is to be appointed ambassador to the Lantooan sector (where quadrupeds live). Tom's is to be offered a test-pilot job in Australia. B'Elanna's hope is that the Maquis faked their own deaths. When they get home, Janeway intends to land the ship at Starfleet HQ.

Qatai has been hunting the creature for 39 years 2 weeks and 4 days, since it ate his family (and 3,000 other people). The creature has been eating ships for 200,000 years, though.

(Lack of) Continuity: Earth was placed in Sector 001 in *TNG* episode 'Best of Both Worlds'.

Neutrino flux has long been established as a sign of wormhole activity.

The crew are again searching for deuterium (as in 'Demon' etc.).

Mark's engagement was mentioned in 'Hunters'.

Naomi still has the Flotter doll created by Harry in 'Once upon a Time'. She also still plays Colliscott with Seven ('Infinite Regress').

The Hirogen, Malon, Cardassians, Romulans and Ferengi are all mentioned.

Tuvok and T'Pel meet with the same finger-touching seen in *Star Trek III*.

Neurogenic fields caused hallucinations among the crew in 'Waking Moments'.

Ye Canna Change the Laws o' Physics: *Voyager*'s sensors show the wormhole as having a transkinetic vector leading directly to Earth. But they also show massive bioplasmic activity, suggesting a life form, and erratic neutrino flux.

Once inside the creature, *Voyager*'s hull is 'demolecularising'.

The creature is 2,000 kilometres across and consumes antimatter and biomatter. It uses psychogenic manipulations (telepathically sensing the victim's desires and making him think they've come true) to lure victims in. This is later changed to neurogenic telepathy and a neurogenic field, which caused heightened dopamine levels among the crew. It can also move under its own power. The creature has highly evolved instinct, but no sign of sentience.

A pitcher plant, according to Naomi, catches insects by mimicking pheromones.

A tetryon beam fired into a pocket of antimatter released from the warp core will explode and cause an electrolytic reaction, making the ship 'taste bad' so the monster will spit it out.

Violent contractions in the digestive chamber sends the ship out through the oesophageal opening. Wouldn't these bursts blow the ship up too?

Puzzles: Is Seven's Aunt Claudia a total creation of the creature, or was the name plucked from her subconscious memory?

When Security is called to the Cargo Bay, only Tuvok arrives. Isn't that odd?

Hey, how do we know the ship really got out? Maybe the rest of the series is a neurogenic hallucination . . .

Learn Your Lines: Naomi: 'My mom says two heads are better than one; isn't that the Borg philosophy too?'

Highs: Seven takes the ship, alone!

Lows: Naomi is already flying the *Delta Flyer*. It's Wesley syndrome, I tell you.

Verdict: Some nice little touches – like Seven's expression when Naomi doesn't want to be alone (to a Borg, being alone is obviously a nasty prospect). Ryan is excellent, as is W. Morgen Sheppard (Qatai). Nothing spectacular, but good, solid entertainment. 7/10.

#209/210: 'Dark Frontier'

by Brannon Braga and Joe Menosky

Directed by Cliff Bole (Part I) and Terry Windell (Part II)
Music by David Bell
US air date 17-02-99

Plot: Stardate 52619.2. After an attack from a Borg scout ship, Janeway decides to attack a Borg Sphere and steal its transwarp coil, which could vastly cut down on the journey time home. To prepare, Seven researches her parents' logs, learning about how they studied the Borg before being assimilated. Contacted by the Queen, who offers Seven *Voyager*'s freedom in return for her return to the Collective, Seven stays behind when the raid on the Borg Sphere is completed. The Sphere then takes her to Unimatrix zero one, a Borg city in space, where the the Queen welcomes her home.* Subsequently, Janeway, Tom, Tuvok and the Doctor attempt a rescue mission in the *Delta Flyer*, while Seven learns some home truths about herself.

Déjà Vu?: The music when the Hansens first detect a cube is reminiscent of the V'Ger theme from *Star Trek: The Motion Picture*.

The transwarp effect is new, and different from those seen previously.

The effect of assimilation tubules was seen in *First Contact*, and is directly derived from the effect of the Cybermen's toxins in the *Doctor Who* story 'The Moonbase'.

Behind the Scenes: The coffin-shaped Borg oblong was originally designed as a possible replacement for the cube in *First Contact*, but rejected and not built. Eventually the design was resurrected for this episode.

The Queen's assembly was also in a draft of *First Contact*, and works quite well.

Note that both parts of 'Dark Frontier' were aired on the

---

* This is where Part I ends in the syndicated version.

same night in the US. Unlike the previous year's 'The Killing Game', the episodes were actually edited together into a double-length feature, rather than simply shown one after the other. In the UK, Sky showed it as two separate episodes on the same night, and caused palpitations for thousands of fans when the continuity announcer joked after Part I that Part II would be postponed because the tape had broken. From this episode on, all episodes shown on UPN have been cut by an extra two minutes to squeeze an extra commercial into each ad break, thus increasing revenue.

None of the Hansen family are the same actors from 'The Raven'. The interior set is also slightly different. The *Raven*'s transporter has also been given the older *TNG* visual and sound effect.

The transwarp corridor interior is the slipstream effect from 'Hope and Fear' and 'Timeless' tinted green instead of blue.

Voyager **Database:** The fact that the Hansens were pursuing the Borg before the events of 'Q Who' has led many fans to speculate that this is a continuity error, since Starfleet were unaware of the Borg prior to that episode. However, great care was taken to ensure that there was no continuity conflict.

The Queen claims to be a member of Species 125. This is interesting, since logic suggests the original species that evolved into the Borg were either Species 0 or Species 1. Presumably this means that either the Queen is an anthropomorphic personification of an internal command function – to which any drone can be adapted for use – or the Borg didn't go around assimilating cultures until Species 125 took them over.

An astounding number of people seemed to be under the impression that the Queen was Annika's mother, in spite of being from a different species, and being played by a different actress!

Seven gets a new burgundy catsuit.

Money became obsolete when the New World Economy took shape in the early twenty-second century, and now Fort Knox is a museum (which two Ferengi tried to rob a decade earlier).

Magnus and Erin Hansen were exobiologists who shadowed a Borg cube for three years before being detected and assimilated. The cube detected by the Hansens measures 28 cubic kilometres, with 129,000 Borg aboard.

The Queen says Seven is the only Borg to return to a state of individuality – she means and then be returned to the Collective: numerous Borg have been separated (Locutus, Hugh etc.).

The tactical Borg monitored by the Hansens was once Three of Five.

There are trillions of Borg in Unimatrix Zero One.

Humans are Species 5618 (and have below average cranial capacity).

(Lack of) Continuity: As stated in the entry on 'Scorpion' Part II, it was necessary to retcon the implication that Chakotay's willpower was stronger than that of the entire Borg Collective. The answer I had developed, which the Borg Queen gives here, is that Seven was quickly programmed to be a sleeper agent or fifth columnist, and deliberately disconnected by the Collective themselves.

A Borg transwarp coil could shave twenty years off the trip, though Seven didn't seem to think of them in 'Day of Honor'.

Janeway refers to having staved off the Borg twice – 'Scorpion' and 'Drone'.

The Hansens' trip in the USS *Raven* was first mentioned in 'The Raven', and this episode follows up on that one in great detail.

According to Janeway it's been two years since Seven was on a Borg ship.

Naomi asks if the Borg have kids – in 'Q Who' they do.

Spatial charges are like limpet mines here, but were the name of the Malon weapon in 'Night'.

Species 10026 wear stock costumes, including Romulan civilian costumes from *TNG* two-parter 'Unification'.

The Hansens try to hide from the Borg in another Mutara-Class nebula.

The Doctor again isolates the translink frequency of

Seven's interplexing beacon (as he did in 'Timeless').

The Doctor says Annika was four – presumably he means when the Hansens set off, as she was six when assimilated, and the mission lasted three years.

Seven torpedoes used (a full spread is six). One shuttle lost.

Ye Canna Change the Laws o' Physics: The autoregeneration unit is made of polytrinic alloy.

Tom says Fort Knox was the largest gold repository in Earth history, with over 50 metric tonnes of the stuff, worth 9 trillion US dollars (1998 prices).

Eight light years is said to be three days' journey at maximum warp, when they detect the damaged Borg scout ship.

Triquantum waves are subspace disruptions measured in teracochranes, and are signs of transwarp conduits.

Bioelectric interference gets in the way of Magnus's transmissions from the Borg cube.

A neural processing adjunct increases synaptic efficiency.

Triaxillating shields counter modulating phasers.

A biogenic charge will spread Borg nanoprobes in the form of a virus, assimilating by stealth gradually.

The transwarp coil requires at least thirty teradynes of power to operate. A torpedo spread on to the conduit threshold destabilises the matter stream and implodes the conduit for a light year.

Puzzles: So, about this old habit Janeway has of rubbing her combadge when ready to make an unpopular decision – it never happened before!

The Borg Sphere pulls the shuttle in to assimilate it? Normally they'd beam drones aboard and assimilate from within.

Why does the Borg image of a human male need a pair of Y-fronts on? Modesty can hardly be relevant to the Borg.

Janeway has a clear shot at point-blank range, and hasn't fired a shot for the Borg to adapt to, so why doesn't she just kill the Queen?

In Act One, the Borg Queen refers to 'our previous attempt' to conquer Earth – there have in fact been two attempts: 'Best of Both Worlds' (*TNG* Third-season Finale) and *First Contact*. And it doesn't occur to her that, since the Borg assimilated the Hansens, they'd know about the multi-adaptive shielding.

Why does the Queen verbally instruct the drones to assimilate Janeway? Don't they all act on collective thoughts?

Bloopers: The *Raven* was a civilian vessel, and so should be referred to as the 'SS *Raven*' and not 'USS'.

When the Doctor says the biodampeners are stable, he's on the bridge without his mobile emitter.

The Borg city is referred to at various points as Unimatrix Zero One and Unimatrix Zero.

Learn Your Lines: Janeway (re a damaged Borg sphere): 'What we have here, in two words, is Fort Knox.'

Janeway: 'There are three things to remember about being a starship captain: keep your shirt tucked in, go down with your ship, and never abandon a member of your crew.'

Seven (to the Queen) 'I am Annika Hansen, human.'

Highs: Impressive Borg-point-of-view opening.

Better than average threatening music score.

The Holodeck rehearsal for the robbery, and the real one after it.

The Borg city (Unimatrix Zero One).

Lows: Young Annika is about on a par with Naomi.

Verdict: Janeway wants to attack the Borg to assimilate their technology? A Borg is dismantled on screen – creepy. The Queen has an intriguing plot and role, right from her first message to Seven. Seven is more valuable with individuality and uniqueness intact. Susanna Thompson is actually more chilling a Borg Queen than Krige was, though not as sexy. The whole thing's a kind of tug-of-love story between Janeway and the Borg Queen. Janeway shows some more solidarity with Tuvok (Mulgrew and Russ working well, like when she pats him on the shoulder – not in the script). If there's another CD soundtrack release, it should be this one. 8.5/10.

#211: 'Disease'

by Michael Taylor
from a story by Ken Biller

Directed by David Livingston
Music by Dennis McCarthy
US air date 24-02-99

Plot: Stardate not given. Harry breaches Starfleet protocol by having sex with Tal, a member of the Varo race, whose leaders are xenophobic. While he is disciplined for this infraction, he can't keep away from her. Unfortunately, she is not as innocent as she appears, and is a member of a dissident group which has sabotaged the Varo ship.

Déjà Vu?: That old staple, a generation ship. Hints of *TNG* episode 'The Outcast' as well.

Behind the Scenes: This week's aliens have a pattern at the back of the neck rather than bumps on the forehead.

The Varo control room is a revamp of the Queen's chamber from 'Dark Frontier'.

Voyager **Database:** The Varo have been travelling on their generation starship for 400 years. They don't want any contact with outsiders, and deliberately avoid travelling near inhabited systems. There is a rebellious faction aboard who feel like prisoners because of this, and would like to stage an uprising.

(Lack of) Continuity: Now Starfleet has lots of protocol against sex with aliens – since when? This contradicts, well, just about every other episode of every *Trek* series.

Subspace vacuules were what caused the transfer between dimensions in 'Emanations'.

Ye Canna Change the Laws o' Physics: And how likely are humans and a Delta Quadrant species to be able to mate anyway?

Harry feels wonderful because his beta endorphins are abnormally elevated, and there's unusual synaptic activity in his cerebral cortex – possible signs of an alien virus.

Harry glows because his heart and Tal's are becoming one. There's no indication of how that works. Tal has infected Harry with artificially created silicon-based parasites which consume duranium from ships' hulls.

The nebula has a subspace vacuole at the heart, acting as a gravitational anchor. Harry was captain of the Academy Velocity team.

Voyager extends its structural-integrity field to reinforce the Varo ship's shields.

Puzzles: What is with Janeway's sudden Harry-bashing? And, if she's so hard on him, why doesn't she sentence him to the brig like Tom?

How did *Voyager* pick up the parasites? Did Harry bring them? And how are they prevented from eating through the hull? They're discovered but no mention of a solution is made. How and why did Harry and Tal get gastroenteritis.

When Harry says he's got a disease at the end, does he mean it simply as a reference to the Borg attitude, or that he actually caught something from Tal?

Bloopers: Janeway's Connery impression: 'I shet the shame shtandardsh for all of my offishersh.'

Learn Your Lines: Tom (to Harry): 'You are such a lousy liar; haven't you learned anything from me in five and a half years?'

Harry (on similarity of species): 'I would've never guessed when it came down to the basics . . . Well, let's just say the birds and the bees would be very confused.'

Highs: Beautiful opening shot, and the design of the Varo ship, being modular, is very sensible – you could add as many or as few extra modules as you wished.

Seven's description of love, which the Borg view like a disease, having encountered it in 6,000 assimilated species.

Lows: More sledgehammer lecturing, this time about thinking first before having sex. A worthy cause, but, as Mark Twain said, you should *covertly* preach and teach, not overtly.

Janeway admits she wouldn't have reacted this way if it had been anyone other than Harry (she's protective of him).

Verdict: Harry still can't look like he's in a mature relationship – he's like a teenager getting his first kiss. Wang's OK, though, especially when acting like a wounded puppy dog. Plotwise, though, it doesn't have much going for it. Wang always seems to get lumbered with rubbish. At least he and Tal have almost-chemistry, and she's fairly pretty.

Frankly it's boring, in a major way – protocol, protocol, protocol. I could barely sit through the whole thing and stay awake. The best thing in the episode was the trailer for *The Corruptor* and *Payback* that aired in the last two commercial breaks. Tal asks what about the rights of the minority. What? At the expense of the majority? How fair and democratic. Mulgrew and Wang are great in their confrontation – shame the whole argument is about such a dumb plot. 4/10.

#212: 'Course Oblivion'

by Bryan Fuller and Nick Sagan
from a story by Fuller

Directed by Anson Williams
Music by Paul Baillargeon
US air date 02-03-99

Plot: Stardate 52568.3. Shortly after Tom and B'Elanna's marriage, the ship undergoes molecular disintegration, and the crew are subjected to what seems like a plague, with the same results. Investigating further, Tuvok and Chakotay discover that the source of the problem is in their own history – and that they are not who they think they are.

(Since this episode features a duplicate *Voyager*, and not the real one, all continuity and background given in it can be taken with a pinch of salt.)

Behind the Scenes: The dress uniforms are *TNG* pattern.

***Voyager* Database:** 'Here Comes the Bride' is still played at Federation weddings.

This ship has modified engines, and is taking a direct route through the centre of the galaxy, which should take only two years. Assuming they don't smash into the Great Barrier (*Star Trek V*).

Neelix gives as a wedding present a holoprogram with aphrodisiac crickets.

Tom expresses a desire to try a holonovel set in 20s Chicago. He seems to think Earth has the best vacation spots in the galaxy.

Eight months earlier, the duplicate *Voyager* was sabotaged by the Kamada. Nine months ago the Nekri tried to conscript *Voyager* into a battle fleet.

Janeway was born in Indiana.

(Lack of) Continuity: This *Voyager* and crew are in fact all duplicates created by the Silver Blood on the Y-Class planet in last season's 'Demon'.

Chakotay suggests checking B'Elanna's blood for deuterium, hydrogen sulphate and dichromates – which was the atmosphere from the planet in 'Demon'.

The duplicates gradually forget they were copies, and take up the real *Voyager*'s life. They're falling apart because radiation from the warp core, though harmless to humans, is deadly to the biomemetic compound.

All the previous captains have performed weddings: Kirk in 'Balance of Terror', Picard married O'Brien and Keiko, and Sisko married Rom and Leeta.

Seven is left in charge of Engineering again (as in 'Extreme Risk').

The Y-Class planet is said to have been in the Vaskin sector – the Vaskin being one of the two races in 'Living Witness' – and was visited eleven months ago.

Ye Canna Change the Laws o' Physics: Captains performing marriages is a myth.

It's thought that the centre of the galaxy is composed of gigantic black holes – this ship may be in for a shock.

The ship and crew lose molecular cohesion, breaking down

the molecular bonds. The crew's chromosomes are breaking down at the molecular level.

Tom wants to honeymoon in 1928 Chicago's Greystone Hotel, dance the Charleston, and ride in a vintage Duesenberg.

The Doctor uses a cortical stimulator to inflict an iso-synaptic pulse.

The Silver Blood was a biomemetic compound.

A polaron burst would knock out the mining ship's shields.

Puzzles: Isn't it convenient that the duplicate Tom got demoted just like the real one?

How did the Silver Blood duplicate the ship, the Doctor's holoemitter, etc.?

Would you take Chakotay as your best man?

Where do crewmen go while on leave?

Janeway is too dumb to stop heading for Earth, even though she's never been there.

Though they left the Demon planet eleven months ago, it takes only five weeks to get back.

Learn Your Lines: Tuvok: 'When it comes to affairs of the human heart, it is wise to look beyond logic.'

Janeway: 'I promised the crew I'd get them home.' Chakotay: 'Home isn't Earth.'

Highs: The vows are quite nice.

Seven's attitude to relationships.

Tuvok and Chakotay work well together.

Lows: Tuvok and Chakotay telling each other what happened in 'Demon' – very crude exposition, that is.

Tom's reaction to B'Elanna's death just doesn't look convincing, the way Janeway's to Chakotay's death does.

Everybody looks rather silly with the slime on their face.

Demolecularised sounds like something out of the *Proton* program.

Verdict: The slow-motion shots are getting a bit overused by now – it worked in 'Timeless' and almost worked in 'Bliss', but it's getting to the stage where you start looking out for them, even though it works here again. This is more interesting than 'Demon', with lovely effects, but it's essentially forgettable, and Janeway's attitude is strange – Chakotay is dead right when he tries to point out that things can't be the same now the truth has come out. Only Tom's reaction to the truth is believable.

A strangely sad ending – it's bold to have the cast fail and be destroyed, but in the end it means the episode was – and I don't mean this as a real criticism – a waste of time. Not of the viewer's time, but it ends up being little more than a time filler, as the very nature of the story and its resolution means there is no development to the characters. 6/10.

#213: 'The Fight'

by Joe Menosky from a story by Michael Taylor

Directed by Winrich Kolbe
Music by Jay Chattaway
US air date 24-03-99

Plot: The ship becomes trapped in a region of chaotic space, where the laws of physics break down. Meanwhile, after some holodeck boxing, Chakotay is starting to hallucinate about being in the ring again. He fears this is a sign of hereditary dementia known to exist in his family, but in fact he is being contacted by aliens, who use his hallucinations to speak from chaotic space. The aliens hope to tell the crew how to escape, but Chakotay must overcome his fears to understand the message.

Déjà Vu?: The shardlike effect when the chaotic space aliens appear is reminiscent of the effects in *TNG* episode 'Frame of Mind'. The aliens in chaotic space are a similar concept to the ones in the Tyken's rift in *TNG* episode 'Night Terrors'.

Behind the Scenes: Robert Beltran had asked for several weeks' notice when this episode was due for filming, so that he'd have time to get in good shape for it. Sadly, with the schedule being disrupted by the fire earlier in the season, he didn't get the three weeks' advance warning, but only the usual ten days.

Chakotay gets a new hairstyle, very like the one the evil Chakotay has in 'Living Witness', but only for this episode.

The music makes use of Chakotay's spirit theme from 'Tattoo'.

The actual communication from the aliens is shot exactly like the Orb/Prophet experiences in *DS9*, but cut in faster sequences.

Voyager Database: Chakotay's grandfather went crazy (his words) – and Chakotay has the genetic marker for a cognitive disorder. The family doctor switched off the gene before he was even born, but somehow it has been reactivated.

Chakotay was coached in boxing by Boothby at the Academy, and spars against a Terallian. He saw Price Jones fight Gul Tullet in the Neutral Zone.

Seven suggests that Federation vessels have been destroyed in patches of chaotic space. Of several Borg vessels to have encountered it, only one cube survived to alert the Collective.

The only question that prevented Janeway getting an A in exogenetics in her senior year – the nucleotide frequency.

(Lack of) Continuity: When Chakotay does his little vision-quest speech, he says 'powerful being' when he normally says 'spirit'.

A spatial sinkhole ('Gravity') appears along with increased graviton shear.

Ye Canna Change the Laws o' Physics: While *Voyager* is stuck in chaotic space, the graviton shear is buckling the hull. These shear forces are caused by changes in the gravitational coefficient.

Chaotic space itself is two light years across, and filled with enough energy for a dozen stars, as well as subspace flux and graviton waves. According to the Borg (Seven) it's an area where the laws of physics don't apply, or at least are in flux. All physical constants are shifting, so sensors can't function. The phenomenon has been encountered by the Borg throughout the galaxy, and it moves.

Aliens stuck in chaotic space are reconfiguring Chakotay's neural pathways so they can understand each other. They strip the optic and auditory neurons of protein encillation, causing hallucination. After his holodeck bout, Chakotay has an oedema beneath the anterior fauca of the cranium and a hairline fracture of the septum. Ganglia in Chakotay's optic nerve are hyperactive – the Doc thinks this is a sign of being fired at by an energy weapon. His sensory cortex is hyperactive, too.

Sensory tremens is the condition that Chakotay refers to as the 'family curse'.

A vision quest taps directly into the frontal cortex.

Chaotic space intersects with alien space at the eighteenth dimensional gradient – *Voyager* entered through a trimetric fracture. The way to escape is to modify the warp field to rentrillic trajectory. Later, more details are given: the main deflector must be modified (again) to induce a paralateral rentrillic trajectory. This is done by routing the deflector through the sensor array, putting the deflector to maximum amplitude and bringing the sensors on line, then going to maximum impulse. The signal from chaotic space is transmitting on the nucleotide frequency and is designed to affect DNA and realign its molecular bonds.

Puzzles: Given that 'Gravity' also featured gravitational shear and a sinkhole, did chaotic space cause the subspace sinkhole in that episode?

Learn Your Lines: Boothby: 'It's not against him, it's against your own natural human desire not to get hurt – that's the real fight.'

Highs: Boothby's advice on boxing – I don't know whether it's accurate, but it's intriguing.

The hallucinatory Doctor's description of the dangers of boxing is great – and accurate too.

When yelling at the Doctor, Beltran finally displays something of the promise we saw in the first season, for his best role in years.

Kid Chaos is impressive when he turns round to reveal his face.

Lows: Chakotay looks a bit podgy to be doing this.

The dead alien ship is designed to look exactly like a giant flea.

Verdict: Since I like surreal episodes, I must confess to finding this one intriguing. Chakotay is best used in a violent role, and this episode certainly qualifies. Better than might be expected. Probably the best Chakotay episode since 'Initiations' – and certainly better than any of his biannual romance episodes.

The perception of chaotic space as the opposing boxer Kid Chaos, with Chakotay fighting him, is surreal and clever – the purse the aliens put up is freedom. 8/10.

#214: 'Think Tank'

by Michael Taylor
from a story by Rick Berman and Brannon Braga

Directed by Terence O'Hara
Music by Jay Chattaway
US air date 31-03-99

Plot: Harassed by Hazari bounty hunters who want the ship, the crew take up an offer of help from Kuros, a member of a think tank in space. His price for calling off the bounty hunters is steep – he wants Seven to join his group. As if that weren't bad enough, there is also the matter of who hired the Hazari.

Déjà Vu?: Very reminiscent of the *Space: 1999* episode 'The Taybor', in which a trader offers to give Moonbase Alpha technology to jump home to Earth, but wants Maya (the show's top girl) in return.

A sphere at the heart of the think tank allows its members to communicate telepathically – just like in the *Doctor Who* story 'Shada'.

Behind the Scenes: A team from *E!* visited the set, to film a behind-the-scenes feature because of Jason Alexander's appearance as Kuros.

***Voyager* Database:** Tom Paris has introduced a puzzle game called Sheer Lunacy to the ship, having previously instigated a shipwide yo-yo craze. Nobody seems to bother that Harry plays with it at his station while on duty.

The Hazari (Species 4228) are bounty hunters who make excellent tactical drones, and are hired to capture vessels, and have 23 ships (with more on the way) in the hunt for *Voyager*.

Luridians keep subspace mesomorphs as pets.

(Lack of) Continuity: When the dilithium-rich planet explodes, *Voyager* is engulfed in a cloud of metreon gas – presumably a substance used in the Metreon Cascade ('Jetrel').

Chakotay suspects either the Malon or Devore ('Counterpoint') of hiring the Hazari to capture *Voyager*.

Kuros says an isomorphic projection is not as crude as a hologram, though the terms were interchangeable when B'Elanna and the Doctor met the crazed isomorphic projection in 'Revulsion'. This one, however, seems to be able to move around independently, without holoprojectors or a mobile emitter.

Janeway says that Starfleet has only theorised about such materials, though *Voyager* has met several before! The Borg haven't been able to build it either.

The think tank recently cured the Phage, and Kuros says Janeway would hardly recognise them.

The group's founder is a bioplasmic entity who launched it 100 years ago. I presume it doesn't eat ships like the one in 'Bliss'. Their last recruitment was seventeen years ago.

Seven's implants are again described as bionetic technology, as in 'Counterpoint'.

Kuros says that Seven contains all the knowledge of the Borg in one individual – directly contradicting several previous episodes.

Ye Canna Change the Laws o' Physics: Warp drive is useless while in the metreon cloud, but setting the gas off with phasers throws them clear.

The Sheer Lunacy puzzle operates on a fractal regression.

Puzzles: Why bring Seven to this strange ship instead of Tuvok, for safety?

Was the think tank destroyed or taken away for a bounty?

Learn Your Lines: Tuvok: 'The Malon are financially motivated; there's no profit in revenge.'

Highs: A clever triple cross.

Lows: Kuros is annoyingly bland.

Verdict: Kuros looks worryingly like Colin Baker . . . He's played quietly, but somehow he's rather irritating. The plot would probably have been better spread over two episodes, to give the bounty-hunter element more time to become established. As it is, this isn't a very interesting or exciting episode. 5/10.

#215: 'Juggernaut'

by Bryan Fuller, Nick Sagan and Ken Biller
from a story by Fuller

Directed by Allan Kroeker
Music by Dennis McCarthy
US air date 21-04-99

Plot: *Voyager* answers a distress signal from a Malon freighter whose cargo is dangerously unstable. When it explodes it will destroy everything within three light years, and the radiation has collapsed *Voyager*'s warp field so that it can't escape. Chakotay, B'Elanna and Neelix accompany two Malon survivors to try to stabilise the ship, but B'Elanna is having trouble keeping her temper around the Malon.

Déjà Vu?: The visual look of the episode – dark, grimy and filled with gas – is reminiscent of the *Babylon 5* story 'Grey 17 Is Missing' but with a much better 'monster'.

Behind the Scenes: I can't help wondering if it's a deliberate joke on Braga's part, that, using Jeri Taylor's stepson a couple of times a year, he casts him as a purveyor of garbage.

The Malon freighter is a redress of the Borg interiors from 'Dark Frontier' and the helm console is from the *Dauntless* in 'Hope and Fear'.

Alex Enberg (Malon Number 3) usually plays Vorik.

***Voyager* Database:** Tuvok is teaching B'Elanna to control her violent emotions.

Malon freighters have 42 decks.

Legend has it that radiogenic waste in the theta radiation tanks creates Vahar – poisonous monsters that wreak havoc on Malon ships.

Hallucinations are the first sign of theta poisoning.

Neelix knows about waste management from spending six years on a Talaxian garbage scow.

The Malon homeworld is called Malon Prime, and is a beautiful paradise.

Malons call the radiation blisters Freighter Blight. It's an occupational hazard, and when blisters appear you've already got a fatal dose.

The Vahar is actually a rebellious core labourer who wants revenge for being poisoned.

We get to see a sonic shower working, with B'Elanna's second topless scene of the season.

(Lack of) Continuity: B'Elanna destroyed the Doctor's holocamera, but made a new one.

B'Elanna thinks Tuvok must have been a cute child.

Danny Byrd used to bully B'Elanna about being half Klingon at school, and called her Miss Turtlehead – Byrd was later Harry's best friend at the Academy ('Non Sequitur').

The Malon dump theta radiation itself, not radioactive waste. A couple of minutes later it's antimatter waste they're dumping (as in 'Night').

The Malon ship is full of metagenic particles.

Tricorder energy creates an electrostatic field that ignites it.

Ye Canna Change the Laws o' Physics: When 4 trillion

tons of antimatter waste explodes, the blast will destroy anything within three light years.

Theta radiation disrupts subspace and collapses warp fields. Theta radiation contamination will liquify visitors in minutes. Liquify? Presumably they mean heat-blistering.

The Doctor is able to inoculate the away team against theta radiation for a couple of hours.

Metagenic particles cause viral mutations, at least according to *TNG* episode 'Chain of Command'.

If the freighter exploded in the corona of an O-type star, it would absorb the radiation.

An analeptic compound can reverse cell damage.

Puzzles: How are they still in Malon space? 'Night' indicates that their space is relatively small, and the ship gets another ten years further away from it in 'Dark Frontier'.

When sensors can't penetrate the control chamber, why doesn't Seven use the neutrino scan she used on a Malon ship in 'Night'?

Learn Your Lines: Tuvok: 'The flame, like emotion, is a primitive force. Left unchecked, it's chaotic, destructive. But if controlled it can be a powerful tool.'

Tom: 'Getting B'Elanna to control her temper is like getting a Ferengi to leave his estate to charity.'

Highs: Tuvok teaching B'Elanna about emotional control.

Chakotay's forcing B'Elanna to behave.

The Seven/Tuvok scene.

Lows: Pelk playing with a toy spaceship.

Neelix's radiation remedy.

Verdict: Not a bad episode by any means, but rather empty. There's some more lecturing about the Malon being filthy, and some nice tension, but no real originality. The identity of the 'monster' is intriguing, but not developed enough. It would have actually been interesting to see a positive side to the Malon, who would be more effective with one, while the likes of 8472 are more effective without a good side. It's a wonderful make-up job on Dremk too.

Overall, nothing special, but entertaining, and in no way the remake of 'Dreadnaught' that the press release and trailer implied. 7.5/10.

#216: 'Someone To Watch Over Me'

by Michael Taylor from a story by Brannon Braga

Directed by Robert Duncan McNeill
Music by Dennis McCarthy
US air date 28-04-99

Plot: Stardate 52648. The Doctor is tutoring Seven in the social skills related to dating. When Tom makes him a bet that she won't have a date for a visiting ambassador's reception, the Doctor finds himself feeling a romantic attraction to her – in spite of her first date ending up in sickbay with a busted shoulder. Meanwhile, Neelix has his hands full with the ambassador – a monk who is very keen to sample the delights of life outside the order.

Déjà Vu?: Well, it's Pygmalion, isn't it, right down to the bet? With the Doc as Professor Higgins, and Seven as Eliza.

Behind the Scenes: Yes, that really is Picardo and Ryan singing.

***Voyager* Database:** Tom has taught Harry to drive a 69 Mustang.
The Caati don't approve of spices, and are easily offended.
Species 8472 have five sexes.
Borg have unimatrices instead of families.
Ensign Berkowksi plays the accordion (badly).
Seven decides there are no potential mates for her on the ship, and gives the Doctor a 'thanks for the memory' gift (a medical tricorder with its efficiency raised by 33 per cent).

(Lack of) Continuity: Sandrine's returns! Tom wasted most of his Academy years there (and now notes that the pool table was deleted, in favour of a piano; the program is now called Paris 3).

The Doctor designed casual clothes for Seven at the same time as her catsuits.

The Doctor asks Tom for advice on how to handle his feelings for Seven – a word-for-word replay of his asking Tom about handling his feelings for Denara in 'Lifesigns'.

Ye Canna Change the Laws o' Physics: *Rosa rubifolia* is a red rose.

Seven claims her wonderful singing voice is due to a vocal subprocessor designed to facilitate the sonic interface with Borg transponders.

Caati don't have the enzymes that break down synthehol. Luckily Borg nanoprobes can assimilate synthehol.

Learn Your Lines: Doc: 'Small talk is a vital dating skill: it helps to establish a rapport with your companion.' This leads Seven to say, 'Perhaps there is something to be said for assimilation after all.'

When Harry says, 'I didn't know you had any interests,' Seven replies, 'Neither did I!'

Highs: Any Seven/Doctor scene, but especially his lecture on courting rituals, and their practice.

There are lots of funny lines, but mainly it's Picardo and Ryan who carry a merely OK script.

The duet.

Seven's chat-up attempt.

Tubing's hysterical binge.

The date.

Lows: The stuff about the Caati ambassador is not very interesting.

The Seven/B'Elanna thing is annoying.

Trek never does religious orders well, though it gets away with it this time, in a most unexpected fashion.

Verdict: Seven's being open about spying on Tom and B'Elanna is out of character – and the whole thing between them is a throwback to Season Four, but all this stuff was over by 'Extreme Risk' (and mostly by 'Demon'). It's no classic, but very amusing. Seven finally knocks Harry back.

You can see where the Seven/Doc rapport is leading, and it's a great shame they haven't left it open for further development – they're a far better pair than Janeway and Chakotay or Tom and B'Elanna. But Tom's such a bastard when he deliberately tells Seven about the bet.

This is a lovely change of pace, and, dammit, it's great to see Sandrine's back. 8/10.

#217: '11:59'

by Joe Menosky
from a story by Menosky and Brannon Braga

Directed by David Livingston
Music by David Bell
US air date 05-05-99

Plot: 27 December 2000. Shannon O'Donnell is an ancestor of *Janeway*'s who was reputedly an astronaut who was specially selected to head up the Millennium Gate company. In fact she was just an aerospace engineer looking for a new job with the company, who ended up persuading the last remaining landowner to sell up to it.

Déjà Vu?: Space travel in stasis – *2001*, *2010*, *Red Dwarf*, *Alien*.

Behind the Scenes: The street is the same Paramount backlot seen in the *DS9* two-parter 'Past Imperfect'.

The Apollo moon-landing module hanging from Shannon's driving mirror is a commercial model kit.

During the third commercial break, Picardo appeared as himself on the sickbay set, in an ad for the Planetary Society, encouraging children to design Mars colonies for 100 people. You can view some of the responses on www.mars2030.net.

***Voyager* Database:** The Millennium Gate was a self-contained ecosystem visible from orbit with the naked eye – a kilometre high and 3.2 around the base, and covered with reflective solar panels. It was built in the US in the twenty-first century. It was a model for the first Mars colony (an arcology) and Janeway's ancestor helped build it. She supposedly worked on all the early Mars projects – but in fact didn't, as we discover. Shannon was also a caffeine junkie.

Henry Janeway is obsessed with the Roman age. There were two Millennium Eves! When no disasters happened at 1 January 2000, everybody decided the real millennium (and disaster) would be 1 January 2001. I bet this really happens!

Eleven years ago a Ferengi businessman collected a database of historical information on Earth's space programmes, for a part of a gift set.

Tom's ancestors were salt-of-the-earth farmers, except for one test pilot, who made the first orbital glider over the lower Martian plateau.

Tom's interest in history extends to knowing all the early Mars programmes from the 1970s onwards (presumably starting with Viking).

Neelix's newly devised holiday of Ancestor's Eve is 22 April.

The Millennium Gate was dedicated in 2012, and the photo of the new Janeway family was taken in 2050.

(Lack of) Continuity: Vulcans saw first contact with humans as with a race of savages; Ferengi saw Wall Street as almost holy; and Bolians lamented Earth's inadequate plumbing. (We already heard hints about Bolians and plumbing in 'Bride of Chaotica!')

Janeway claimed in 'Future's End' to know nothing about her twentieth-century ancestors, but here she was brought up on stories of Shannon O'Donnell.

Ye Canna Change the Laws o' Physics: 'E-mail every computer within a hundred miles'? Since when was there a range limit?

Neelix's facts on the Great Wall of China – made when the first emperor united several other walls to keep out nomadic invaders from the north: 2,400 kilometres long, and until the twenty-second century it was the only man-made object visible from orbit with the naked eye.

We're told that the Millennium Gate was the first ever artificial experimental biosphere – overlooking Biosphere I and Biosphere II in real life.

Space travel in stasis is a valid theory, but in real life the Russians tried freezing in stasis, and it doesn't work – the test subjects died.

If there really is a replica of da Vinci's *The Last Supper* in corn somewhere in Indiana, I don't want to know.

Puzzles: Though Janeway is fifteen generations removed and has only a fraction of the DNA of Shannon, they look identical!

Bloopers: Though the backlot is convincingly wintry at night, it's too summery during the day. Mulgrew sounds amazingly like Marge Simpson when she tells Henry, 'Well, I might have a few connections.'

Learn Your Lines: Doc: 'My cousin was a prizewinning chess program.'

Various people: 'Nobody here but us galloforms' (chickens).

Highs: Henry Janeway.

Lows: Shannon sets a very bad example by sipping coffee while driving through snow – she's asking to crash.

Verdict: It's not a very interesting story – Kate is fine, Henry is great (though his surname is an obvious giveaway to the outcome). None of it adds anything to *Trek* or *Voyager*, and they even get the contemporary technology wrong! That said, it's a relief that Shannon is a reasonably normal person, and not the heroine her descendants think she is. There is a point, in the sense of looking at how history is not always exactly accurate, but still, the whole thing is thoroughly inconsequential. And yet . . . I dunno what it is, but it's somehow just . . . nice. 7.5/10.

#218: 'Relativity'

by Bryan Fuller, Nick Sagan and Michael Taylor
from a story by Sagan

Directed by Allan Eastman
Music by Dennis McCarthy
US air date 12-05-99

Plot: Stardate 48308. At *Voyager*'s launch, Seven of Nine discovers a temporal disruptor, having been put there by Captain Braxton of the twenty-ninth century USS *Relativity* to search for it. When she has to be pulled out abruptly, the strain kills her. Stardate 52861.274, and our Seven is abducted shortly before the ship is destroyed by temporal fragmentations. She is then sent three years into the past, to complete the mission her previous self was attempting – to find out who planted the device, and prevent it.

Déjà Vu?: Time running at different rates in different areas – Brian Aldiss's *The 80 Minute Hour*.

Behind the Scenes: Maybe a blooper, but it's not the same actor playing Captain Braxton as in 'Future's End'.

The bun of steel returns.

The uniform design and combadge of the twenty-ninth century are from 'Future's End' as is the twenty-ninth century phaser issued to Seven.

The bridge of the *Relativity* is a revamp of the *Enterprise-E* bridge.

The prop in the Jeffries tube, to which the device is attached, is a holomatrix, or so Tuvok says in the next episode (it's directly above sickbay).

Voyager Database: Janeway has nightmares about the fractal calculus exam imposed by Admiral Patterson.

Seven poses as Ensign Anna Jameson, service number 890790.

Seven's ocular implant can detect irregularities in space-time, so she can see things others can't.

There are different names for the various types of time paradox – the Dali Paradox, or Melting-Clock Paradox, is a temporal fissure which slows the passage of time to a gradual halt. The Pogo Paradox is a causality loop in which interference to prevent an event actually triggers it – Seven quotes *First Contact* as an example.

(Lack of) Continuity: As in 'Caretaker', *Voyager* has fifteen decks, bioneural circuitry, and a maximum cruising speed of warp 9.975.

The EMH has knowledge of over 5 million medical procedures, and the medical knowledge of over 3,000 cultures.

Seven is put on to the ship during a Kazon attack on Stardate 49123.5621, which is three years six months and two days before 52861.274. The temporal disruptor is planted shortly after this.

Voyager uses spatial charges as mines against the Kazon (though these weapons were never mentioned until this season, in 'Night').

Braxton refers to having been stuck on twentieth-century Earth for thirty years ('Future's End') and to a yet-to-occur temporal inversion in the T'kara Sector (though this is where the ship crashes in 'Timeless').

Janeway and the admiral briefly examine the EMH during their tour of the ship prior to its launch. Presumably this is the activation on Stardate 48308.2 that he referred to in 'Projections' and 'Lifesigns'.

Janeway says time travel gives her headaches, as in 'Future's End'.

Ye Canna Change the Laws o' Physics: The threshold of the H2 molecule is 14.7 electron volts.

The third brightest star in Orion's Belt as seen from Earth is Gamma Orionis, or Bellatrix.

Space sickness? Maybe caused by fluctuations in inertial dampeners – so perhaps it's a form of motion sickness. Inaprovaline deals with it (as with most things – it seems to be the twenty-fourth century's aspirin).

Temporal fractures are causing time to run at different rates in different areas of the ship.

The force-three temporal disruptor is designed to fracture space-time.

Temporal distortions demolecularise the hull.

The *Relativity*'s temporal transporters have a chroniton flux signature of 0.003.

Braxton says Janeway has been responsible for three major temporal incursions which he had to repair. He says she has a knack for sticking her nose in where it doesn't belong, especially where time travel is concerned.

Puzzles: Wouldn't Janeway recognise Seven four years after having seen her as an ensign?

What happened to Carey prior to Season Four? Seven doesn't recognise him from her time aboard.

How are escape pods supposed to reach a planet from deep space – they're not warp-capable.

If the bomb was placed during Season Two, then why did Seven find it at the time of the ship's construction?

Braxton can be arrested for something he hasn't done yet (which will presumably lead to the rehab that makes the future version so bitter, and causes him to sabotage *Voyager* while suffering temporal psychosis (a Pogo Paradox).

How exactly would the three Braxtons and two Sevens be 'reintegrated'?

Learn Your Lines: Doc: 'You try being funny after treating 37 cases of nausea.'

Braxton: 'I gave up trying to keep my tenses straight years ago.'

Highs: The Utopia Planitia Yards.

Ryan is excellent.

The *Relativity*'s exterior.

Braxton's analysis of Janeway.

Lows: The interior of the *Relativity* has too many recognisable designs from *Voyager* and the *Enterprise*.

Verdict: I love time-travel episodes and this is a lovely, complex set of puzzling and complex alternate timelines. It's confusing, but cleverly done. It's also very exciting, with a fast pace and some great twists. Not to mention some neat touches in the different time zones. It's a shame it's a different actor playing Braxton, when they're supposed to be the same person. (Or is he a Time Lord who regenerated?) 10/10.

#219: 'Warhead'

by Michael Taylor and Ken Biller
from a story by Brannon Braga

Directed by John Kretchmer
Music by Jay Chattaway
US air date 19-05-99

Plot: Answering a distress call, Harry and the Doctor find a device with an artificial intelligence whose memory is damaged. While Harry and B'Elanna work on it, they discover that it is actually a bomb, capable of flattening 200 square kilometres of ground, and was aimed at a military base on Selenia Prime. When they try to disarm it, it takes over the Doctor's holomatrix, and traps the pair in sickbay, insisting that it be delivered to its target – but the war ended three years ago, and the inhabitants there are no longer an enemy.

Déjà Vu: A sentient talking bomb to argue with and try to persuade not to go off? Someone's been watching *Dark Star*, not to mention the Season Two episode 'Dreadnaught'.

The Doc turning evil, of course, follows up on 'The Darkling'.

Behind the Scenes: The holomatrix above sickbay is where Braxton planted the temporal disruptor in the previous episode.

***Voyager* Database:** The bomb was launched by mistake – a common fear during the Cold War.

Tom takes B'Elanna a Mouton Rothschild 2342, Terallian pheasant and asparagus soup for his anniversary dinner with B'Elanna.

The Doctor can understand the bleeps of duotronic

algorithms (à la Threepio understanding Artoo).

Janeway implies that the whole of Deck 5 can be jettisoned, or at least the sickbay section.

The bomb can't be transported far enough to spare *Voyager* from the blast – isn't transporter range over 10,000 kilometres?

B'Elanna's first command was against what she thought to be a Cardassian supply dump – but the signs were merely unstable minerals, and there was a cave in it from which it took three days to dig their way out.

Starfleet Officers' Manual, Section 1–26, states that when taken captive by a hostile force, seek out any opportunity to engage the assailant.

Ye Canna Change the Laws o' Physics: The device is made of paratinic shielding, a dense energy matrix and bioneural circuitry.

The other bomb's explosion left radiogenic decay in the walls of the crater it caused.

Third-degree burns in real life are the most severe, causing damage to dermal and subdermal tissues.

Learn Your Lines: Tom: 'Do well in this mission, Neelix, and the captain may promote you to chief beautician.'

Highs: Picardo is much better than as the Darkling, probably because he's not trying to be 'evil', just cold-blooded. Wang is also good, trying to talk the bomb round with some good logic.

There's an intriguing moment when the bomb says it will detonate, but refuses to kill the crew, insisting they abandon ship.

Lows: The most unconvincing planet we've seen since TOS.

Verdict: The Doc's chats with the bleeping bomb are very R2/3PO-ish. Unlike Darkling, the Doc isn't evil – merely being used as a mouthpiece by the bomb. In essence it's a separate character. It's a nice reversal of *Dark Star* – the bomb has been programmed with propaganda and develops a human philosophy that prevents it from destroying its target. 7.5/10.

#220: 'Equinox'

by Brannon Braga and Joe Menosky
from a story by them and Rick Berman

Directed by David Livingston
Music by Jay Chattaway
US air date 26-05-99

Plot: *Voyager* receives a distress signal from the USS *Equinox*, a science vessel under attack by aliens, and comes to its rescue. The *Equinox*'s skeleton crew – one of whom is B'Elanna's ex – work together with the *Voyager* crew to create a multiphasic force-field generator that will protect them against the aliens. The Doctor discovers that in fact the aliens were attacking in self-defence, as the *Equinox* crew have thrown the Prime Directive out of the airlock, and are killing them for extra warp power. Janeway confines the *Equinox* crew to quarters, but the Doctor accidentally activates the *Equinox*'s EMH, whose ethical subroutines have been deleted.

Seven is knocked out while trying to shut down the *Equinox*'s engines, and the *Equinox* EMH replaces the *Voyager* one, to free his crew. The *Equinox* escapes with Seven and the field generator, leaving *Voyager* defenceless as the aliens invade the bridge. To be continued . . .

Déjà Vu?: Some similarities with the previous episode – another 'evil Doc' opus!

In essence the *Equinox* crew are what the *Voyager* crew was accused of being like in 'Living Witness'.

Despite Braga's instructions to the effects crew to create a monster that would give nine-year-old nightmares, the aliens look like Slimer from Ghostbusters.

Behind the Scenes: The *Equinox* is little more than half the size of *Voyager*, but is clearly derived from the *Enterprise-E* design, at least where the identical warp nacelles are concerned. The bridge is a revamp of the *Defiant* bridge, and the research lab is a revamp of *Voyager*'s sickbay.

B'Elanna has a new wavy hairstyle.

***Voyager* Database:** The *Equinox* is Nova-Class, a science ship designed for planetary surveys and with a maximum speed of warp 8. It got ahead of *Voyager* through a wormhole.

Burke is an old flame of B'Elanna's (whom he calls BLT) at the Academy, ten years ago.

The Shrieks can exist in normal space for only a few seconds, like fish out of water. Multiphasic force fields can hold them.

Ransom lost half his crew to the Kirtonan Guard, who accused them of violating their space.

The ships are 35,000 light years from home – halfway there (or about 25 years).

Starfleet Regulation 191, Article 14: In a combat situation involving more than one ship, command falls to the vessel with tactical superiority.

The Doctor is immune to thermionic radiation.

Starfleet Regulation 3, Paragraph 12: In the event of imminent destruction, a captain is authorised to preserve the lives of his crew by any justifiable means.

Ransom swapped an energy converter for an Ancari summoning device which summoned their spirits – actually nucleogenic lifeforms radiating high levels of antimatter.

The *Equinox*'s Doc designed the experiments, after Ransom deleted his ethical subroutines.

(Lack of) Continuity: Ransom is an exobiologist who made first contact with the Yridians (such as the one seen in 'Birthright'). Yridians are Species 6291 to the Borg, who thought they were extinct.

The *Equinox* was also pulled to the Delta Quadrant by the Caretaker, which means Janeway's knowledge in 'State of Flux' (where she says no ships are missing that she knows of) is incomplete.

Ye Canna Change the Laws o' Physics: The Shrieks come through interspatial fissures.

A synaptic stimulator fits behind the ear and sends images to the optic centres – a poor man's holodeck.

The stasis chamber in the *Equinox*'s research lab has been modified into a matter/energy-conversion unit, using a polaron grid and submolecular resequencer to convert the aliens into a crystalline compound. This is then biochemically altered, extracting the base proteins, which hold nucleogenic energy – a power source to upgrade the warp drive. Energy-vampirism, by any other name.

Puzzles: Why is Janeway so cold to Ransom's crew – some of whom clearly oppose the experiments.

Learn Your Lines: Janeway: 'How many lives will it take to get you back to the Alpha Quadrant?' (63 more!)

Janeway: 'It's never easy, but, if we turn our backs on our principles, we stop being human.'

Highs: An exciting teaser.

Noah Lessing (Rick Worthy) has a good rapport with Seven. He's a nice guy – I hope he stays next season.

Good cliffhanger – and the sound effects are spine-tingling, even if the Shrieks' appearance isn't.

Lows: The monsters look like a slimmed-down Slimer.

Burke seems to think he's a Vulcan . . . Very flat delivery. He looks like a slimeball too.

Naomi's utterly pointless appearance.

Verdict: Ransom is a real throwback to the barking captains of Kirk's day. It's not as good as it could have been, what with the reshoots and all, but this still manages to be an exciting season finale. The acting is mostly good, and the sound effects are scary. At least this time, Janeway using diplomacy on the Shrieks won't be a letdown after a great villain, since they're supposed to be the victims rather than mean opponents. It'll be interesting to see how it all turns out . . . 8/10.

Interlude

In the hiatus between Seasons Five and Six, it had been intended that the *DS9* producer Ronald D Moore would join the production staff of *Voyager*, as *DS9* had just finished. In the event, however, Moore quit his executive producer's position after one week, and Ken Biller took his place, with Robert J Doherty moving up to become story editor. Rumours abound as to the reason for this, but perhaps it was simply because Moore felt uncomfortable being under another producer, after his time as top man on *DS9*.

Shooting on Season Six began on Tuesday, 8 June 1999, and is slated to premiere on 22 September. At the time of writing, the first half of Season Six looks like this:

Sixth Season

#221: 'Equinox' Part II

by Brannon Braga and Joe Menosky

Seven of Nine must try to stop Captain Ransom from getting too far away from *Voyager* from within the *Equinox*, where she was left stranded at the end of Part I. However, Ransom removes the Doctor's ethical subroutines and gets him to torture her.

On *Voyager*, Janeway tries to establish communication with the Shrieks in order to prevent the *Equinox*'s continued exploitation of them. . . . Some crew members come aboard *Voyager*, stripped of their rank, and will have to earn the trust of *Voyager*'s crew before they are allowed to participate on the ship.

Noah Lessing (Rick Worthy) and Marla Gilmore (Olivia Birkelund) and two other *Equinox* crew members, James Morrow and Angela Tassoni, will be the crew members to come aboard. Despite Bryan Fuller's promise of 'less Seven this year', the first scene shot was her in a pink swimsuit on the *Equinox*'s holodeck.

#222: 'Survival Instinct'

by Ronald D. Moore

Directed by Terry Windell

Seven encounters a number of drones who left the Collective with her eight years ago, and whom she forced to rejoin (see 'One'). The three ex-Borg are disconnected from the Collective but are still linked with each other. They are named Two, Three and Four of Nine respectively.

The episode is rather slow and talky in a *DS9* sort of way, but very good.

Vaughn Armstrong (Two of Nine) was Telek R'Mor in 'Eye of the Needle'. Scarlett Pomers returns as Naomi Wildman.

#223: 'Barge of the Dead'

by Ron Moore and Bryan Fuller

B'Elanna goes on a vision quest to the barge of the dead, which takes Klingon souls to Sto Vo Kor, to confront her Klingon heritage and make sure that her late mother can get to into Sto Vo Kor. Of course, the first thing I want to know is, 'how did she know her mother was dead?' and 'how does she know she didn't get into Sto Vo Kor' – the last we heard was that B'Elanna thought her mother was on the Klingon Homeworld, in 'Eye of the Needle'. Eric Pierpoint (*Alien Nation*) guest stars as the barge operator.

#224: 'Tinker, Tenor, Doctor, Spy'

by Jeri Taylor and Lisa Vallely

Originally as in 'The Secret Life of Neelix', where Neelix's daydreams took on a life of their own as aliens started dismantling the ship. However, here this has been rewritten as a Doctor episode, and the aliens believe the Doctor's delusions are reality – can we say 'Bride of Chaotica'? Highlights include a Tuvok pon farr scene, and the fact that the aliens are incredibly like *Doctor Who*'s Sontarans.

#225: 'Alice'

by Michael Taylor

Voyager is visited by a junkyard salesman who sells Paris an old shuttle that is flown by big-neural interface, which allows the vessel to interface directly with its pilot's mind. Paris dumps B'Elanna to deal with this spaceship. Unfortunately, the ship turns out to be possessed by evil, and makes Paris do things that not only endanger himself, but also the safety of V*oyager*. 'Alice' is the name of the ship. This episode was originally entitled 'The Genie'. It is clearly influenced by Stephen King's novel *Christine*.

#226: 'Dragon's Teeth'

by Brannon Braga and Joe Menosky

Originally the November Sweeps movie, it's now a single episode. Centuries ago, the Delta Quadrant was ruled by a race of humanoids capable only of Warp 2 and armed with machine guns. *Voyager* discovers them frozen in stasis, and Seven (wanting to help a civilisation, having helped destroy so many as a Borg), wakes them up. They then try to re-conquer their territory, and only *Voyager* can stop them. Whether or not these villainous aliens will return to threaten the Delta Quadrant in either the February Sweeps movie or the season finale depends on viewer reaction to this episode. Note that this doesn't air sixth in the season – 'Riddles' does.

#227: 'Riddles'

by Brannon Braga and Robert J. Doherty

The first episode to be directed by Roxann Dawson (B'Elanna). Tuvok is hit with a brain-scrambling beam, which causes him to forget what it's like to be Vulcan. Tuvok must be cured to survive this away mission with Neelix, so Neelix tries to each him how to be Vulcan. Tuvok, however, doesn't want to be Vulcan again, and would rather have fun with Neelix. Meanwhile, a very Mulder-ish investigator is tracking the aliens responsible.

#228: 'One Small Step'

by Mike Wollaegar, Jessica Scott, Bryan Fuller and Michael Taylor

Directed by Robert Picardo

What drove Chakotay as a young man? We find out when *Voyager* encounters evidence of a lost early expedition to Mars, and the crew build a Mars command module for this episode, making it as detailed and accurate as possible based on real NASA projections. Bryan Fuller says, 'We decided to focus on the next big conquest in space – which is obviously Mars. I don't think there's a person working on *Star Trek: Voyager* that isn't a fan of the space program. We're all anxious to see the next steps taken. The episode is our way to nudge the American public and remind them of the importance of space exploration and its impact on the collective future of the planet.' Oddly enough, life imitates art here, as NASA's Mars Climate Observer was lost recently, in what appeared to be a navigational malfunction.

#229: 'The Voyager Conspiracy'

by Brannon Braga

Seven discovers that not only is the Caretaker still alive, but *Voyager*'s abduction was no accident, with a cunning plan stretching from Starfleet HQ to the Borg Homeworld. Scarlett Pomers returns as Naomi.

Voyager Merchandise

As always, there's plenty of stuff out there for fans to buy.

VIDEOS

In the UK, the series debuts on video, with two episodes per tape, in the order they're presented in this book. In the US, Columbia House releases them as part of a mail-order collection, with one episode on each tape.

BOOKS

The novel series:

1. *Caretaker* (novelisation) by LA Graf
2. *The Escape* by Dean Wesley Smith and Kristine Kathryn Rusch
3. *Ragnarok* by Nathan Archer
4. *Violations* by Susan Wright
5. *Incident at Arbuk* by John Gregory Betancourt
6. *The Murdered Sun* by Christie Golden
7. *Ghost of a Chance* by Mark A Garland and Charles G McGraw
8. *Cybersong* by SN Lewitt
9. *Invasion* Book Four: *The Final Fury* by Dafydd ab Hugh
10. *Bless the Beasts* by Karen Haber
11. *The Garden* by Melissa Scott
12. *Chrysalis* by David Niall Wilson
13. *The Black Shore* by Greg Cox
14. *Marooned* by Christie Golden
15. *Echoes* by Dean Wesley Smith and Kristine Kathryn Rusch
16. *Seven of Nine* by Christie Golden

17. *Death of a Neutron Star* by Eric Kotani and Dean Wesley
    Smith
18. *Battle Lines* by Dave Galanter and Greg Brodeur
19. *Captain Proton!* by Michael Jan Friedman

Also, there are the following novels, which aren't part of the
numbered ongoing series:

Flashback by Diane Carey (novelisation)
Day of Honor by Michael Jan Friedman (novelisation)
Equinox by Diane Carey (novelisation)
Mosaic by Jeri Taylor (hardback)
Pathways by Jeri Taylor (hardback)
Day of Honor 3: Her Klingon Soul by Michael Jan Friedman

Then there is the Starfleet Academy junior series:

Lifeline by Bobbi JG Weiss
The Chance Factor by Diana G Gallagher and Murray Cohen
Quarantine by Patricia Barnes-Svarney

And some miscellaneous:

A Vision of the Future: Star Trek Voyager by Stephen Edward
    Poe (this is a book about the creation of the series, and the
    making of 'Caretaker'; in fact Poe is the real name of
    Stephen E Whitfield, who wrote the original 1960s *Making
    of Star Trek*)
Becoming Human: The Seven of Nine Saga – a collection of
    Season Four scripts

AUDIOS

Caretaker, original TV soundtrack by Jay Chattaway (GNPD
    8041)
Heroes and Demons suite by Dennis McCarthy on the *Star
    Trek* thirtieth-anniversary CD, *The Best of Star Trek*
    (GNPD 8053)

Caretaker by LA Graf, the novelisation read by Robert Picardo, Pocket Books, 1994

Mosaic by Jeri Taylor, the novel read by Kate Mulgrew, Simon & Schuster Audio, 1996

Pathways by Jeri Taylor, the novel read by Robert Picardo, Simon & Schuster Audio, 1998

ACTION FIGURES
from Playmates

All of the regular characters, in various outfits. Also various guest aliens. If I listed them all I'd be here all week.

MODEL KITS
from Revell

The USS *Voyager*
USS *Voyager* mini
USS *Voyager* hi-tech (more accurate)
Kazon Torpedo
Maquis Fighter
Maquis Fighter mini

SOFTWARE

Apart from some semi-licensed Windows utilities, March 2000 sees the release of '*Voyager: Elite Force*', a 3-D shoot-'em-up using the Quake 3 Arena engine. You play a security officer who must fight alien invaders, including the Borg. It looks stunning.

MISCELLANEOUS

The usual calendars, ties, pins, posters etc.

A Victim of *Star Trek*'s Success?

Even the most casual fan probably knows that *Voyager* is the least popular of *Star Trek*'s incarnations. Although it has a few diehard fans who rate it as the best of the Treks, it garners far more criticism, and far fewer viewers than the others. Why is this?

Well, as far as the US audience figures are concerned, it's hampered by being on the US equivalent of Channel 5 – a new network that many regions don't actually receive. *Voyager*'s ratings are a far cry from the way *The Next Generation* dominated the ratings at its peak. In fact the last two seasons of *Voyager* each got fewer first-run viewers in the US than *Red Dwarf VIII* got in the UK. To be fair, audience figures have fallen generally with the advent of VCRs, DVD players, more TV channels and console games.

I suspect *Voyager* suffers from the success of previous Trek series, and on several different levels. At its most basic level, it competes directly with a more established Trek – *Deep Space Nine* – and this has split fandom to a certain extent. There are frequent flamewars on the Internet between fans of *DS9* and fans of *Voyager*, over who has the better show. This squabbling also occurred when *TNG* debuted (between its fans and *The Original Series* fans), but in that case *The Original Series* wasn't still in production, so both groups had to be content with *TNG* for any new Trek. In the *DS9/Voyager* situation, both shows were running simultaneously for four years. This was detrimental to both shows: *DS9* lost some of its viewers to *Voyager*, and *Voyager* simply never gained the rest. It'll be interesting to see whether the ratings improve in Season Six, now that *DS9* is over, or whether it is too late for *Voyager* to recover that audience.

There are, however, other factors at work to make *Voyager* a victim of its predecessors' success. For one thing, each of the previous Trek series had a distinctive 'voice'; a style and tone all of its own. *The Original Series* was, of course, original, with likable characters engaging in SF parables from week to week. *The Next Generation* developed this further, introducing character development arcs, and making its *Enterprise* crew more three-dimensional. In many ways it was a soap opera of sorts. So too was *Deep Space Nine*, but that series also had a new take – the epic story arc that made you feel that the situation you were watching could change, as the producers weren't afraid to kill off characters unexpectedly for dramatic effect.

Then came *Voyager*. What *Voyager* did, right from the start, was take the best elements of those three shows – *TOS'* weekly status quo, *TNG*'s 'soapier' characters, and *DS9*'s potential for arcs – and combined them. However, no new element was added to the mix, and this was disappointing for viewers who had expected the next stage of Trek evolution. The concept of *Voyager* does leave room for development, such as discord between two antagonistic factions aboard the ship – but this element was quickly buried under *TNG* philosophy that the crew should be one big, happy family. From that moment on, *Voyager* was essentially fated to be what it is – an entertaining extension to its predecessors, but not a new evolutionary stage.

Fandom itself has possibly contributed to *Voyager*'s conservative style. I'm not about to suggest that the fan base has deliberately harmed *Voyager*; far from it. What happened, and still happens, is that fandom almost subconsciously makes demands: 'We want more Borg', or 'We want a sequel to this episode', or 'We want a new alien' . . . These requests have at times influenced the producers. Instead of having a unique voice that concentrates on being the best it can, *Voyager* consequently has too many cooks in the kitchen.

Having said all that, *Voyager* can produce the goods when given the chance. But, compared to *TNG* and *DS9*, it achieves this less frequently. Fear of losing the fans has led to accusations of playing 'safe', and it prevents *Voyager* from taking the chance to sing in its own voice. And that's a chance it should take more often.